Whalsay

LHBEC

Anthropological Studies of Britain
General Editor: Anthony P. Cohen

Belonging
Identity and social organisation in British rural cultures

Symbolising boundaries
Identity and diversity in British cultures

Also by Anthony P. Cohen

The management of myths
The symbolic construction of community

Whalsay

Symbol, segment and boundary
in a Shetland island community

Anthony P. Cohen

Manchester University Press

Copyright © Anthony P. Cohen 1987

Published by
Manchester University Press
Oxford Road, Manchester M13 9PL, U.K.
27 South Main Street, Wolfeboro, N.H. 03894-2069, U.S.A.

British Library cataloguing in publication data

Cohen, Anthony P.
   Whalsay: symbol, segment and boundary in
   a Shetland island community. –
   (Anthropological studies of modern Britain).
   1. Ethnology – Scotland – Whalsay Island
   2. Whalsay Island (Scotland) – Social life
   and customs
   I. Title II. Series
   306'.09411'35   GN585.G8

Library of Congress cataloging in publication data applied for

ISBN 0 7190 2339 4 *hardback*

Photoset in Linotron Sabon by
Northern Phototypesetting Co., Bolton
Printed and bound in Great Britain by
Biddles Ltd, Guildford and King's Lynn

Contents

Illustrations

Acknowledgements

We had not been in Whalsay long before my wife, Bronwen, and I came to regard it as a home rather than as a base for our academic studies. To have known its people, and to be able to count so many of them as our close friends, has been the rarest privilege and good fortune. They could not have received us with greater kindness and generosity. They may judge this book an unworthy offering in return. Many of them will disagree with its opinions and some may regret its very existence. I can only ask them to accept it as a token of my genuine respect and esteem. By their example they have instructed us, like other soothmoothers, in many virtues, not least those of friendship and community.

Our debts to Whalsay folk are too many and too personal to be requited by the mere expression of gratitude; they are irredeemable. But of all our friends (none of whom would wish to be named here) I cannot let the opportunity pass without thanking our neighbours in Whitefield, Sodom, *an' alang da road*, for their countless kindnesses and their forebearance. Among them, and with seemingly unlimited patience, Jimmy and the late and so sadly missed Bella Arthur, with Peter and Mary Hughson, have given us support of every kind without which we could not have stayed in Whalsay, and guidance without which we would have learned nothing.

Beyond Whalsay, and over so many years, I have been helped by more colleagues and friends than I could possibly acknowledge here. At the very outset of the research, I was fortunate to make contact with Bob Storey, then Social Research and Development Officer at the Highlands and Islands Development Board in Inverness, and, earlier, Shetland's first County Development Officer. His advice, encouragement and unerring judgement have been invaluable throughout. His long-time friend, Robert Paine, had already helped me through my previous research in Newfoundland. It was his enthusiasm for the Islands which initially turned my thoughts towards Shetland. The most constructive of critics, he has always asked the correct (awkward) questions and has refused to be content with the sloppy answer. He continues to teach all of us, by his example, that academic excellence and

personal commitment are wholly compatible in the enterprise of anthropology. In the planning and organisation of the project I received great support
from Peter Worsley, whose own commitment to 'the present as anthropology' has long been an inspiration to me, despite his scepticism about my
decision to pursue it in Shetland rather than in Latin America. My colleagues
and students at Manchester have struggled valiantly to remedy the more
glaring deficiencies in my thinking. Nigel Rapport, in particular, has given me
the benefit of his unflagging critical energy and his unfailing eye, and Marilyn
Strathern kindly read, and commented on, the entire manuscript.

From 1973–78 my work in Shetland was supported by two grants from the
Social Science Research Council. The University of Manchester has been a
most generous patron, allowing me a year's fieldwork leave in 1974–75, a
sabbatical year in 1985–86, without which I could not have written the book,
and several awards from the staff travel fund to assist my return visits to
Whalsay.

I am most grateful to G. P. S. Peterson for permission to reprint verses of his
poem, 'Da Shetland Tongue'; to William J. Hunter for permission to reprint J.
J. Hunter's poem 'With Apologies to Thomas Moore'; to Dennis Coutts and
to Robert Johnson, for permission to reproduce their photographs.

I am most grateful to Alastair Hamilton and his colleagues in the university's Audio-visual Service for their help in producing the artwork of Figs 1–7,
9–10, 13 and 14. I thank Vimalan Jesudason for his skilful transcription of
'The Tune with no Name'. I am indebted to Gordon Craig of Symbister
House JHS for tolerating my nagging with such equanimity and for producing such excellent photographs. I wish space could have been found for all of
them. Last, but by no means least, I humbly and sincerely thank my son,
Liam, for his splendid maps and drawings (Figs 8, 11 and 12).

Above all others, my debt is to my wife, Bronwen Cohen, historian of
Shetland, who has shared with me the experience of Whalsay and whose
greater insight has taught me so much. My sternest critic, she would disagree
with almost every page of the text which follows. But she alone will know
how much worse it would have been without her influence. With humility,
and in some trepidation, I dedicate this book to her.

A.P.C. September 1986.

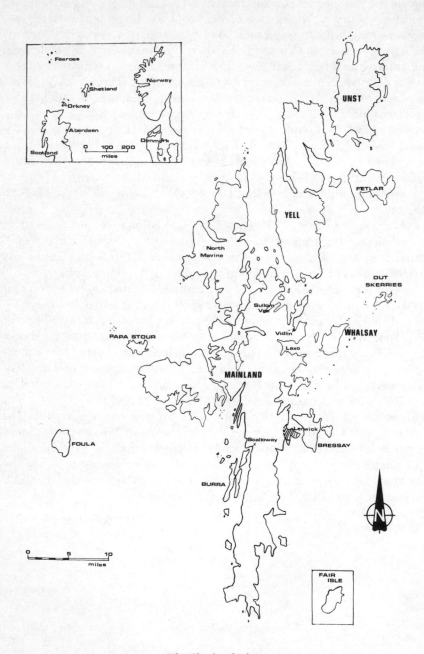

The Shetland Isles

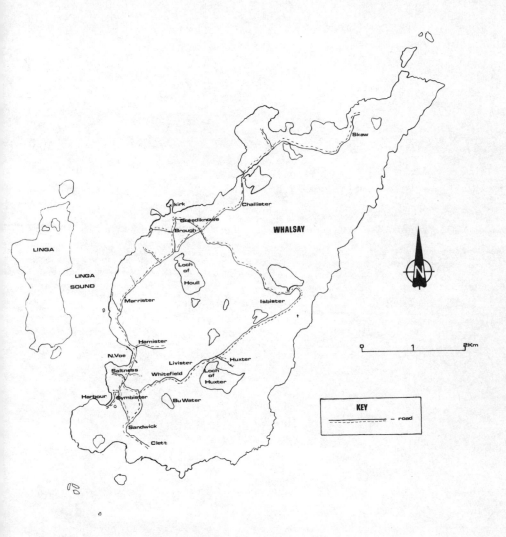

Whalsay

For Bronwen

Introduction

Versions

11th April 1973, a day of quirky, eccentric weather, typical of a Shetland winter. When I boarded the MV *Earl of Zetland* in Lerwick as first light was breaking, a moderate wind was blowing from the west, and continued in this benign manner during our ninety-minute passage. An invigorating morning. The steamer slipped out of the Nort Moot of Lerwick harbour as the fish market was beginning to stir. Like an aromatic counterpoint to the *Earl*'s familiar signature of diesel fumes, the seductive smell of frying bacon wafted from the galley, and there promised also the tempting prospect of steaming hot porridge.

We steamed steadily northwards, passing the gauntly cliffed bird sanctuary of Noss to the east, and the fjordal coastline of Nesting parish to the west. Then, out of the cloud sitting over its south end and encircling the wartime hilltop camp at the Ward of Clett, there loomed the island of Whalsay, 'the bonny isle', the object of so much of our earlier anticipation and speculation.

Waiting on Symbister pier for the boat were the postman, Peter, there to collect the mail; Tammy, the steamer's agent; Angus, with tractor and trailer, ready to haul milk and groceries up to the Co-op; some of the other shopkeepers – Jamie, Ertie, Wilf, Henry and Robbie – all expecting supplies; and a few other individuals hoping, perhaps, that their parcels, sacks of sheep nuts, spare parts, would be aboard. It was an apparently placid scene. What, to the outsider, was the romance of the steamer's arrival was merely a routine chore for the islanders. The steamer called three times a week. Its unloading, though easier now with a pier than it had been with the old 'flit boat', was slow, cumbersome and, in bad weather, distinctly uncomfortable. If a south-easterly was blowing, the steamer might be unable to dock at all. Spoilage of goods through breakages, damp penetration and rodents was a continual irritant. But on that day, and to this observer's then still naive eyes, all was in place and seemingly as it should be.

I walked along the pier, full of the trepidation and self-consciousness which always dominate the anthropologist as he intrudes upon the 'field'. But my near-paralysing self-doubt was distracted by the scene of apparent chaos which soon confronted me. One of Whalsay's new purse-seiners was in harbour, her huge net partially slung over the side, engulfed in what looked like a thick and unsavoury porridge. The wheelhouse, deck and all the men aboard were covered by the same silvery-grey mess. The men were playing hoses over everything in sight, including each other, in an appalling effort to sluice away the ordure. Some were grimly systematic; some shouted in the struggle to make themselves heard in the bedlam of pumps, winches and hoses. Some convulsed with laughter as they tumbled in the slime. This boat, testing its gear for the forthcoming herring season, had fouled its net on a huge shoal of young sprat, and had had to make for home to clear up the consequences.

Into the midst of this frenetic activity stepped a squat, wild-haired, bespectacled and boiler-suited figure, holding a small polythene bag. He wanted some sprats for a 'fry', the customary gift of fish which returning fishermen would always make to those ashore. This was Henry, ever the optimist, seeking at least a modicum of virtue out of adversity.

Years later, reflecting on this scene, I found in it a metaphor for Whalsay life: a veneer of harmony, order and agreement masking, and only barely containing, a ferment of opinion, argument, debate – sometimes dissensus – an ordered chaos. But this was the luxurious product of an occasion for reflection. We shall return to it repeatedly in the pages which follow. My immediate attention was now absorbed by a demented battle to keep my feet as the wind suddenly screamed out of the north-west. I was dimly aware of being lifted bodily by the gale and flung, fortuitously, into the front porch of a house. The door opened immediately and I, sodden and bedraggled was greeted quite matter-of-factly:

'Oh, guid mornin', guid mornin'. It's a bit breezy.'

Having restored me to a semblance of life with hot tea and bannocks, my phlegmatic host gave me a guided tour of the island.

Though again it was some time before I realised it, his tour was highly instructive, for he identified each house, croft and township in terms of their genealogical and social referents, frequently focused upon his own family. 'Yon's a hoose me faither helped to *bigg* [build] tae his cousin –.' 'Dat croft ower by belangs to de faither o' me son's wife.' 'Dis is where my wife's mither stayed as a girl.' 'Dis where da son o' me faither's eldest brother bides. . . .' Even relatives at a further remove were classified genealogically. The detail was bewildering and awesome. Its factual content need not concern us. But it suggested to me, first, the importance of genealogy to Whalsay people as a means of mapping their social knowledge; and, second, a demographic fact which later and more systematic research would confirm, the remarkable intensity of kinship in the island. I was to discover that the entire island-born adult population could be interrelated by going back no further than four generations. Three-quarters of the population could be related to each other through their grandparents' generation. This is explained by two factors: the historical preponderance of local endogamy; and the much lower rate of out-migration from Whalsay than occurred in other areas of Shetland. This, in turn, has produced a powerful sense of historical continuity in which the present and the past are curiously merged. The past is ever-present, in yarns about characters of old, in the minutiae of place names; in the historical association of families with their crofts and parts of the isle. Walls, dykes, rocks, *geos* (deep narrow inlets in the shoreline), *crüs* (sheepfolds), *crubs* (circular stone enclosures within which seedlings were nurtured) may all be known by personal or family names dating back perhaps three hundred years. Conversation thus spans and concertinas the centuries. In this and in the extensive knowledge of genealogy and kinship history there is a pervasive sense of rootedness, of belonging, as if people were as immovably and inherently part of the island as the very features of its landscape.[1]

There thus rests on individuals the weight of history and tradition. Sometimes this is experienced pleasurably; on other occasions it seems to be a burden, compromising people's sense of their individuality. But I cannot – indeed, *must* not – generalise. In the realm of attitude, opinion and belief there are no truths about Whalsay. People may express apparently similar sentiments, or may use shared terms for their expression. But they plainly understand them in very different ways. They mean different things by them. The terminology of consensus is only a skin drawn over the dynamism of debate, of competition, of diversity. Every one has his own versions of the truth. The anthropologist can report other people's versions; but his own judgements are simply the product of *his* version and are in no way privileged. I therefore make no pretence here of objectivity. Most of what is offered should be regarded as interpretation rather than as fact, and any statement for which factual status is inadvertently claimed should be treated with the greatest scepticism.

This *caveat* is not offered as a token of academic humility. Perhaps the contrary is the case. The stance I take in this book, known to social anthropologists as 'interpretivism', places the self of the anthropologist at the very centre of his observations. I do not offer any contribution here to the attempts of contemporary anthropologists to theorise their position as one of 'reflexivity'. I can say only that I have written the book in this manner because it was the only one honestly open to me: it replicates the manner in which I have conducted my observation of Whalsay life over the last twelve years. I could not have done it in any other way.

I suspect that many Whalsay people have long since abandoned any expectation that the book would be written. Year after year when I returned to the island they would ask, 'Have you written the book yet?' I had continually to reply, 'No,' and they were always kind enough not to press for the reason. I tried many explanations on myself. I was not yet ready; did not know enough; kept changing my mind; was too close, and so forth. The real reason was that the task was too difficult. Without claiming any particular expertise, I know I could have written the classic style of monograph, with chapters on Whalsay kinship; economics; politics; religion; symbolic, ceremonial and ritual life; dialect, etc. But whilst that might have been of some interest to scholars of Shetland, it seems to me an approach now properly redundant in anthropology, very little more than an alien conceptual matrix imposed uncomfortably and misleadingly upon a body of rather superficial data which masquerades as fact. Mine was the more elusive quarry of modern anthropological discourse: 'culture', meaning, thought. I despaired of hunting it down. Whenever I thought I had it sighted it disappeared, changed shape, or altered direction. So much of the talk within Whalsay is about the complexity of the island's people that it seemed to me absurd to claim any authority for my view, achieved after such a relatively brief period. Moreover the depiction of such complexity in a few thousand words was, as I am still too well aware, far beyond my competence as a writer, and could be achieved only at the cost of gross simplification.

But, eventually, I recognised that if the book was ever to be written it could not be further postponed. First, I felt that I had begun to lose that intuitive ethnographic sense that comes with intensive fieldwork. Secondly, I wanted to amend the impression of Whalsay that I had given in many articles and papers during the preceding years. I have previously spoken too generally, too dogmatically and have failed to temper my remarks with the caution that the more I learn about Whalsay the more I realise how limited is my knowledge of it. That realisation, though, is a kind of knowledge in itself, and was complemented by the reactions of some Whalsay people to what I had already published. These confirmed my earlier suspicion that whilst, of course, they knew much that was not known to me, I was also privy to information which they did not have. It also became clear to me (or is this wishful thought?) that, whilst my version is not privileged, neither is it *less* privileged than any of those current on the island. As I have said, there is orthodoxy of expression, but not of content. So, mindful of my responsibility to be as accurate as possible, I am also relieved of the search for any ultimate truth. I offer my *version* to them. It differs from theirs in two formal respects. I have to make it intelligible to an audience which is not so fortunate as to know Whalsay at first hand. Secondly, I have to attempt to formulate it within the terms of anthropological discourse. I am not a journalist or a novelist. If I have anything to contribute to Whalsay, in insubstantial return for what it has given me, it must be my competence as an anthropologist, such as it is. But I do not claim that my anthropology constitutes a warrant for the truth of anything I say about Whalsay. Nor do I seek in it a licence to make any such claim. If my account is found in Whalsay to be wanting, then my critics there must say of me what my professional colleagues will: that I have not looked properly, have not understood sufficiently, have not written adequately.

Perspectives

The early 1970s were years of economic and structural transformation in Shetland. The earlier history of the islands has been told well and frequently, and does not require reiteration here.[2] When historians turn their attention to the last twenty years, they will show that the turning point in Shetland's fortunes was not marked only by the discovery of oil in the East Shetland basin of the North Sea, but also by the earlier and surprising resurgence of the traditional industries, fishing, crofting and knitwear.

As is well known, Shetland has been significantly influenced genetically, demographically, linguistically and culturally by its Norse period, which began around A.D. 800. But when the islands passed into the ownership of the Scottish Crown in 1469 the pattern was laid for their development over the next 500 years. It was not just the influx of Scots themselves, nor the Scottish dilution of the Norn language (see Barnes, 1984) but, rather, the alienation of lands and imposition of absolutist rule by the Scots lairds, operating under royal patronage. As tended to be the case throughout the Highlands and islands of Scotland, the lairds wielded enormous power within their own estates, indenting labour, clearing habitations, taxing and confiscating produce as they wished. It was a power which depleted the economy, for its profits were frequently invested or expended elsewhere. Moreover, it was sustained only by creating conditions for, or directly enforcing, the export of vast quantities of people (see Hunter, 1976). Between the mid-nineteenth and mid-twentieth centuries the population of Shetland was halved through out-migration.

During this period the economy came to rest almost entirely on fishing. Shetland's waters were among the most prolific in Europe and the North Atlantic. Herring, haddock, whiting, cod, saithe, Atlantic pollock, halibut and ling were all to be found. Fortunes were built out of the herring industry in particular.[3] The abundance of fish made Shetland a target for Dutch, German and Scandinavian fishermen (see Goodlad, 1971). In addition, at various times Shetland boats and men were involved in the Faroese and Icelandic fisheries. Until well after the second world war Shetland men were recruited to serve on Norwegian vessels in the South Georgia whale fishery. But the prosperity of the Shetland fishery was subject to extreme fluctuation. In some years the market was glutted; sometimes the fishery failed completely through the absence of fish. Shetland was always too peripheral, too remote politically and too dependent economically to exercise any control over the market.

During the late eighteenth and nineteenth centuries Whalsaymen were active, if involuntary, participants in the *haaf* fishery, fishing upwards of forty miles from the coast in 30 ft, six-oared open boats, *six'erns*. During the season they lived in spartan stone 'lodges' on Grif Skerry, to the east of the island, their entire working regimen closely superintended by the laird's bailiff and, later, by the merchant's weighmaster and manager. They fished with baited long-lines in a routine of astonishingly skilled seamanship and appallingly arduous labour. Towards the end of the century the British white fishery was being revolutionised by the advent of steam trawlers, a technology with which Shetland generally was quite unable to compete. Shetland's remoteness from mainland markets meant that white fish still had to be salted and dried for export much farther afield at low prices. The white fishery simply failed to develop and, indeed, remained little more than a subsistence activity until well after the second war.

The near cessation of fishing during the first war permitted a substantial replenishment of the herring stocks, and in the years following the herring fishery went through a period of boom. Although its own boats still fished under sail and, therefore, at extreme disadvantage in relation to the steam drifters from the east-coast ports of Scotland and England, Shetland rebuilt a considerable industry, salting, barrelling and exporting herring. Whalsay had an important herring 'station', in which the now prominent Lerwick firm of J. & M. Shearer Ltd originated as coopers and, later, as boat owners. The herring fishing provided a crucial introduction for Whalsay fishermen to independent fishing and ownership. But it was seasonal, ill paid and incapable of generating the capital necessary to build a modern fishing fleet.

Like most Shetland communities, Whalsay suffered terrible losses during the first world war. The viability of the customary domestic economy required large families in order to exploit the multiple sources of subsistence. The depletion of the island's manpower, during and after the war, together with the depression of the early 1930s, caused the local economy to stagnate. Fishing, crofting and the general standard of life lay in a trough. In Shetland as a whole, out-migration increased again. Apart from permanent migrants, many men left the islands to join the merchant service, staying away for years on end (cf. Jamieson, 1949, pp. 147 ff.). Many of these settled around the home port of the line for which they sailed. The problem was essentially one of remoteness. Shetland was far from mainland markets and lacked the capital to contrive an economic means of bridging the distance to export its produce. Its lack of capital also made it unable to compete with the vastly superior catching power of British and foreign fishing fleets which exploited local waters. So far as crofting was concerned, easily cultivable land was in short supply on Whalsay, as also was labour. Cultivation for livestock and human subsistence decreased, and the deteriorating land was turned over increasingly to non-profitable grazing.[4] An injudicious decision excluded Shetland from the Wool Marketing Board so that even the export of the fine Shetland yarn became difficult. Finally, in the mid-1960s, the local herring fleet was dealt a devastating blow by the arrival of the huge Norwegian purse-seining armada which made the Shetland drift-netters, on which hundreds of men depended for seasonal income, completely uncompetitive and was to lead, within a few years, to the decimation of North Sea stocks. The indigenous packing industry disappeared.

Throughout this long period of decline and despair Whalsay suffered a much lower rate of out-migration than was typical of Shetland communities.[5] Indeed, not only was its population retained but it seemed determined to do more than merely subsist. Between the wars Whalsay maintained a small herring fleet, but white fishing was relatively unimportant. After the second war large numbers of young men joined the merchant navy, and many eventually returned to invest their savings in fishing boats. These boats, novel in the history of Shetland fishing, were dual-purpose white-fish seine-netters, for use during the long winter season, which were simply converted to drift-netting for herring during the summer. Their versatility made investment in boats more viable, and paved the way for a substantial expansion of fishing as a full-time occupation.

A parallel development occurred in Burra Isle, which, hitherto, had long been one of Shetland's major fishing centres – certainly of greater significance historically than Whalsay (see Byron, 1986). But, unlike the Burra men, Whalsay fishermen quickly began what has now become their characteristic strategy of continual investment in new boats and gear. In the late 1960s it became clear that the drift-netters could not compete with the new purse-seiners, capable of taking in one good *shot* what might previously have been a season's catch. The first Whalsay purser was built in 1969. By 1974 there were three; two years later there were five. Now, in 1986, there are eight, ranging in size from 80 ft to a massive 187 ft. In addition there are twelve first-class white-fish boats, all but two of them less than twenty years old. The pursers, fishing for herring and mackerel, range as far as Cornwall and the Rockall bank. Even when they fish locally they often sell their catch, according to the state of the markets, in Denmark or mainland Scotland. The first pursers were dual-purpose vessels which could be converted for trawling. The new boats are equipped with bulk tanks, making them less suitable for white fishing. But, like the white-fish seiner-trawlers, they can also engage in the 'industrial fishery' for sand eel and pout, species which are rendered for fish meal.

The new boats have not changed the customary structure of ownership in which all owners, including the skipper, hold equal shares and all are members of the crew. But it has transformed the scale of ownership. Whalsay's first purser, the *Serene*, was built for £80,000. The new boats have all

costs upwards of £1½ million. Crews not regularly double their original
investment by modifying their boats, perhaps by lengthening them, or by
installing shelter decks, new winches, and so forth. When I began fieldwork in
Shetland in 1973 the 'Shetland Fish Gutter', designed by a Scalloway man,
was installed on boats throughout the world. But it was used by hardly any
Shetland boats. I learned later that it was regarded as insufficiently adaptable
to the varied local catch. But I was told at the time by a Burra skipper that
'Shetlan' men are gey cautious aboot yon new technology.' There is no such
reticence in Whalsay today. The capital value of the Whalsay fleet has at least
quadrupled over the last twelve years and must now (1986) be worth between
£25 million and 30 million. To appreciate the enormity of the sum one has to
keep in mind, first, the rapidity with which the fleet has developed[6] and,
second, the size of Whalsay's population: 1,064 in 1983 (Stewart, 1985, p.
117).

This transformation in the island's economy during the recent past has
been matched by change in other aspects of social life. The fish factory,
established in 1970 and run for many years with a small, largely male,
full-time work force, has now expanded to seventy-three full-time and
twenty-one part-time and casual jobs. It provides a vital element in the
foundations of economic life. It has met the aspirations of many local women
to paid employment, and provides a much-needed niche for men who, for
various reasons, have given up fishing. Crofting has become much less
labour-intensive and much more specialised. In 1985 only three crofters still
kept cows, and the demise of *da kye* has decreased the need for substantial
arable crops. It is partly a consequence of the shift to full-time fishing. Only a
tiny proportion of croft land is now under cultivation, mostly for staple
household vegetables. The rest is used for hay and grazing for sheep, animals
which were not commonly farmed in Whalsay before the last war.

With the prosperity which has accrued from fishing, the housing stock has
been transformed. Few houses now contain more than one 'household'.
Frequently a newly married couple will live with the parents of bride or
groom for a year or so while they await the chance to build their own house or
for a council house to become available. They will usually build in close
proximity to their kin, often on the family's croft. But, whilst crofting
townships are aggregates of close kin, the houses themselves reflect a greater
nucleation in the population. Moreover the spread of car ownership to every
family has meant not only that the population is more mobile than it ever was
before, but also that the distinctive townships – of which there are twenty-one
– are becoming conflated. Skaw, in the north-west of the island, is no more
than ten minutes by car from Sandwick, in the south-east. Before the advent
of cars and of the road itself in 1947, the return journey would have been a
day's undertaking.

Mains electricity was installed in 1964, and UHF television reception in

1974. The consequent advent of colour television and the video recorder has substantially inhibited, though not yet eliminated, the widespread casual visiting that marked the shore life of Whalsay people, especially during the winter. Domestic visiting has been further diminished, especially among the younger population, by the opening in 1983 of licensed premises owned and run by the sailing club. Mains water, installed in 1954 and substantially improved in the early 1980s, has revolutionised the domestic and social lives of the women, now liberated by the washing machine and spin dryer from the arduous, but sociable, lochside laundry.

Perhaps most dramatic of all these changes was the introduction of a continuous roll-on-roll-off car-ferry service, linking Whalsay to the Main-land of Shetland. This followed the final demise of the *Earl of Zetland* in 1975. There is now constant movement across Whalsay Sound. Lerwick, previously a special expedition away, is now only an hour distant. It has become practicable for people to commute from their island homes to work on Mainland. Similarly, children can now attend the high school in Lerwick as weekly boarders, without having to reconcile themselves to months on end away from home. Many more children now attend the Lerwick school than was the case ten years ago. Previously the handful of children who went to Lerwick were effectively cut off from island society, and rarely returned home to settle at the end of their school career. Now, returning home, they bring the town's youth culture with them.

This mobility has also made it common for Whalsay families to travel to the mainland of Britain and farther south in Europe for the summer holidays. When I began my fieldwork many Whalsay people had never set foot in Yell or Unst, the most northerly of the substantially populated islands in the archipelago. In a very real sense Whalsay was then the centre of their world. Everywhere beyond its physical boundaries was peripheral. Now the relation has been largely inverted.

These introductory remarks reveal one of the temptations which attend the attempt to write up the results of a long period of observation – the 'then and now' syndrome. The temptation should be resisted, for it is borne of a retrospective view, whereas the observation itself has been continuous. Retrospection implies some kind of disjunction between t_1 and t_2, even if occasioned by the observer's absence from the field.[7] It also lends itself to causal explanation, an arbitrary and, at best, probablistic linking of events separated in time. In the hurly-burly of social life, events are not so neatly ordered. Their causal arrangement is the product of analysis rather than of history itself: it is the observer's deconstruction, and reconstruction, of social process. My aspiration for this book is to avoid intruding such analytic rearrangement on to the record, in so far as that may be possible. I should like to capture for the reader some sense of how events just 'happen', of how the bits and pieces of social life just flow out of each other in a seamless web which makes the retrospective question 'Why?' manifestly inappropriate. In so far as I have indulged in the before-and-after game, and will do so further, it is only to give the reader some inkling of the scale of change which has occurred during the years covered by this study.

I shall not treat the period chronologically. Rather the text will wander back and forth across the years, identifying particular moments and, thus, contextualising people and events historically but in a manner which may flout the discipline of serial form. This is not to make history merely incidental. It is an attempt to replicate the way in which history informs and is recreated by people's experience of the present.

There is, however, one respect in which a retrospective and analytical perspective provides the basis of my principal argument. In this book I draw particular attention to the symbolic dimension of social life in Whalsay. I shall discuss the theoretical aspect of this emphasis shortly. But my focus is not just the product of current anthropological fashion. It has been generated also by the continuing process of change in Whalsay, a process considerably accelerated during the last twenty years by infrastructural improvements, the oil era, and the condition of the fishing industry. Change is, of course, continuous. One may delve into the Shetland literature published at any time during the last 250 years to find authors lamenting, on their own or their informants' behalf, the passing of the old ways. The demise of Norn, under the impact of lowland Scottish, is a matter of particularly frequent and regretful mention.

But recent change has been qualitatively different from that which preceded it, for it has breached the insularity and effectively decreased the remoteness of Shetland in general and of Whalsay in particular. During a recent trip north to Shetland I overheard an elderly man from Burra Isle, in the east of Shetland, telling some English tourists about the construction of the bridges in the early 1970s which link Burra, via Trondra, with Mainland. Burra was previously a day's journey by sea and overland from Lerwick. (See Byron, 1986.) Now the distance has shrunk to a mere fifteen minutes by road. The immediate response of the interested tourist was revealing: 'That must be better for you.' It is easy for the outsider to romanticise the enchantments of remoteness (as will have been evident from my own seduction by the *Earl*). 'Better for you?' Yes, it puts the services and employment opportunities of the town within easy reach. It makes the school and the hospital accessible. It opens up opportunities for novel kinds of economic and leisure activities, for travel and so forth. But it also threatens the community's indigenous structure and the vitality of its culture. How can rural shops and services compete with the lower prices, modern fashions and wider choice in the towns? How can the arduous labour of anchoring the fishing boat in Hamnavoe harbour, then having to row ashore and beach the *foureen*, compete with the convenience of tying up alongside the pier and stepping ashore in Lerwick or

Scalloway? And if the boats are kept in the town harbours, how long can it be before their crews follow? How can the neighbourly yarn round the winter fireside survive the ease of a drive down to the pub – or even of the intrusive television and the seduction of the soap operas? When a basic resource of communality is close personal knowledge, how can it accommodate and monitor the continuous movement of people in and out, over the bridge or by ferry? The cultural integrity of a community does not inhere in its insularity alone. But distance certainly protects its boundaries from incursion. When that distance shrinks, the *structural* bases of the community are attacked and progressively weakened. In order to maintain itself the community must throw up a new line of defence, one which is impervious to the insinuations of infrastructure and the central dissemination of 'culture' and information. I shall argue that the new fortifications are symbolic (with all the fraught anthropological difficulty which that proposition entails) and that they are being continuously built and tended in the course of social life in Whalsay.

Symbolism

Anthropologists have long agreed that there is a character of vagueness about the interpretation of symbols. The very notion of symbolism is itself imprecise. Clearly, we use the word to refer to something more than 'emblem', something a little different from 'sign'. One of the most often quoted, though not brilliantly illuminating, formulations has been that symbols are 'things which stand for other things'. It is in the relationship of 'thing' to 'thing' that the difficulty lies. By and large, anthropologists of symbolism are not very interested in unvarying relations, such as those which link technically a word to an object – say, 'ball' to spherical bouncing object. What causes their ears to prick up is when the symbol (word, or whatever) appears to have a rather more tenuous relationship with a 'thing', or when it appears to do more than merely 'stand for' something else. Turner (e.g. 1967) illustrated two such competences of symbols: their capacity to 'condense' complex statements or sentiments in a shorthand expression; and their ability to stimulate emotion. With earlier anthropologists and psychologists, he thus sees symbols, once projected into cultural discourse, as having a life of their own. In the functionalist tradition, their vitality has usually been related to the expression and enhancement of social sentiments, and subsequent analyses treated symbols *as if* that were what they do.

In a way this was to treat symbols as a discrete class of phenomenon, as if our means of expression could be divided between symbols and other things. Structuralist and semiotic approaches to language and meaning reinforced the view that symbols express in rather different ways from other media. Specifically, they are imprecise, ambiguous and vague, not because people are sloppy in their use but because (*a*) there are some things that can only be expressed in such ways; and (*b*) it is socially expedient to have imprecise means of expression available. There were two major problems which confronted anthropologists in their interpretation of symbols: the first was to establish their meanings; the second was to ask whether one could actually have access to their meanings.

It may look as though these difficulties should have been stated in reverse order. I have given them in the sequence in which they appeared on the agenda of anthropological debate. From Durkheim and Freud, to Sapir, Turner and Lévi-Strauss, the analytical question was how to make sense of symbols: what can they mean? But, more recently, it has been recognised that there is a logically (if not historically) prior problem: much of what symbols 'mean' or express may be beyond or behind consciousness; much of what they 'mean' may not be expressed explicitly at all: it may be secreted away, 'private' (Firth, 1973), 'tacit' (Sperber, 1975), 'implicit' (Douglas, 1975) or 'unconscious' (Needham, 1980), either because these meanings are so inchoate as to be inexpressible, or because their value depends upon their being left unstated.

We have come to think of symbols, therefore, as very amorphous indeed. Their meanings are elusive, and their interpretation is problematic. Moreover, if symbols themselves are the property of the unconscious, *our* assertion of other people's symbols is tantamount to postulating what they do not know themselves: to assert symbolism or symbolic significance is to make a hypothetical claim whose justification can rest not upon scientific demonstration but, rather, upon plausible interpretation.

The meanings of symbols – of the ideas behind the words – is not merely a problem of anthropological analysis. It is a problem which confronts everybody in the course of everyday social life. We are all engaged in a continuous struggle to understand the meaning of other people's behaviour. Sometimes we may not struggle very valiantly but, instead, presume that the other person means what we would have meant if we ourselves had behaved in similar fashion. Sometimes, perhaps, we struggle too hard, and end up by mystifying other people's behaviour, or by imputing to it meaning and significance which were not intended. In everyday life meaning is a hit-and-miss affair. When we speak, or otherwise 'present' ourselves, we strive to effect the greatest possible congruence between the meaning we intend and the meaning received by our audience. Recent political ethnography has closely examined the use of codes (Bloch, 1975), rhetoric (Paine, 1981), passion (Bailey, 1983) and other techniques (e.g. Atkinson, 1984) with this kind of calculation in mind. More generally, the work of Erving Goffman alerted us to the ubiquity of such tactical devices in social behaviour.

So we grapple with the problem of the relations between meaning intended and meaning conveyed. Part of the intractability of this problem is due to, and is exacerbated by, the ambiguity and imprecision of symbols, for they also mask the degree to which speaker and audience may differ in their interpretation of the 'same' words. This is because, whilst the *form* of symbols may be common to those who bear the same culture, the *meanings* of the symbols, their contents, may differ. The crucifix, the clenched fist, the word 'love', the handshake, are all symbolic forms which we regard as commonplace and intelligible. But they do not carry their meanings inherently: in using them we impute meaning to them. Because of their very commonness we can use them competently with other people, exchange them – for that is what communication is – and yet mean different things by them, often being unaware of such differences. (See Rapport, 1986; also Stromberg, 1986).

This problem is not peculiar to industrialised societies, in which the explicit forms of symbolic expression are attenuated, and in which the same 'language' must serve 'instrumental' and 'symbolic' purposes simultaneously. The anthropological literature is replete with accounts of the most marvellously complex and mysterious symbolism, sometimes in myth or ritual or visual form, of which awesomely lucid explanations and interpretations are offered. But so often they are offered as if their compelling plausibility is a guarantee of their orthodoxy. The two should not be mistaken. All too often these accounts originate with an indigenous expert who, by virtue of his very expertise, is unusual. Or, of course, as in structuralist expositions, they may be the product of the anthropologist's own ingenuity. In neither case should they be regarded as having any universality within the culture. In our own experience we would not confuse the doctrinal sophistication of the theologian with our own religious sentiments, any more than we would mistake the intricacies of musicological analysis for our enjoyment of a symphonic performance. Similarly, the arcane devices of Buddhist cults, of Nilotic sacrifices, or of the Kwakiutl cannibal dance mean different things to their participants, and among their participants, than they do to their official or authoritative spokespersons. People may enjoy the dance, thrill to the drumbeat, laugh at the grotesque decoration. Whatever their doctrinal significance it is these things which constitute meaning in the minds of the participants. Just as two communicants can share liturgy but differ in their religious experience, just as neighbours in the conference hall can listen to the same speech and understand it differently, so people seemingly habituated to an endless cycle of the most esoteric symbolism can experience it with such diversity that the imputation of generalised meaning to the symbolism becomes futile, an academic travesty of reality.

This really seems to be the essence of the phenomena which we have categorised as symbolic: that we hold their forms in common, we *communi*cate with them; but we also invest them to some extent with meaning, rather than have their meanings imposed upon us like Durkheimian social facts. This argument does not offend Wittgenstein's denial of the possibility of a private language. It suggests only that it is the symbolic *form* which has currency, and not its contents. It is this very pliability of symbolic form which makes it so useful, so effective a means of marking boundary and identity.

Symbolic boundaries and the community[8]

It would be both tedious and unnecessary to rehearse here the old debates about the definition of 'community'. The word is no more capable of general, precise and theoretically neutral definition than are any of the terms imported from ordinary language into the discourse of social science (cf. Gusfield, 1975). Suffice it to say that my use of the word in this book seems to me consonant with the ways in which Whalsay people employ it: first, to refer to the people residing within the place; and, second, to express a relational concept. This latter point needs only a little elaboration. 'Community' suggests that its putative members have something in common with each other which distinguishes them in a significant manner from the members of other groups. The term thus seems to imply simultaneously both similarity and difference; hence its relational character: it suggests the opposition of the community to others or to other social entities. Frequently the very salience of the word lies in its use by people to express just such a distinction. In a sense, therefore, we might see the essential meanings of the community – those propagated as a collective rhetoric, and those imputed to the collectivity by individuals through the medium of their idiosyncratic experience – as invested in its *boundaries*, those ideas which discriminate the community from other places and groups. It is in precisely this sense that I suggested above that boundaries might be regarded as symbolic entities. Like other symbols, they can be thought of as common in *form* to their members, who can invest them with their own pertinent meanings.

The boundary is thus more complex than its physical, legal or administrative bases; more complex than the ethnic, racial, religious or linguistic differences which it may enclose. Many of the elements which constitute the boundary may not be objectively apparent at all but, rather, exist in the minds of their beholders. Like other symbols, the boundary does not entail given meanings. Rather, it provides people with forms which they may then invest with meaning. But to say that community boundaries are often symbolic in character is not only to suggest that they imply different meanings for different people. It also suggests that boundaries perceived by some may be utterly imperceptible to others.

When, as outsiders, we encounter a community about which we know little, we are bound to perceive it and make sense of it in general, perhaps stereotypical, terms. We have not the information on which to base more subtle discriminations. We can begin to discern internal variations only as we grow increasingly familiar with the community. Frequently outsiders never bother to qualify the generalisation: they may be uninterested in so doing; they may judge them to be inexpedient, or they may just find it too difficult. People who regard themselves as peripheral with respect to those who have power frequently feel that they are misunderstood, their needs, views and aspirations stated so generally as to be grossly innaccurate. The subtle differences which distinguish them from others are often more important to them than their similarities. Writing about villages in the Andalusian sierra, Pitt-Rivers (1971) noted that they were often paired by outsiders in terms of geographical and social proximity. Yet villagers reserved their greatest loathing and contempt for those in their 'pair' village. Earlier, Evans-Pritchard (1940) had described a similar intensity of feeling within the segmentary structure of Nuer society.

Such stereotyping is not borne only out of animus and adversity. Often in political interaction the detailed representation of a community would be too difficult to convey, too difficult to comprehend and too difficult to satisfy. In consequence the representation is made in terms of a lowest common denominator. Charles Tilly, describing the Vendée counter-revolution, observed that the counter-revolutionaries were more notable for their internal disparities than their similarities. How, then, could they be mobilised behind a common campaign? Tilly (1963, 1964) presents the Vendée as the paradigm case of the complex social movement for which the leaders' rhetoric and the campaign platform provide the necessary hooks on which to hang together a wide variety of hats. The rhetoric, though it may advocate specific demands, is formulated in terms sufficiently general that all the diverse constituencies of the movement can identify with it. Similarly, a community may gather behind its collective, overgeneralised rhetoric for the purposes of communicating with some extraneous party. It does not signify its homogeneity – although the other party may well suppose, or pretend, that it does. Theoretically, it indicates that communication between levels of society is invariably simplified in content; while communication within a given level or entity is relatively complicated. Empirically, it suggests that members can find at least a minimal degree of affinity with the collective statement.

Members of a community thus orient to its symbolic boundaries in two distinct ways. First, like participants in great social movements, they gather behind a highly generalised statement of the community's character, in order to advocate the distinctive interests of the community or to promulgate its collective identity. This does not necessarily entail their subordination by a collective ideology because, secondly, in their 'private', internal discourse they render this generalised statement meaningful in terms of their particular interests, experience and identities. Their own interests are refracted through the collective statement of identity. Whalsay people all use the idiomatic shorthand of 'being Whalsa''; '*wis*' (us); 'here . . .'; 'the way *we* do things. . . .'

Their shared use of these forms absolves them from the need to explain themselves to each other – and leaves them free to attach their own meanings to them.

Moreover the symbolic character of the boundary – its location in the mind – often accounts for its invisibility to outsiders. It may be a useful invisibility, for if outsiders are unaware of it they cannot attack or subvert it. Remote communities, whether their remoteness is geographical, cultural, or both – have a keen sense of their own anomalousness. Their members see themselves as marginal, as powerless to alter the course of events, vulnerable to all the pressures exerted from the centre: pressure to think like those at the centre, to consume like them, to live like them. They see their distinctive ways of life being steadily eroded by the irresistible force of modernity. The insularity is bridged; the language is suppressed (see, e.g., Mewett, 1982a; Dorian, 1981); the economy stagnates; the culture atrophies. Superficially the remote periphery begins to take on the appearance of metropolitan society. It responds to the latest fashions, changes its diet, travels abroad, gets absorbed in the latest soap operas. Yet, beneath the surface, it harbours a powerful sense of self, an almost ironic view of these alien styles which it appears to embrace but which, in reality, it transforms by assimilation to that sense of self. The sense people have of 'being Whalsa' ' and, thereby, different may have changed greatly from the sense which their grandparents had, but is no less authentic. It is just that sense which constitutes the boundary, which is expressed symbolically in the ideas behind the words and actions – perhaps, sometimes, beyond consciousness – and which, in its mental invisibility, is impervious to the burgeoning influences of the 'mass' society.

Symbols do not carry meaning inherently. They give us the capacity to make meaning. The same is true of symbolic boundaries. It has long been noted that those items which are hardest to categorise are often hedged around by the most ambiguous symbolism (e.g. Leach, 1964; Tambiah, 1969). In such cases the content of the categories may be so unclear that they exist largely, or even only, in terms of their symbolic boundaries. Such categories as justice, goodness, duty, and so forth, are impossible to spell out with precision. But their range and diversity of meanings can be glossed over in a commonly accepted symbol, precisely because it allows its adherents to invest it with their own meanings. The same is true of the community: it is just such a boundary-expressing symbol. It is held in common by its members, but its meaning varies with its members' unique orientations to it. In the face of this variability of meaning the consciousness of community has to be kept alive by manipulation of its symbols. The reality and efficacy of the community's boundary – and, therefore, of the community itself – depend upon its symbolic construction and embellishment.

The ideas behind the words[9]

But what of the philosophical objections raised earlier? If people are unconscious of their own symbols, or are unwitting in their use of them, how can the anthropologist justify asserting their existence? I think the answer must be that we are reluctant to treat events simply as events in themselves and as signifying nothing beyond themselves. This reluctance does not merely beg the question. Rather, it is rooted in the basic conviction that cultures require more for their sustenance than rules of behaviour. They also need the inexpressible which lies beyond the empirical and the concrete: the ideas or meanings behind the words – the area we conjure through our category of the symbolic. In a brilliantly iconoclastic discussion Sperber argues against the view that symbolic thought is an evolutionary precursor of, or a lesser intellectual form than, 'rational thought'. He maintains the opposite: that symbolic thought is built upon rational or 'directed' thinking: 'Symbolic interpretation does not consist of recalling or reconstructing a strong or weak connection between a symbol and a sense; it is rather a particularly creative form of problem solving' (1980, p. 43). In Sperber's view the symbolic element copes with problems raised by, but not resolvable by, the rational device. In the particular case of Whalsay such a problem might be the difficulty of preserving a sense of distinctiveness, of collective self, in the face of its subversion by modernity. Why should a community need to resolve the problem? The answer is twofold. The first, theoretical, answer is 'the compulsion of identity'. As individuals we recognise our sense of identity as the premise, the *sine qua non*, of all social interaction, and its loss as pathological. Why should not the same be true for *groups* of individuals also, especially since their individual constituents so obviously relate their own sense of their selves in some way to the collective sense? The second, empirical, answer is that such a sense of self is the most crucial and most effective defence against disintegration. Remote communities face a perennial threat of depopulation. Indeed, we saw earlier the extent to which Shetland was decimated by its long history of out-migration. In the late twentieth century islanders recognise that their continued residence in Whalsay involves the acceptance of limited occupational opportunities for themselves and their children, which can be exceeded only by emigration; limited recreational facilities; a substantially higher cost of living than on the mainland of Britain;[10] a geographical remoteness which prejudices their investment opportunities; and, above all, the strain of continuous scrutiny of and by neighbours which characterises life in the small, intimate community. When we first went to live in Whalsay we were continually asked whether we did not find it 'too quiet'. It was not just the lack of noise, nor the putatively slow pace of life, to which reference was being made. It was the sheer effort of living in a remote area where services were sparse, the climate so severe as to dominate the conduct of life, and whose insularity precluded any escape from the tension or *ennui* of the same few faces, the inescapable obligations, the grind of social life and of the calendar. It was as if islanders were really questioning the reasons for their own continued commitment to life in Whalsay, an introspective query which may have been made inevitable by the influx of outside people and influences in the hectic development of North Sea oil-related facilities (see Cohen, 1978b).

Such cultural accounting was not peculiar to Whalsay. It can be seen in almost every assertion of localism, ethnicity and sectional interest which has coloured politics during the last twenty years. Describing the unprecedented resistance by the Norwegian Saami to the Norwegian government's plans for a hydro-electric scheme on the Alta river, Robert Paine wrote that they had reached their culture's 'to be or not to be', a question he compares to 'asking about the importance of a right arm to its left – a question one really asks after the left has been amputated' (1982, pp. 90, 71).

Although perhaps not so diminished in number, nor so despised by the host society as the Saami, many peripheral communities, Whalsay certainly among them, perceive this crunch question in almost every major crisis. This is not because of any inclination to over-dramatise, nor because of an inherent fatalism, but because the security and continuity of their lives is felt to be so very tenuous. Government Ministers and bureaucrats, who tend to approach international negotiations as a diverting, but not terribly important, game, seem to be continually bemused by the passionate commitment which Shetland fishermen bring to their lobbying whenever the details of the EEC Common Fisheries Policy are on the table in Brussels. The cataclysm awaits the unwary, and is kept at bay only by constant vigilance.

A crucial component of such vigilance is the maintenance and continual reconstruction of a sense of self. It is this sense – intangible, tacit – which renders so deceptive the apparent similarity to some idealised metropolitan norm of the members of bounded communities. Despite superficial appearances, such people must be acknowledged as occupying their own worlds of meaning – their own cultures. As these cultures lose the protection of structural boundaries and become more and more constructs of the mind, so they become more difficult for the anthropologist to document. They have to be the subject of ethnographic claim rather than of scientific demonstration. They are recordable by intuition rather than by direct observation or statistic, and must be thought of as the ideas behind the words rather than the words themselves. It is precisely these ideas, the *intentionality* of meaning, which sustains a culture, and in these tortuous depths that we locate symbolism.

Let us think of these behind-the-scenes sentiments as the realm of meta-meaning. It is that realm of consciousness which we occupy when we are aware of some 'added value' in our behaviour: when we know that there is something more to what we are saying or doing than there appears to be.

Durkheim supposed that, if common structures of behaviour and categories of knowledge were imposed upon individuals with sufficient insistence, they would think and behave in similar ways. He was wrong, for, as Malinowski realised, *social* forms leave room for individual (or 'psychological') constructions (Malinowski, 1948). Communities within great centralised metropolitan societies can thus live with the *forms* engendered by these societies whilst finding their own distinctive and idiosyncratic ways through them – paths through which they preserve their distinctiveness. Whilst these forms, categories and constraints may be shared, the meanings which people find in them – their contents – are not. Moreover, they are variable not only as between groups and communities, but also within them. The forms may 'signify', but much of what they signify is a matter of the individual's construction. Just as it is through such creativity that individuals preserve a sense of self (cf. Abner Cohen, 1977, p. 123), so also it is the means whereby *communities* contrive and preserve a sense of collective self as a counterpunch to the subversion or penetration of their structural boundaries which had previously held at bay external cultural influences.

So this book is about an anthropologist's claim that behind much of the ordinary activity of Whalsay people there is a realm of meta-meaning whose components will be called, for want of a better word, 'symbolic'. The symbolism refracts Whalsay's condition: its peripherality; its remoteness; its recent transformation; its need continually to reconstitute its sense of collective self. This symbolically constituted collective self presents a fairly undifferentiated, 'typical' image to the outside world. But in reality it is composed of the highly diverse, and disparate, experiences, aspirations and needs of Whalsay people and their forebears. The image they have of themselves is one of great complexity, of an immense variety of character, skill, humour and propensity; of rich history, of acutely felt difference.

This theme will be illustrated through ethnographic sketches of social life, of people and events, which will be presented as details from a larger canvas. Anthropologists may recognise in this programme the influence of the 'text–context' paradigm, employed and advocated by Geertz and others of the 'interpretivist' school. I happily acknowledge this influence, whilst also accepting the essentially contingent and hypothetical nature of the model. This acceptance does not extend to the contention that the postulation of context, because it is always *claim* and is inherently undemonstrable, amounts to a confidence trick (Hobart, 1985). Symbols, the ideas behind the words, are accessible to us only through text, and are interpretable by us only through their contextualisation (cf. Rainbow and Sullivan, 1979, pp. 12–13). But let us conclude this preview by recalling to mind its early caution: what passes here as context should not be regarded as anything more than 'version'. It has no essential truth, but is just a way of looking.

Programme

The structure of this book resembles the formulation of an anthropologist's perspective on the society he or she studies, moving from naive observation, through increasing contextualisation, to the endlessly ramifying connections among ethnographic data. At the outset of fieldwork the things we observe appear to be simple: isolated individuals, discrete events. As our familiarity with the culture deepens, so we become increasingly adept at connecting these phenomena, until we have a picture which is so complex that, in order to convey any sense of it to others, we have to risk its distortion by extricating bits of it from their context. Here I begin in chapter two by presenting a set of sketches each of which introduces some of the issues which I see as fundamental to people's sense of belonging to Whalsay, the sense which they refer to as 'being Whalsa''. I follow each of these sketches with suggestions about the significance of their issues for the general conduct of social life in Whalsay.

In chapter three I attempt to give this elementary contextualisation fuller theoretical and ethnographic bases. The discussion focuses on the ways in which people oscillate between association with the community as a whole and with its various parts: the former producing relatively simple forms; the latter, forms which are much more complex. The issues encountered earlier are shown to be related to each other in the ways in which people manage these internal and external boundaries, and in the conceptual models they have of each.

As has already been suggested, the historical context of the discussion is a period of intensive change in the circumstances of Whalsay society. Chapters four and five examine in detail some of the dimensions of this change, attempting to show how people locate the community in 'tradition', and how their reconstruction of this tradition, and their perceptions of the present, bear upon each other. In this way I hope to convey some impression of how this intensive change is managed by being continuously subjected to people's sense of cultural stability. I try to show how this sense is itself maintained by people's use of the Whalsa' themes and models identified earlier, to process and mediate their interpretations of people and events and, thereby, to buttress the local boundary.

Thus my ambitious claim is that in the progression from chapter two to chapter five the reader is moved from the outsider's naivety to an interpretation which more closely approximates to that of Whalsay people themselves. This progression is tested in chapter six, in which the reader is invited to apply the full battery of interpretive themes elaborated in the preceding chapters to a final selection of ethnographic sketches. These themes are then brought together in a brief conclusion to the descriptive part of the book.

Finally, in chapter seven I raise some points about the nature of this study as an anthropological exercise, and speculate on its more general applicability.

Notes

1   A noted local student of Shetland history and tradition attributes this orientation to the past to the circumstances of life in the early nineteenth century: '. . . the feeling of continuity produced by folk memory, reinforced by the fact that often three generations lived together under one roof: the awareness of the world of love and legend which invested the daily round with significance.' (Graham, 1983, p. 230.)

2   The published historiography of Shetland is extensive and easily accessible through the Shetland collection in the county library. The Shetland Islands Council also maintains a Shetland Archive, founded on the transfer of local documents from the Scottish Record Office. Recent unpublished historical work of particular interest includes B. Cohen (1983), Smith (1972) and Wills (1975).

3   An impression of the scale of the herring industry may be gauged from an anonymous report written a little earlier in the century: 'The herring fishing, last season employed in Shetland about *five hundred boats*, manned by *two thousand five hundred men and boys*, one hundred and thirty coopers, and about one thousand six hundred old men, women, and boys, were also employed in cleaning and packing the herrings' (anon., 1834, p. 11; italics in original). By contrast, at the peak of the herring fishery in 1905, a million barrels were cured and 20,000 men on 1,700 boats were involved. (Donaldson, 1983, p. 16.)

4   As early as the late eighteenth century Whalsay folk were reported as reluctant cultivators. The account for the parish of Nesting, which included Whalsay, stated, 'The people direct their sole attention to the fishing, and consider the cultivation of the lands as only a secondary object.' (*Statistical Account*, 1978, p. 450.)

5   See, e.g., *Census 1971 (Scotland): County Report (Zetland)*: table 5c, p. 6; *Shetland in Statistics*, 9 (1980), p. 27.

6   In 1961 the County Development Officer valued the Whalsay fleet at £250,000. (R. J. Storey, personal communication.)

7   See, for example, the exemplars of so-called 'long-term' fieldwork in Foster *et al.* (1979).

8   Parts of this discussion previously appeared in Cohen (1985a).

9   Parts of this section draw on Cohen (1986).

10   In 1986 the Rural Scotland Price Survey, commissioned by the Highlands and Islands Development Board, showed retail prices in rural Shetland to be between 14% and 24% higher than those obtaining in Aberdeen. (*Shetland Times*, 28th February 1986.)

Chapter 2

Lives from a scene: sketches of Whalsay

T., and the Earl's last voyage

Until February 1976, Whalsay's lifeline to the rest of the world was the MV *Earl of Zetland*, a diesel-engined ship of 548 tons, built in 1939 (see Robson, 1982, p. 190). She would leave Lerwick at 8 a.m. on Monday, Wednesday and Friday, calling at Whalsay on her journey north to Yell and Unst. On Wednesdays she made the complete round trip. On the other two days she would also call at Fetlar and the Out Skerries, and would berth in Unst overnight before sailing for Lerwick. The *Earl* carried the mail, passengers and virtually all supplies to the island, from cases of jam to building materials. She brought in animal feedstuffs and took out livestock. Until the opening of a new pier in 1961 the *Earl* had to discharge her passengers and cargo for Whalsay into a flit-boat, jointly owned by local shopkeepers, in an arduous and time-consuming exercise that was frequently aborted by severe weather. Even after the pier was opened, a severe gale would sometimes prevent her from docking. But, these occasions apart, she provided a link without which the island's isolation would have been even more critical.

Despite this, islanders' attitudes to the *Earl* were ambivalent: a strong sense of loathing, tempered less by affection than by resignation. Women complained that her diesel fumes and rolling motion made them seasick. There were frequent complaints about damaged cargo due to dampness, rodent infestation and poor handling, and allegedly exorbitant freight charges were attributed largely to the Lerwick dockers' restrictive practices. Anything that threatened the tenuous viability of continued life on the island gave understandable grounds for anger, and the freight charges considerably increased the cost of goods – already far higher than those obtaining in mainland Britain. It was commonly supposed that prices in Whalsay were substantially higher than on the Mainland of Shetland which were themselves some 10% higher than in Aberdeen.[1] The *Earl*, mediating between Whalsay and the outside world, might well be seen as a focus of the fearful resentment islanders had of their dependence upon external support. Superintending their relations with this unpopular medium was T., the steamer's agent.

The MV *Earl of Zetland* leaves Whalsay for the last time

Perhaps it is instructive that T. is an outsider in origin, a Fife man who, after war service in Whalsay in the radar camp, married into a local family and has since lived in Whalsay with only a brief interruption immediately after the war. A man of warmth and kindliness, he is regarded with the greatest affection. His small stature and broad Fife accent (eccentrically mixed with Whalsa'), his modesty, lack of pretension and widely recognised proclivity for unremitting hard work have all made him a 'character', more accepted in Whalsay society than almost any other outsider. As steamer's agent it was his unhappy lot to collect the hated freight charges, a task he undertook with tact and with an obvious sympathy for the islanders' attitudes to the *Earl*.

Whatever the weather, if the *Earl* was due, T. would be there, ready to tie up the boat, to store goods, to superintend the movement of cargo on the pier, to carry sacks, to load vans, generally to ease the fraught relationship of steamer and client with an energy and helpfulness beyond the call of duty. The job was burdensome, and he looked forward to the *Earl*'s demise without apparent regret. Besides his job with the North of Scotland Orkney & Shetland Shipping Company, T. was also the local water engineer, chief of the local volunteer fire brigade and an active crofter. Always bedecked in peaked cap, frequently muffled in green oilskins – 'Whalsay tartan', he called them – T. was a lynchpin in Whalsay's relations with the outside.

On the occasion of the *Earl*'s last visit to Whalsay before her replacement by the new roll-on–roll-off car ferry, one might have expected to find T. a little regretful. In all its other ports of call the *Earl* had been feted, her departure marked with appropriate ceremony and, in Lerwick, serenaded by the brass band. She arrived for the last time on 21st February 1975, carrying many of her retired crew, including ex-skippers, and a company which had clearly been celebrating for some considerable time. But her visit to Symbister harbour must have been distinctly anticlimactic, for she was greeted with a display of profound indifference. Three or four people had come down to the pier to photograph the occasion, and only a handful of elderly islanders, among them a couple taken down by my wife and myself, seemed at all moved. The ship was full, the convivial atmosphere on board sustained by whisky and music. The *Earl* stayed a little longer than usual to allow a proper opportunity for bottles and glasses to circulate.

T., an habitual teetotaller, stoutly resisted all urging to imbibe. Such regret as her crew had about the *Earl*'s last voyage clearly owed more to their need to bid T. goodbye than to their imminent estrangement from Whalsay. He had helped them in innumerable ways, had given them hospitality, and had coped uncomplainingly with their own tantrums. But he was glad to see them go. As the *Earl* pulled away from the pier and turned southwards she saluted Whalsay and him with a series of long blasts on her siren and foghorns. T. stood on the pier's edge, hand raised in farewell – and muttered, 'Good riddance,' a sentiment echoed by others around.

Whalsay is an island. To the west, a mile and a half of water separate the community from the Mainland of Shetland. To the east across some 200 miles of the North Sea lies the Norwegian coast. These simple geographical facts have complex cultural ramifications. The island's boundaries are secured, on the one hand, by the sea; but, on the other, by a densely knit web of kinship and a powerful sense of historically founded discreteness. Its insular history has placed the community at the very centre of Whalsay people's conscious-ness. Any breach of its boundaries threatens serious disorientation, a threat which islanders attempted to neutralise and defuse by keeping the breach under what they felt to be, their own control.

This does not signify parochialism so much as a deeply ingrained view of the outside world as the source of unpropitious influences. The larger world was not seen as inherently malevolent but as ignorant of the circumstances of life in Whalsay – for which it could be excused if it did not interfere continuously and complicate those circumstances to the extent of appearing to subvert islanders' best efforts to cope with them. The line of external domination runs through Scottish landlordism to nineteenth-century mer-cantilism and on into the political and bureaucratic regimes of the present day.

Not *everything* which comes across the boundary is negative: but most negatively regarded things *do* originate elsewhere. Certainly Whalsay beliefs and practices are positively valued relative to those of the outside. But the comparison is qualified and the discrimination may be illustrated by the differing attitudes people had to the steamer and to her local agent as personifications of the outside. In a sense T. and the *Earl* are analogues of each other, outsiders who, in their different ways, implied the permeability of the boundary. But T. was the object of esteem and the recipient of affection; the *Earl*, of loathing. Of course, it could be argued that the comparison is improper: it would be quite reasonable to expect that different judgements should be applied to the *Earl* — a thing — and to a person. But the *Earl* betokened people — shipping company executives, seamen, dockers — all of whom were outsiders. Moreover, other outside people, especially if they are not Shetlanders, *do* tend to be regarded with as little sympathy as was the *Earl*. That T. is not so regarded was obviously due in some measure to his unique personality. But it also requires the observer to qualify his remarks about the relationship between Whalsay and the symbolic 'otherness' of the world beyond its boundaries, and this may be accomplished by pursuing the comparison a little further.

There was a clear difference between the orientation of each to Whalsay's boundary. The *Earl* was manifestly 'outside'. She could not penetrate the geographical bounds of the island. The pier, extending like a limb from the western point of Symbister Bay, figuratively kept her at arm's length. Symbolically her connections with the island were tenuous. She was halted physically at the boundary, which was manned by islanders themselves, for it was they who hitched and unhitched her fore and aft ropes to the pier's bollards. The arrival and departure (boundary transactions) of her passengers were easily monitored, for they (and outsiders generally) had no other avenue to and from Whalsay than the *Earl*'s gangway. There were no *social* grounds for identification with the ship, for there were no Whalsaymen among her crew. Indeed, the seamanship of her skippers was frequently contrasted unfavourably with that of local men. As suggested earlier, she was an emblem of the island's resented dependence on the outside world, and thus of the loss of self-sufficiency. But the attitude of Whalsay to the outside was certainly not that of a supplicant and dependent client to a demeaning patron. For it was the outside, *da sooth*, which was denigrated for its incompetence, its false values, its arrogance (see Cohen, 1978b). The ship thus betokened not merely dependence, but dependence upon an inferior. Moreover, salt was rubbed into the wounds of this humiliation by the seemingly careless manner in which cargo was shipped; by its unpunctuality, which frequently left people waiting on the pier in miserable weather, which delayed the mail, and which exacerbated the crush in the shops that always followed the *Earl*'s arrival as people rushed for the scarce fresh fruit and vegetables, meat, bread, milk and the previous week's newspapers. The ferry would be an altogether different prospect. It would be manned by a Whalsay crew, would be based in Symbister (in an *inner* sanctum of the harbour) and, running in each direction every two hours throughout the day, would suit the convenience of the islanders rather than of the Lerwick dockers or the shipping company. The *Earl*, by contrast, was spatially and conceptually 'outside'.

T. was not so. He had penetrated the boundary, not just by his mere presence (for, after all, he, like many others, had been stationed on the island during much of the war) but by anchoring himself socially through marriage. In due course these roots would be deepened still further by the marriage of his sons into local families. His grandchildren are the second generation bearing his name to have been born in the island. His commitment to Whalsay was proved in the most valued way of all, by the reproduction of her population.

It is just possible to read some consequences of T.'s outsiderhood into his working career in Whalsay. Lacking fishing 'blood', he might have had difficulty in securing a good berth, even if he had aspired to one. He took such jobs as were available, some of which might be regarded as socially exposed and, therefore, as entailing certain risks. For example, he *could* have been a focus of islanders' resentment about the inadequacies of the *Earl*'s service. In the minds of some islanders he might conceivably have been held responsible in some way for the flawed water system installed in 1954 and only brought up to standard during the 1980s. The supply was frequently discoloured, was believed by some to harbour malign bacteria, and in summer was often meagre. The faults lay, of course, in the design of the system rather than in T.'s management of it. Nevertheless, many a tale of woe was communicated over his telephone. Should a tractor fracture the main, T. would be summoned to witness a householder's distress. In the even unhappier event of a fire, he was charged with the hopeless task of coping with the pathetically inadequate fire-fighting equipment made available by the Northern Joint Fire Brigade.

These are speculations, of course. However, it may not be mere coincidence that T. held several of these novel posts of responsibility. They differ from the political roles observed in other rural communities to have been thrust at outsiders (e.g. Frankenberg, 1957, especially pp. 98, 131; also Cohen, 1975, pp. 85 ff.). Nevertheless, their performance could have been considerably complicated by the kinds of social tie from which T. was free by virtue of his outsiderhood, and the exposure which they entail is one which Whalsay people would have been inclined to avoid.

It should not be supposed that T.'s occupational career can be attributed in any way to ill will on the part of Whalsay people. That would be a gross misreading. Rather, an established niche in the kinship system is the sole means of cognitively placing people in the scheme of things. Without it, one has to contrive identity, status and position for oneself, albeit with the support and goodwill of islanders. I would suggest that T. could not have achieved more: the measure of his success, and of the esteem in which he is held, is his apparently complete integration into the community.

As a minimal condition of acceptance into Whalsay society the outsider must make Whalsay itself the centre of his or her existence. As recently as our arrival in 1973, people's experience of other places aroused only limited interest: it was experience which might be added to their public personae, rather than treated as interesting in itself. Early in our stay we concluded that people's enquiries about our lives elsewhere were principally expressions of politeness. If one responded with any alacrity, eyes quickly glazed, attention wandered and the subject was changed. But I hasten to stress again that this response did not indicate our audience's parochialism. Rather, it demonstrated our impoliteness in responding to their courtesy, for we were expatiating on experience which they could not share; to respond in that way was to distance oneself when the enquiry had been an invitation to enter their discourse. T. has clearly committed himself utterly to Whalsay. He made only infrequent visits to his native Fife. Instead, his relatives would visit him in Whalsay, and he took a manifest delight in introducing them into Whalsay society and in observing their enjoyment of it. His voluntary submission to the locality neutralised his outsiderhood, in so far as that is possible.

The outside world, amorphous entity though it may be, is the ever-threatening presence in Whalsay's life. In the past, even as recently as the *Earl*'s demise, it was held at bay by a subtle inversion. The powerful centre was treated as inferior in terms of local values and as peripheral to local interests. The relationship could be managed in this way provided that Whalsay could regard itself as controlling transactions across the boundary. That is why the *Earl* was unlamented, for it was an instance of their lack of control. It explains also the reserved attitude they might have to outsiders who wished to carry the outside into their own local world.

A Whalsay event: the anglers' annual general meeting

A cold February night in 1975, and eleven of us are seated on a bench in front of the peat stove in the ante-room of the Isbister Public Hall. The occasion is the annual general meeting of the Whalsay Angling Club. The club has brought the exclusive rights to fishing in all the island's lochs from the Symbister estate.[2] It charges a small annual fee for membership. It restocks the lochs, sometimes buying in fry from Orkney, maintains the spawning burns, and keeps the main fishing sites in good repair. More recently (1984) it has purchased a fibreglass dinghy for use on Huxter Loch, the largest expanse of water, and has built a boathouse for it. It organises competitions, and arranges reciprocal visits with clubs elsewhere in Shetland.

For twenty minutes the company sits chatting. No one seems to want to take the initiative in calling the meeting to order and getting the business under way. Eventually J.–J., the secretary-treasurer, asks, 'Now, boys. How do we proceed? What order do we do things?' He is advised by J., his cousin, a stalwart of many such committees, local crofters' Assessor, and voluntary scribe on all manner of affairs involving relations with the 'outside'. J. says quietly, 'Well, first you read the minutes; then you elect a committee; then you talk about any business – and that's it!' In fact J. himself begins by distributing the prizes for the previous season. Tammie's second son has won the Hill Cup for the largest basket of fish caught in one day. Gibbie has won the prize for the opening catch of the season. He says, 'Boys, it must be a mistake!' Everyone laughs. Gibbie, a man in his early sixties, is nearly blind following an accident in his youth and subsequent glaucoma. Despite his handicap, he was a marvellously skilled line fisherman, handling fathoms and fathoms of baited hooks with uncanny certainty, a dexterity he still brings to the *eela* fishing in the summer, to his fly fishing, and to his household joinery. J.W. asks him, 'Does dü tink da flee [the fly] mad' a mistake, Gibbie?' More laughter. 'Na. Da fish must hae tocht it wis anidder body's line!'

J.–J. then reads the minutes. When he reaches the item dealing with the negotiations J. has conducted with the Water Board on the club's behalf concerning compensation for damage inadvertently caused to the club's boat by the Board's workmen, he expresses thanks to J. for everything he does for the club. 'An' I hope aabody'll endorse that.' J. looks away during the murmurs of assent with evident discomfiture. He conducts all the club's negotiations – for compensation, for the purchase of rights from the estate; for restocking; for the reciprocal visits, and so forth.

The committee is re-elected with just once change – the competitions secretaryship. The incumbent has written to ask that he be excluded, as 'I've been out of work for a year, boys, and now I'm trying to get on my feet again.' He has been on a retraining programme and now works in Lerwick. There is anecdotal affirmation from various members about how well he is doing now, and many expressions of goodwill are to be heard.

We all pay to the treasurer our subscriptions for the new season. J. then rises, takes from his pocket a tumbler and a bottle of whisky, and offers the company a drink in the conventional manner. The tumbler is filled to the brim and offered to each person in turn. After each has taken a sip it is refilled. The donor is the last to drink, after quietly wishing the company 'Guid health' or 'Guid luck,' and returns the whisky remaining in the glass to the bottle. Everybody present except one embarrassed man has a bottle and, as is the custom, each offers his whisky in exactly the same manner in turn. As the evening proceeds the intervals between offerings get shorter.

There is some discussion about restocking two or three of the lochs, and about whether spinning should be allowed. Brown trout are the only species present in Whalsay, though rainbow trout have been caught in one loch in the past. Sea trout are occasionally caught in the voes. The fish do not grow to a great size in Whalsay conditions. A weight of 1–2 lb would be considered substantial, although very occasionally rather larger specimens have been taken at the seldom fished loch of Stanefield and in Huxter loch. There is concern about conserving the stock, and spinning would be definitely pre-judicial in this regard. So Gibbie says, 'Spinning? Boys, dü might as well stand a' banks [on the sea shore] an' catch piltocks' (young saithe, a basic staple, and the most plentiful species found around the shoreline). There follows a good deal of talk about what should be done if anyone were caught spinning. J.–J. says, 'We must be careful. You might do more harm by being unpleasant than the spinners would do.' This earns general agreement. The anglers also console themselves with the observation that children who are given spinning rods usually exhaust their enthusiasm after about three nights. Gibbie tells a story about fishing on Huxter loch, getting a fish, and immediately being joined by young D. with his spinning rod, thinking that he too would get a fish at the same spot. Gibbie moved off. To D.'s enquiry where he was going, Gibbie replied, 'Awa' frae you.' This receives much laughter. As is the usual practice, Gibbie repeats the punch line. J.–J. has already begun to speak. Should they permit the use of worms? J. says, to general amusement, 'That's as bad as spinning.'

It is agreed that each of us will contribute prizes for a raffle. Would Muckle Peter, a retired joiner of highly regarded skill (and one of our number) make a prize? Would he make a ship? No, he didn't think he could do that. They try hard to persuade him. A jumper board? He is not keen. Eventually he agrees to make a yarn winder.[3]

More drink circulates. The talk loses its fishiness. Although no one has so declared it, the business seems to have been completed. 'Someone said the ferry isn't very seaworthy.' 'Na, I heard it was as good a sea boat as any.' J. says, 'These aald men round here, they've got to find something wrong with any boat. It's the same with just a *foureen*:[4] if there are two boats identical, one man'll always think his is better than the other one.' J.–J. reports on his trip to Bridlington to inspect the second-hand fishing boat that he and his crew are to buy. Much of the information they received there was grossly misleading. They brought the boat up to Shetland, where his cousin, a marine engineer, cured many of her faults. 'He's first-class. He'll not leave a job until he's absolutely satisfied with it. Absolutely first-class.' They comment that such people are rare nowadays.

By this stage of the evening several people have weakened and left for home. Those of us who remain now tumble down the road to the house of the club president. He brings out his mandolin-banjo, hopelessly out of tune. He brings out rum. He brings out whisky, and presently he falls asleep in his chair, so we go elsewhere. Gibbie plays his mandolin, but despite all our urging Muckle Peter will not sing. 'Peter, sing "Da Four Walls".' 'Na, na. Yon's nae use avaa'.' 'Well, sing dü some ting other.' 'Na, man, I canna' sing.' The conversation turns to local delicacies – *tattie crüse* (fish livers baked in hollowed-out potatoes) and *spjulkins* (the livers of *sillocks* – saithe up to a year old – roasted in the gutted fish). Then they reminisce over the fishing of years ago – the 'turbot line' (turbot usually referring locally to halibut). J.–J. says, 'Man, yon was exciting fishing! Really exciting,' and Gibbie agrees enthusiastically.

Then Gibbie says he is beginning to feel *suir* (sadly sober) – and we disperse for the night.

In Whalsay fly fishing, like sailing, completely lacks the class connotations it carries farther south in Britain. Competition sailing is the most popular summer sport. Many of the young men now sailing have revived the old local art of boatbuilding, and have designed and constructed their own craft. Others commission boats from builders elsewhere in Shetland. It has a winter companion: the sailing of model yachts, also locally built, from point to point round Houll loch. Fresh-water angling is not so widely practised but has no restrictive associations whatsoever with income or generation. It is an entirely democratic, if all-male, activity. It may seem eccentric that men who spend most of their lives on the water fishing for a living should turn to the fishing for their leisure activity as well. Yet the *eela* fishery in spring and summer – fishing from *foureens* with rods and hand lines close to the shore – is very popular, while 'Haa'in' a swap ipo da waater' for trout has an enthusiastic following too. One can only speculate about the reasons. It may be that, the more sophisticated the technology of modern commercial fishing becomes, the more difficult it is for men to identify themselves within its process. Much of the work now involved in fishing is operating machines, whether the electronic wizardry of the wheelhouse, or the winches, power blocks and other labour-saving machinery of the deck. With the shelter decks of the modern boats, the men are even considerably less exposed to the elements than they were formerly. One man put it to me in 1985, with some exagger-ation, that 'You can fish all day, every day, in your shirtsleeves.' The pitting of personal skill and stamina against the fish and the sea has thus become highly specialised.

Whalsay people rarely give the impression of thinking of themselves as masters of their environment. Such an attitude would be regarded as foolish. The seas are treacherous, and the Shetland climate, especially in winter, can be as severe as anywhere in northern Europe and the northern North Atlantic, with violent storms and frequent gales. To claim *mastery* of such conditions would imply a lack of respect for them. It is a sense of respect which best characterises their attitude. They do not risk lives and boats in the reckless displays reported for some other North Atlantic fishermen (see, e.g., Warner, 1984; van den Hoonaard, 1977; Tunstall, 1962). Historical disasters which occurred when fishermen had no choice but to follow orders and put to sea have made a deep impression, and are frequently recalled in conversation and in articles in the local press. Whalsay people *cope* with natural conditions which they know intimately and study endlessly: they do not attempt to trounce them. Perhaps it is in that proper humility that real mastery lies.

Angling in Whalsay is a paradigmatic instance of their respectful relationship to nature. The fish are scarce, the weather is often cold and wet. It is an activity in which all one's experience and judgement can be brought into play, man against fish, wind direction and so forth, aided only by the ingenuity of rod and fly design. In this sense it recaptures something of an earlier mode of life when success was largely dependent upon one's own resourcefulness. A catch is exciting, and widely discussed among the anglers. The details of flies, the weather at the time, the size and condition of the fish, may be rehearsed repeatedly for years. But there is no sense that a barren night suggests failure. Without any expression of fatalism, it is just 'one of those things'. In days when deep-water technology has run so far ahead of the fish stocks' ability to reproduce themselves, with the consequent need for the imposition of catch quotas on all manner of species; and when the entire catch is subject more to the politicking of European governments and bureaucrats than to the genius of the fishermen, the unadulterated contest of human canniness and natural phenomena may be particularly enjoyable.

This may seem rather theoretical as an explanation of what is essentially entertainment. There are, of course, many ways of accounting for the pleasure people obtain from fishing. As children Whalsay boys used to handle sillock *waands* (long poles made from bamboo) almost as soon as they could walk, and would be found around the shores filling buckets with the little fish. At the *eela* itself the use of a rod for drawing fish is still preferred by many for the sheer exercise of skill which it entails. For these men the fishing rod is almost a third arm. Further there are respects, other than the technology, in which this recreational fishing belongs to a quite different conceptual category from the occupational fishery. It is, literally, peaceful, undisturbed by the perpetual throb of diesel engines, the periodic clatter of warps, chains and trawl doors, the intrusive VHF radio chatter, the blipping of sonar. It is also quite devoid of the pressures of the professional fishery: the scramble for the market, ahead of the next boat; the anxiety about covering expenses to make interest payments; the irritations of shipboard life, and all the fraught aspects of the relationships among the crew.

For years now the pressure which bears upon crews has been quite unlike the earlier struggles to wrest a living from the sea. Herring, mackerel and white fish species are now limited not by what a skilled crew can catch but by the restrictive quotas imposed by external agencies. Fishing and investment strategy is thus now oriented towards such political and fiscal considerations, rather than to the competition of the hunt (see Andersen and Wadel, 1972). Many fishermen may justifiably regard themselves as innocent in these rarified calculations of financial management and political manoeuvre. They are largely dependent on advice and guidance for success in a game whose stakes are now very high. Such dependence is wholly at odds with the long-cherished and much vaunted ethic of 'independence' which has been used to explain the nature and development of the Whalsay fishery since the last war, a value whose flavour must now be savoured in other aspects of life.

This loss of control over one's economic destiny may thus find its relaxing complement in the attempt to maximise one's control with respect to natural resources, without even supposing that the outcome could be anything more than 'holding one's own'. It is this which explains the anglers' anxiety about conservation, evident, for example, in their discussions about restocking and the thorny problem of spinning. The condition of the stock is carefully monitored, and, while not given to the perversity of making fish more difficult to catch, the fishermen reject methods which make them *easier* to catch if, as a consequence, the stock might be seriously endangered. It has to be emphasised that they have a similar attitude to commercial fish stocks but find themselves frustrated by ill-informed government policy and the destructive vested interests of the non-Shetland fleets and companies, British and foreign.

Associated with these related themes of conservation-mindedness and resourcefulness is a pronounced antipathy to waste of any kind. Whalsay people pride themselves on their happy knack of recognising potential utility in what others might carelessly dismiss as debris. Sheds are full of odd bits of wood retrieved from the beaches, parts of now derelict machinery, pieces of net, coils of twine. Anything which might conceivably have a use in some unspecified future usually does eventually find one. This inclination to harbour and exploit resources extends beyond material items. People will talk animatedly about the news, about a television programme, a newspaper article, about some information gleaned from somewhere, until it has been wrung out and squeezed dry. To allow it all to float unremarked into the ether would be wasteful. By the same token, to dissipate energy needlessly is regarded as foolish. To rush when there is no need, to run when walking would be adequate, to tear around aimlessly, all cause eyebrows to be raised. The key idea is one of purposeful activity.

The anglers' concern to protect the resource is thus not specific to their interest in the trout; it is born out of a much more extensive attitude. But the problem posed by spinning was not just one of conservation. It also evokes a similarly extensive concern to do things 'correctly' in the Whalsa' way. I often received the impression that the outcome of an activity was less important than the way in which it had been conducted. A premium is placed on ingenuity – a spin-off, perhaps, of the commitment to resourcefulness. Thus the size of the basket at the close of the night's fishing is less significant than the manner in which the fisherman overcame the difficulties with which he was confronted. Doing things the Whalsa' way is exhibiting the proper skills, and this may preclude the convenient short cut to the same end result.

Spinning is thus denigrated not only because it is destructive but because it eschews the recognised skills of fly fishing, especially when, as is widely the case, the flies are local creations.

But the issue of how to deal with people caught spinning poses a delicate problem. People in Whalsay go to some lengths to avoid behaviour which might generate conflict among themselves, and take a very dim view of public confrontations. Legal action is rare. When it has occurred during the last fifty years it has usually been over the tangled issue of croft boundaries.[5] Until the early 1980s divorce was unknown. Fights are rare and, when they do occur, are almost always a consequence of drink. Routine incidents such as road accidents or a dog worrying sheep are dealt with quietly and personally without recourse to external agencies such as an insurance company or the police. Even when the compensation in question involves the cost of a new car, it is likely to be paid direct rather than through an insurance claim. In recent years there have been occasional instances of strained relations over the wish of a shareholder in a fishing boat to sell his share. Frequently the rest of the crew-owners would buy him out. But as the value of boats and gear has fluctuated during the recessionary period since the late 1970s, agreement over the value of a share has become difficult. These cases seem to have been dealt with either through the arbitration of the Lerwick fish salesmen, who act as agents for all the crews, or through the simple passage of time. Not until 1980 was there a policeman permanently stationed on the island. The suggesion had been made occasionally in the past, especially during the previous six or seven years, but had been resisted. Eventually the proposal attracted support largely as a means of coping with the nuisance of teenagers coming over from Mainland on the ferry on weekend nights, and causing some havoc on the local roads. Perhaps through emulation, local youths were also causing irritation with their motor bikes and occasionally careless use of air rifles. I would suggest that the advent of a policeman was originally resisted precisely because it introduced externality into local conflict, and thus took the management of such disputes out of islanders' hands. Those who eventually campaigned for a police presence had only a limited appreciation of the ramifications of police responsibility, believing that the object of the exercise would be to eliminate under-age and intoxicated drivers rather than to check the condition of tractor tyres, scrutinise excise licences, sheep-dipping procedures, and so forth. (See chapter five).

The avoidance of behaviour which might induce dispute runs right through island life. Unlike other Shetland communities, there is no sectarianism in Whalsay, the Church of Scotland being the sole denomination.[6] Whalsay people explain this as a conscious obviation of religious conflict. Moreover, they are manifestly indifferent to the Church, and do not lightly tolerate interference or criticism by its ministers. Church congregations rarely number more than seventy on a Sunday. Although people profess belief in

God, they also express the view that even without sectarianism the church is divisive, inviting interference in each other's affairs through the scrutiny of their religiosity. The Church elders, each assigned to a district of the island, are not accorded any prestige by the non-Church folk, and their position is often treated with mild derision.

Whalsay people's sensitivity to potential conflict could be described as sophisticated and unremitting peacekeeping. This sensitivity does not reflect any squeamishness about argument. It is a product of long experience of the tensions which inhere in close social life in circumstances from which escape or retreat are well nigh impossible. People do experience as stressful the continual mutual scrutiny which generates social 'knowledge'. As if the insularity of the island was not itself sufficiently confining, the men spend most of their lives crammed into the still more claustrophobic space of the fishing boat, living at very close quarters with the same few men year in and year out. The possibility of continuing a pleasurable existence on the island depends upon maintaining peace, and on suppressing whatever other inclinations people may have from time to time. A decision to police the lochs against spinners, and to penalise them when caught, would constitute a threat to peace over a matter which, in the general scheme of things, was relatively trivial. That is what J.–J. meant when he cautioned that punitive action 'might do more harm . . . than the spinners would do.'

The commitment to peace should not conjure up the picture of an idyll. Its concomitant is a considerable measure of resentment and competition which bubbles away under the surface. In private people are less than restrained in the views they express about each other. Moreover, it could be argued that avoidance of dispute induces a kind of conformist stultification in the public life of the community. There have been major disputes. One in particular, concerning the location of the harbour, raged for years and created intense divisions at every level of the community. Indeed, the example it provided of the strife which could be engendered by the relaxation of customary and collective self-control may well have persuaded islanders that nothing like it should ever be allowed to recur. Some aspects of this dispute will be discussed in chapter five.

It was suggested above that conflict avoidance could be seen as a discipline imposed upon itself by a community conscious of the tenuous nature of its existence, and of the strains which inhere in the intensity of its social relations. But it might almost be seen as a democratic reaction against the former regime of the laird, dividing the tenant population among itself the better to maintain and bequeath his autocracy. The nature of historical landlordism has been well documented in the Shetland literature, and requires no further rehearsal here. Although the Symbister estate was effectively broken up through insolvency early this century, the folk memory of its cruel and exploitative nature, and of its absolutist power, is kept alive in yarns. The overwhelming presence of the laird's hall (and financial ruin), Symbister House, now the island's school, is also a constant reminder. Folk history is largely the history of oppression: by the Scots lairds; by the press gang; by the fishing merchants; and, now that ruthlessness has given way to incompetence, by the 'authorities' – outside agencies of all kinds. Having shaken off at least the bounds of the lairds, social relations in Whalsay are characterised by a public ethic of egalitarianism which, even though it may only mask inequalities, results in the democratic conduct of life in public and restraint from anything which looks like assertive or superior behaviour.

This quality of democracy is a pervasive characteristic of social life, and we shall encounter it repeatedly. It is apparent in a variety of instances during the anglers' meeting. For example, it is evident in the way J.–J. disclaims knowledge of proper procedure. He apparently invites the company to advise him – 'Now, boys. How do we proceed?' – but knows that J. is the only person present who could give the advice. However, it would not do to single J. out. When he does so, to thank him for his sterling efforts on the club's behalf, J. suffers obvious embarrassment. It is manifest in Gibbie's self-effacing response, which denies superior skill, a superiority that would be readily acknowledged by all present.[7] It is evident also in Muckle Peter's resistance to the company's urging, first, to make a prize and, later, to sing. He is a deeply modest and retiring man, and his response was not contrived. Yet, had he agreed readily, it would not have been well regarded, for it would have indicated his acquiescence in other people's view of his superior qualities.

It is a democracy which also characterises the nature of communal drinking, not just in the sharing of drink but also in the essential egality of the procedure (see also Cohen, 1985b). The offering of drink by each person is spontaneous; there is no urging, nor even any nudging, of someone to offer his bottle. No one would 'jump the queue' by offering his own drink for a second time until everyone else with bottles had offered theirs first. To do so would imply either their stinginess or his greater generosity. Sharing the glass also unites the company, as if the circulation of the tumbler traces the bonds of their solidarity, a unity marked also by the donor's final toast to the entire gathering.

The last aspect of the meeting to which I shall draw attention is the ubiquitous, if tacit, reference to locality. This is made through the demonstration of shared knowledge of people and things, and by the celebration of a common heritage. Community, as a quality of life, does not inhere in place, or population size, nor even in the character of a group *vis-à-vis* other groups, although all these may be significant. It is an *achieved* quality, an accomplishment, a product of effort or of what Wadel (1979) so lucidly called 'the hidden work of everyday life'. Working conditions for the labour of community in Whalsay have changed considerably in the last twenty-five years, as suggested in the previous chapter. Before the building of roads and the extension of car ownership the physical integration of the population was more difficult and called for a definite commitment to effort. People walked a great deal. Sundays especially were reserved for long treks from township to township to share the news and to see people one had not been with during the course of the week. Young people would walk the island together, crossing the difficult peaty terrain of *da hill*, the interior. People would gather in the shops to exchange news and pass the time of day. One Whalsay shop still bears the scars of a dartboard which adorned the wall and testified to its function as a centre of sociability. The shopkeepers ran mobile shops throughout the island, purveying news and information as well as provisions.

Quite apart from the distances involved, the structures of social organisation were far more localised. Fishing crews tended to be based upon more intensive groups of kin than is now the case, and kinship tended to have a territorial dimension. Moreover, until their amalgamation in 1961 there were two schools, one in Brough, serving the west and north-coast townships; and one in Livister, attended by children from the east, south and south-west shores. As a result, youngsters may have grown up having very little direct contact with children from parts of the island outside their school's catchment area.

Life is different now. The schools are amalgamated in Symbister House and a pre-school play group, held in Isbister, brings children together at an even earlier age. The mobile shops have disappeared. Cars have made the distances between townships negligible. Of neccessity, fishing crews have widened their bases of recruitment and no longer have the localised character they had in the past. They are away at sea for much more extended periods. Shopping is now a rushed and hasty business – and, indeed, may often be done in Lerwick. The opportunities for meeting are now more easily contrived but are rarer. The imperative to engage in the work of community thus remains, although the talking can be accomplished without walking. Every household has a telephone. The VHF radios on the boats are frequently used for communicating information which has little to do with fishing. Household visiting remains, though reduced by 'lack of time' and the demands of television. The shops have ceased to be gathering points, but in 1983 the sailing club opened licensed premises which, at weekends, provides a popular centre, especially for younger people. Islanders' attitudes to 'the club' are mixed. Many fear its inducement, especially to the young, to engage in regular drinking – a habit regarded as incompatible with fishing – and resent the move away from the hearth as the focal point of sociability. Many of these people, though not teetotal, have never set foot inside the club's premises. Nevertheless, it is now established as a centre of local activity. Similarly, during the 1980s the fish factory has dramatically changed and expanded its labour force. Most of the packers are now women employed on a casual basis. The work benches and canteen tables thus provide them with the opportunity, absent since the

demise of the herring station, to meet on a regular basis. Both these developments are discussed in chapter five.

So, although circumstances have changed considerably, the work of community through the sharing of information remains a viable and diligently
practised activity. The nature of publicly available knowledge is such as to be
evoked by the merest allusion, and does not require detailed exegesis. 'Everyone' would have known that J.–J. had been south to the Humber to inspect
his new boat. They would have known in some detail about the conversations
he had held there, and about the boat's various reported deficiencies. They all
knew about the position of the former committee member who had asked to
be relieved of his responsibilities. They all share a sufficient familiarity with
his life history so that his situation could be communicated among them by a
kind of shorthand. When J.–J. referred to his engineer cousin who sorted out
the problems on his new boat he was adequately identified simply as 'Harry':
no further elaboration was necessary, even though the man had lived away
from Whalsay for years. Everyone present, fisherman or not, young and old,
could, if pressed, have uttered the stock repertoire of 'Harry' stories. In the
exercise of this easy conversation there is an almost tangible sense of fel-
lowship, one which hangs upon the assumption of shared knowledge and
which would probably be immediately dissipated by such jarring enquiries as
'What do you mean?' 'Why?' 'Who?'

The same kind of mutual assurance extends from knowledge of people to
knowledge of things. The talk about Whalsay food and about the fishing of
the past are cases in point. The traditional Whalsay cuisine has now substantially disappeared from everyday use. Older people would remember the
dishes referred to from their childhood. Doubtless they would recall also the
jugs of *blaand* (buttermilk) on the kitchen table. The oldest among them
might remember drinking *swaats*, a fermented brew made from *sids*,
unhusked oats. They would have eaten the rich *craapin'*, fish livers boiled
with oatmeal. But all these once unremarkable items of the diet have become
rarities, almost delicacies, and exemplify the process, identified in Brittany by
Hélias (1978), in which once mundane items become fetishised emblems,
almost parodies, of their culture. There are indigenous items which remain
prominent – dried fish, *reestit* (salt-cured) mutton, bannock, *hofsa* (cake)[8] –
but the diet has changed greatly through the greater availability of imported
food, the freezer revolution, and outside influences. The recollection of items
such as *spjulkins* and *tattie croose* has to be seen as more than gastronomic
nostalgia: it is a more general evocation of the past in which the essence of
Whalsay was unadulterated by acculturation. Similarly, talk of the 'turbot
line' summons up a vision of the quintessence of Whalsay manhood: man
striving to extract his just share from the sea with only his native wit to help
him. That was 'really exciting!'

Thoughts of the essential Whalsayman are also conjured up by J.'s gentle satire on the commitment everyone has to his own boat, however modest a vessel, and his denigration of everyone else's. For 'these aald men round here' read 'us'.

Angling is a minority pastime in Whalsay. The anglers are skilled and informed practitioners of their art. They could, do, discuss the pleasures and problems of fly fishing with fly fishermen from anywhere else. But, among themselves, talking fishing, doing the business of the club, is inseparable – not reducible to, but inseparable – from the cultural context of the community.

Magnie, and the battle of the water main

Life in Whalsay is always perceived as a struggle against formidable odds: the weather, remoteness, authority, cost, the perversity of local disagreements, petty jealousies, other people's incompetence, shortage of time. No one struggles harder than Magnie. Sometimes known as 'Powster', after the croft on which he was born, Magnie is the physical stereotype of the Whalsayman: powerfully built, with broad shoulders, his strength is prodigious, as is his capacity for relentlessly hard work. Magnie is a heavy equipment owner-operator, using his own mechanical digger to excavate house sites; to dig and maintain croft drainage ditches; to improve and repair roads, under contract to the local authority; to dam lochs, dredge parts of the harbour, dig out channels for water and sewage pipes, and so forth. He runs a haulage tractor with which he transports peat from *da hill*, where it has been cut and cured, to be stacked outside people's homes. He has a range of agricultural machinery, some of it home-made, and takes on crofters' ploughing and mowing jobs. He is one of the most active crofters in Whalsay, and one of only four to have kept *kye* (cows) in the last ten years. He has a welding workshop, principally to maintain his own machinery, but whose amenities he makes freely available to others. His services, therefore, are in continuous demand, though the demand reaches a peak in the summer. One could not imagine Magnie doing anything casually or aimlessly. His pace exhausts onlookers, but is never reckless. His work is deliberate and skilful.

Magnie cannot abide time-wasting. A taciturn man, his facial expressions are anxiously scrutinised by those who may have need of his assistance. A man from Cready Knowe, on the isle's north-west coast, had asked him to cut a ditch along his croft boundary. Magnie went down to measure. What happened? 'He wis jus' waalkin' dat fast. . . . Well, he said some ting or anidder which I didnae understand.' Didn't you ask him again? 'Oh, na! I wis dat feared fer him!' The great bane of Magnie's life is when, for whatever reason, people neglect to discover and clearly mark the routes of under-ground hazards across a site they wish to have excavated. Telephone cables, power lines, water mains, have all at various times been uprooted by his digger, involving him in further expenditure of time whilst he clears the ground for repairs and waits for the appropriate craftsman.

On a July afternoon in 1977 Magnie was digging out the foundations of a new house to be built that summer. He had previously consulted W., the owner of the site, about the location of the water main. W., in turn, had asked his father-in-law, who remembered the main being laid, the croft having previously belonged to *his* father-in-law. His memory was certain: the water main ran in a north-westerly direction, well away from the site. Soon after Magnie began work the inevitable happened, and a wretched fountain spurted skyward. The main actually ran due west across the site. Magnie did not say a word, but onlookers claimed to sense the 'black rage' in his features as, having swiftly bared the now separate ends of the main, he clambered down from his cab to await T.'s arrival. He stood, glowering, silent, whilst the Offending Expert proclaimed his amazement. 'But, man, I mind it gaain' doon yonder, roit in line wi' da lum o' Frankie's cottage.' When T. came he and Magnie went into their well rehearsed routine, without a word needing to be spoken between them. T. looped a rope round the pipe, put a 'Fife hitch' on it, then Magnie trundled his digger over and lowered the bucket so that T. could hook the rope on to it. To W. T. said, 'I mind me an' Aald Davie [W.'s WiMoFa] laying this line.' To the OE he said, 'I mind me and thy wife's faither laying this line!' Only then did Magnie speak. With as clear an expression of personal injury as he could ever make, he said to the OE, 'Dü telled me dere wis nae pipe here avaa'.' 'Na, na. I telled you dere *wis* a pipe. But I tocht it went doon by.' With a just perceptible shake of the head, and a resigned look in the eye, Magnie turned back to his machine and resumed work.

Recalling this incident two years later, someone observed to me that what would have annoyed Magnie about it was not that W. and his father-in-law had been mistaken and thereby caused him loss of time, but that in failing to check more thoroughly the location of the main they had failed to make 'a proper effort'. Effort, work, labour, are the supreme test of a person's worth in Whalsay. More important than accomplishment, they reveal a commitment to coping with the intractable adversities of local life and, therefore, demonstrate a commitment to that life. To be referred to as 'a hard worker' is an accolade suggesting that one applies oneself diligently to everything (Cohen, 1979, p. 264; cf. Crozier, 1985, *passim*). 'Working hard' is seen both as labour towards some specific objective – say, tasks associated with crofting or fishing – but also towards the more general and amorphous goal of 'being Whalsa'. We will return to this later when considering the contemporary significance of crofting. But it is sufficient for now to note the contrast presented by Magnie's encounter with the water main. He is not a fisherman and so might be seen by some as relatively marginal to the local economy. His earnings would certainly not approach those of the successful fishermen. His clients (and unintentional tormentors) in this case *were* fishermen. The intriguing feature of their relationship is not just that they are dependent on him, but that in acquiescing totally in their dependence (i.e. by failing to contribute more effectively to Magnie's work) they emphasise his entitlement to the accolade 'hard worker' (or, quintessential Whalsayman) and diminish their own claims in this regard.

One component of the 'hard worker' ideal is 'knowing what you are doing'. To invest effort without appropriate information would be seen simply as foolish and wasteful. Similarly, quite apart from being self-deceiving, to make an unjustifiable claim to certain knowledge endangers one's reputation. Such hostages to fortune are not given lightly in circumstances in which everyone's performance is continuously scrutinised. The mistake made by W.'s father-in-law was innocent enough. He is himself a man of enormous experience, with a compendious knowledge of local fishing grounds and of local lore. But his mistake was *public*. It was instantly widely known, and entered the treasury of public knowledge about him. Such is the tyranny of community! By and large, people eschew expressions of certainty even though they may *feel* certain. Opinions will be prefaced by 'I may be wrong, but . . .' and concluded with 'Well, that's just my opinion and I may be wrong.'

Magnie's knowledge is not only technical but includes a comprehensive and detailed familiarity with the entire island landscape. Topographical knowledge is generally extensive among the adult population, with all notable features bearing widely known proper names.[9] But Magnie's expertise is much more substantial. It would not be a gross exaggeration to say that he knew every inch of Whalsay. But he would not presume to describe himself in those terms, and would not broadcast his expertise in a way which exposed his reputation and left his opinion vulnerable to refutation. W.'s father-in-law is doubly vulnerable: not only has he claimed certainty in a matter in which he could *not* have had certain knowledge; but he has also trespassed on other people's – T.'s, Magnie's – legitimate area of expertise. Fishermen would be quick to denigrate an assertive statement on a fishing topic by a non-fisherman; here they have been found similarly 'guilty of opinion'. Their comments among themselves which imply Magnie's disregard for man-made hazards can be taken as no more than an attempt at exculpation. But, moreover, they are revealed as less expert in their knowledge of the landscape – a wounding revelation, for, after all, the landscape is the physical expression of community. Authoritative knowledge of it makes a person an authority on the community itself.

Magnie is widely seen as being constantly engaged in a battle with time. People say he gets restless in the spring when the changeable and unpredictable weather exacerbates the demands on him for ploughing, digging, and so forth, and that he relaxes only when the work is well under way. I suspect there is another dimension to Magnie's vexation which has more to do with social than with temporal pressures. The community of Whalsay is a composite of many tightly knit segmentary groups, based upon a combination of kinship and locality. Until the post-war development of full-time fishing and the consequent specialisation of labour, these bases of social association informed almost all social activity. Fishing crews were founded on kinship and neighbourhood, as were the informal groups which co-operated in the labour of crofting, building, peat, child-rearing and domestic life (Cohen, 1982a). For reasons to which some allusion has already been made, and which will be pursued later, the tight containment of life by these groups has substantially diminished and, whilst they are still acknowledged, their importance is much more occasional (Cohen, 1985b). Although people interact far more intensively across these lines, and, of necessity, form working partnerships on quite different social bases, there remains a residual unease about engaging with others. It is an inhibition which may result, firstly, from a sense of unfamiliarity with other people, and, secondly, from a consequent fear that arguments might develop, with serious repercussions.

Both factors underlie the proliferation of fishing boats during the last twenty years. Fishermen would often acknowledge the irrationality of a large number of undercapitalised units chasing each other round the North Sea, and then incurring additional expense because the same fear of formal co-operation dissuaded them from landing their catches for the local processing factory. They made reference to 'independence' to countermand the logic of collaboration. This argument was not a mere rhetorical device, but betokened the deep-rootedness of their reluctance to engage formally with others. There have been one or two collaborative ventures. In 1977–78 a number of crews teamed up briefly to experiment with pair-trawling, with discouraging results. Before the latest generation of purse-seiners two or three white-fish boats collaborated for the season with pursers. One such venture led to the merger of two crews and joint investment in a new vessel – but, significantly, there were ties of close kinship across the crews. Crofters too have long been reluctant to risk any substantial degree of formal collaboration. Occasionally neighbouring crofters may jointly hire a ram, or perhaps share machinery, but it seems to be the unhappy results which are remembered. In 1977 forty crofters did form an association to buy and administer veterinary supplies. They went on to build sale pens and, now, covered premises. But the group's development has been slow.

Magnie is the very personification of the independent spirit. A bachelor, and self-employed throughout his working life, his working routine is related to the demands of his croft and his own predilection. The risks, and costs, of compromising his routine or of foisting it on others create a genuine cause of hesitation about collaboration with other people. In digging out house sites he depends upon the client to mark out the area, to provide supplementary labour, to identify hazards. He may then have to wait upon T. for repairs to the water main, or upon the electricity and telephone linesmen. Each such relation of dependence incurs social risks which, in the small, close and insular community, provide understandable grounds for caution. Magnie is sensitive to the dangers, and therefore contains his anger. The community imposes a discipline on its members which is uncommon elsewhere, and which results in a perpetual understating of personal sentiments.

It is a similar sense of discipline which tempers these strains and stresses by the use of an idiosyncratic and personally directed humour. In the public arena of the community, people are allocated, and acquiesce in, a persona. Whatever private frustrations they may suffer arising from the dissonance between their private sense of self and their publicly allocated identity, there is a recognition of the necessity for at least a minimal compliance with these roles. It is almost as if people recognise that they must spend some time on the community's stage, during which their discretion over performance, script, appearance, is severely restricted by the public's expectations (Cohen, 1978a). Such limitations are stressful but perhaps softened through the use of humour as the principal medium of such public discourse. (See chapter six.) Magnie's reputation for 'fierceness' is never tinged with the slightest suggestion of aggression – he is in fact a most gentle and courteous man – for it has a humorous timbre, and is gently satirised through the endless recounting of slightly deflating stories. One such story goes back many years to the time when an elderly, and somewhat eccentric, neighbour of Magnie and his parents (then still living) would go to their house to take his weekly bath. This old man, Robbie o' Linthouse ('Robbie Linty'), whom we shall meet later, had replied to an advertisement in *Exchange and Mart* for a suit. When, eventually, it arrived he was first disconcerted, then amused, to discover that it was a full-dress suit of tails. He decided to ask Magnie's mother to cut it about and make it serviceable for him, and so took it with him to Magnie's house. But legend has it that Robbie, being an inveterate practical joker, and knowing that Magnie would not refuse an old man's request, asked him to put it on, 'Jus' so's I cin see how yon süd look!' Magnie, furious in his embarrassment, duly modelled the outfit, to the hysterical delight of his mother and Robbie. In the recounting of the incident the anomalous image of a bulky Magnie, habitually clad in outsize overalls and cap, now crammed into a small, satin-faced dress suit, is only part of the joke. The other is his, more easily pictured, painfully suppressed rage.

The football club dance

A Saturday in October 1974. The football club will tonight hold its dinner and dance. After the dinner, the various club trophies will be presented. The event is held in Symbister Public Hall, which is packed with four long tables running end to end of the hall, with seating for about twenty-five people each side of every table. The tables are set with paper plates bearing cold beef and covered by paper napkins, and with candles and bottles of cider. The company – men in suits reserved for such occasions, weddings and funerals, women with freshly set hair, in dresses – sit quietly, most talking only to their immediate neighbours. A sedate, almost funereal decorum, reigns. Various members of the club committee bring round hot vegetables and gravy. At the conclusion of the meal everything is passed down to ends of the tables so that the committee members can collect it all easily.

The trophies duly presented – 'Best Player', 'Best Young Player', and so forth – the company have to disperse while the hall is made ready for the dance. Among the men there is a perceptible sense of relief that the formality of the dinner, with its uncertain etiquette, is over. My companion, a reluctant participant attending at his wife's behest, wipes his brow and comments thankfully, 'Well, dat's da first bit by!'

Everyone retires to various houses; they will not be readmitted to the hall until 9.15 p.m. In the meantime the bottles of whisky, which every man will later take to the dance, are opened and their contents sampled.

When we return the hall has been transformed. Not only have the tables been cleared away to make space for the dance, but the placidity of the dinner has given way to a developing bedlam. Younger men have stationed themselves in the vestibule and are already drunk, or pretending to be. They bar the entrance into the hall itself, making everyone take a swig of whisky from the proffered bottles before they can be admitted. Inside there are two rows of seats around the perimeter of the hall, the front row occupied mostly by women. Most of the dancers also are women; the reels are confused, and nobody seems very sure quite how they are supposed to go.

More and and more people arrive and greet each other, exchanging their bottles for swigs. Some of the men appear to succumb rapidly. Early in the proceedings my neighbour's brother-in-law goes out like a light, defying solicitous attempts at revival, and is laid to rest in the Gents'. A little later, his uncle subsides to the floor, almost in time to the waltz he has been dancing, and is unable to rise. The bottles circulate with increasing rapidity, the surreal character of the scene heightened by the conversation.

'Man, I dinna ken wha's happening tae wis! Dere's dis EEC. Boys, what does dü tink o' yon EEC ting? An dere's dis "social contract". Dat's a queer on-carry. . . .'

'We süd hae listened ta Lenin!'

'Wha's Lenny?'

'Now de're putt'n' across dis ferry. . . .'

'What *feerie* [a contagious 'bug'] is he on aboot?'

'. . . hit's likely da Freemasons 'at's behind it. What's dat word o' deirs? Bosh, or something like yon.'

'Na, it's Boaz, not bosh.'

'Oh, yea, Boaz. Hey, Lowry, how's yer Boaz today?'

'How's me ballast? Dü're surely ower foo' up o' Johnnie Walker!'

As the evening wears on, and the whisky wears down inhibitions, more men join in the dancing, especially in the local version of the Gay Gordons. The band is composed of local men, all self-taught and skilled instrumentalists: Magnie, the accordionist, as much in charge as anyone could be; Alan, a fiddler of reknown; Tammie Arthur on drums. Occasionally they try to catch each other out. As things get more hectic, some of the dancers seem oblivious to the music, and move as if propelled by some inner anarchic tempo. At 1.00 a.m. the M.C. stumbles to the microphone to declare the end of the dance. He is too drunk to make himself heard, and no one seems inclined to listen.

People are now being urged to 'cam alang wir hoose' and those who are still ambulant do so. In the houses the whisky is offered in a tumbler, rather than straight from the bottle. The women of the house, who may well have had to rise from their beds, produce sandwiches, cakes, perhaps some *reestit* mutton. The men conclude the night's ingestion with a few cans of MacEwan's Export, and most seem finally to have retired by five o'clock.

One of the most striking characteristics of Whalsay behaviour is its control and restraint. Men, in particular, tend to be reserved in public, almost shy, invariably courteous. Even when drunk, though language may coarsen, behaviour never becomes abusive. Women do not, and need not, feel any apprehension about being among a roomful of men, inebriated or otherwise.

It is not difficult to appreciate the importance of reserve. Whalsay is no more of an idyll than anywhere else; it is a place which, like any other small and closely knit community, generates great tensions. But the tensions have to be mastered, otherwise the community's ever vulnerable grip on survival would be further endangered. The dangers are exacerbated, but their precautions also assisted, by the physical insularity and dense kinship of the community. Both insularity and kinship amplify the tension but mean, first, that there can be no escape other than through emigration, and, second, that a failure of restraint would harm whole families as well as less intimate social relationships.

The habit of reserve must also have been deeply ingrained among men by their long experience of the circumstances of fishing. In the days of the *haaf* they lived in tiny crude barracks, 'lodges', on the fishing beaches, between their long voyages, often lasting more than forty-eight hours in the open *six'ern*. The dangerous and arduous nature of such fishing must have bred a solidarity; but the cramped accommodation both at sea and ashore, and the endless fatigue and discomfort, must also have threatened the most relaxed of temperaments. While accommodation on fishing boats has improved steadily to their present considerable comfort, men still live cheek-by-jowl. It is only in boats built during and since the 1970s that the cabin has been separated from the messroom. On the older boats, still fishing, seven or eight bunks would be arranged around the walls of the cabin, in the centre of which stood the mess table, with the oil range just at the room's threshold, and the noisy engine room on the other side of the bulkhead. So, while some men were cooking or eating, others, just off watch, might be trying to catch up on some sleep, all within the same few square feet. The potential for shipboard strife has been well observed elsewhere (e.g. Tunstall, 1962). There are few instances of it in Whalsay's collective memory. On the one or two occasions known to me when it has occurred it led to the immediate dissolution of the crew and, in one instance, to the sale of the boat.

Both community and messroom thus impose an unspoken discipline of restraint and reserve, and engender a respect for privacy which balances the public treasury's continual demand for replenishment. This reserve is tested when a person is put into an unfamiliar situation where his ground is uncertain, his clothes are unusual and he is brought into proximity with people he does not know well. This very hallmark of metropolitan society is strange to the members of the remote rural community. Even now that Whalsay people have become so much more accustomed to travel elsewhere, and to having outsiders on the island, they still profess themselves uncomfortable among *unken* (strangers; literally, unknown) folk. Of course, the familiarity of context is a matter of degree. Table companions at the football club dinner are bosom pals by comparison with the other patrons of the Lerwick cafe – who, if met outside Shetland, might themselves be treated as long-lost intimates. But it was clear that the dinner was sufficiently unfamiliar to be uncomfortable, especially for the men, and we can sympathise with Davy's relief when it was 'by'. These formal occasions used often to be parochialised by the performance of a locally written sketch, in dialect, and full of allusions to Whalsay people and incidents. These exercises in self-satire also had their detractors, not least, perhaps, because they tacitly accepted cheap stereotypes. But they had the effect of anchoring the event cognitively in the locality: they were tantamount to saying, 'Well, look at us! All dressed up in our finery, and eating as daintily as we know how. But, bairns, underneath all this nonsense, it really is us.' The football club's celebration did not include a dramatic interlude. But the transformation to the inebriated ambiance of the dance might be seen as expressing a similar sentiment, and as accomplishing a similar result.

We shall encounter drink and drunkenness on several more occasions. But it would be quite wrong to suppose that Whalsay is peculiarly addicted to whisky. Indeed, it is not. It is unusually disciplined for a Shetland community in matters alcoholic and, by contrast with Scottish fishing ports, positively abstemious. Alcohol is not taken aboard fishing boats and, apart from the odd can of beer, fishermen do not drink during the working week. There are people on the island with alcohol problems, but they are few in number and are widely recognised. Drinking such as that occasioned by the dance, by weddings, *sprees* (see chapter three) and other notable events is essentially a *social* act, as implied by the continuous exchange of bottles and, on sprees, by the circulation among the entire company of a single glass. In this respect, taking drink is an expression of mutual belonging, comparable to that of commensality in other cultures. Even people who are teetotal assent to their co-membership by 'layin' a lip in'. Of course, drink is more than figurative; it is also licensed relief from the most stringent constraints of customary reserve and inhibition. It is a support in the socially stressful context. As suggested earlier, all social occasions beyond the bounds of one's customary associates can be stressful. It is also a component in the public construction of identity which we encountered earlier. People's drinking escapades and characteristics are rehearsed repeatedly. There is no *machismo* in being able to take a quantity of drink. Hangovers are recounted like battlefield campaigns. Habitual over-indulgence may well be ill regarded; but to get occasionally 'foo' up', and then to suffer for it, is understandable and unremarkable. People are not pressured into drinking, and the determined abstainer is never mocked. But Whalsay people recognise their own reserve. They are also sensitive to the change in the nature of their social interaction which has breached the old barriers of close social association. If a dram can ease the reserve and thereby facilitate social engagement, then so be it: the alternative might be a divided or, at least, malintegrated place, less community than assembly of mutually antagonistic or suspicious factions.

It is significant that this particular celebration of society, with its stresses and its remedies, is the community displaying itself to itself on public and neutral ground, the Symbister Public Hall. Symbister is in the south-east of the island and, since 1960, has become increasingly the centre of public activities. It has what is now the largest of the island's shops, and both sets of petrol pumps. The main post office is just a quarter of a mile to the south, at Harlsdale, and it has the school and multi-court, and two council housing developments in the immediate vicinity. Apart from being the base for the fishing fleet, the harbour itself contains the fish factory, the net factory and the ferry terminal.

The hall was built in the 1930s at the top of the road leading down to the harbour. There is a smaller and older public hall at Isbister, on the east coast, and the church hall at Saltness, a third of a mile north of Symbister. This gradual concentration of services on Symbister follows the development of the South Voe as the island's harbour in 1960, following a prolonged and bitter argument over its location. The hall belongs to the community, is administered by a representative committee, and is one of very few neutral

Symbister, from the harbour. The Public Hall is in the centre of the picture, at the top of the road leading down to the harbour. The building in the bottom right corner is the Symbister shop, earlier the premises of Hay & Co. The small building to its left is the recently restored Hanseatic trading booth. [Picture by Gordon Craig]

locations on the island. Most other places are associated with particular townships and/or groups of kin, or with other 'vested' interests – the Church, the shopkeepers, factory owner or external agencies. Of course the harbour is itself public territory, but has obvious associations with the fishermen, with the council, and is jointly owned by J. & M. Shearer Ltd, the Lerwick company which originated in Whalsay. By contrast, the hall belongs absolutely to the community itself, and is used by everyone. All local weddings are held there, as are all the major dances. It is the only major meeting place on the island to which everyone has uninhibited access. It is *par excellence* the public stage in the local drama.

We have noted already the unease Whalsay people feel when thus publicly exposed. Their retreat to *private* houses after the dinner and, later, after the dance might be seen as offering a respite from the prolonged need to perform – a chance to rest in the wings, so to speak, and to recover their composure after the prolonged exercise of control or after its lapses. Things do get said in public which ought not to be said – the reference to Freemasonry, for example: a subject not usually mentioned in mixed company because of its divisiveness. There are a number of Whalsaymen, particularly among the fishing skippers, who are Freemasons, and there are many who will have nothing to do with Freemasonry. But the drink provides a degree of excuse for such *faux pas* and, in this particular instance, the subject was raised only among people of like mind. That degree of familiarity with each other's opinions is itself instructive. The nuances of shared localness are everywhere: in knowing what might be said to whom; in the personal knowledge which renders tolerable the excesses of those in drink; in the possessive pride with which people comment on the band; in the reluctance of any of the women to breach the imperative of egalitarianism by offering authoritative direction for the 'eightsome' reels; in the celebration itself – for, after all, it is *Whalsay*'s football club.

A trip to the front

The essence of Whalsay's struggle for survival is its continuing ability to wrest a living from the sea. The fishing grounds are the ever more complicated battleground in which the enemy is not so much the fish, nor even the weather. It is provided by other, less predictable adversaries: international politics, regulations, unfair foreign competition, the inanities of government policy, the fisheries protection officer, fluctuating interest rates, and human (especially skipper) fallibility. (See chapter five.)

It is a Sunday night, early in June 1975. The wind is blowing at Force 6 from the north-east, a bad *ert* (direction), with several more days of gales forecast. At this time of year the fish are inshore, and there is no lee from a north-easter along which the boats can work. Perhaps this accounts for the somewhat subdued atmosphere as the fishermen gather at the pier, and swiftly disperse to their respective boats. The crew of the *Langdale* arrive singly.[10] Barely greeting each other, each man goes straight to his own task without a word of instruction. The *Langdale* has one of the first composite crews, formed by a merger of the crews of two of the smaller seiners. Kinship and affinity provide the core of the combination: Arthur (the skipper); his brother, Lowry (engineer), and their cousin (MoSiSo), Barry (cook), owned the *Zenith*. They are an Isbister family, and the *Zenith* was so closely identified with the locality that it was sometimes referred to as 'the Isbister boat'. James John (mate) was previously co-owner and mate of the *Flourish*. He is married to Arthur and Lowry's sister. The three other co-owners and crewmen were formerly associates of James John on the *Flourish*, and are related through kinship and neighbourhood with James John and their former skipper. (Fig. 1.)

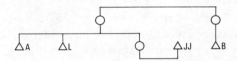

Fig. 1   Kinship and affinity in the *Langdale* merger.

The *Langdale* is presently *tripping* (selling her catch in Aberdeen or Peterhead) and it is assumed that it will take most of the week to *get their trip* – to catch sufficient (approximately 350 boxes) to make the journey south worth while. I ask the skipper where we shall be going. He says he does not know. He obviously has alternatives in mind, but is not yet prepared to commit himself. As soon as we have left the pier James John comes into the wheelhouse and asks Arthur where he is headed. Again, the skipper replies that he does not know: he will have a look at the water south of the Sound, and see. He eventually steers to the north, and enters the discussion being conducted over the ship-to-ship radio among various Whalsay boats about likely locations. Many of the exchanges seem to be focused in particular on the skipper of the *Azalea*, Josie. Everyone rehearses his indecision in a formulaic 'I dinna ken where tae bloody go. I dinna ken *avaa*'.'

The skipper's problem is not just the weather. In the early summer the fish are inshore, within the three-mile prohibited fishing zone. If the boats are to catch anything at all they will probably have to second-guess the fisheries protection vessel which is patrolling nearshore waters in an attempt to forestall such 'poaching'.

Predictably, we make for Balti, off the north-east of Unst, Shetland's most northerly island. The *Ardsheean* is heading in the same direction. Her skipper, Willie, and Arthur talk to each other frequently over 'the box'. James John, meanwhile, fiddles with the echo-sounder and the fishlupe. He tries to find the newly submerged Brent Field oil pipeline with the echo-sounder, but cannot do so. They notice a boat fishing along the banks off Fetlar, and joke about calling up the fisheries officer. Much of the radio talk about the officer is conducted in code so that he will not be able to understand. He is referred to as *da gruelli* (the ghost),[11] an invention by Willie of the *Ardsheean*.

When we have been at sea for a couple of hours most of the crew go below to sleep. Barry is on watch, and the skipper stays up with him in the wheelhouse. Willie is scrubbing out the galley, which still bears the marks of a recently burst water tank. As he works he enthuses about sailing, and about model yachts. A skilled craftsman, he builds and sails models, dinghies and full-size regatta boats. He exudes real pleasure at being close to the water and at everything about the fishing environment. He watches birds with fascination, noticing their different feeding habits, and waxes lyrical over the sight of hundreds of *mallies* (fulmars) flocking around the boat on a calm winter's night. 'Dey seem to gie aff dis great glow.'

By midnight the skipper is ready for the first *shot*. Barry, an ex-seaman, goes below to awaken the crew – 'Right ho, me old fruits' – and off they go. They fish without a break for the next twenty-five hours, until 1.00 a.m. on Tuesday morning. James John and Lowry, the engineer, take respectively starboard and port side duties, setting and hauling the heavy steel trawl doors. They make sure the net and warps are paid out, and hauled, without snagging, and thus ensure that the catch comes aboard, is unloaded, and the net shot again with the least possible delay. The long fishing day is a repeated cycle of shooting the net, trawling, hauling in the catch; then shooting and *dragging* (trawling) again, while the catch from the previous shot is gutted and sorted on deck. Willie boxes the fish, salting, icing and stacking it in the hold. The men eat a substantial cooked breakfast. But for the rest of the day, until we tie up in the small hours, they eat only snacks of crackers, biscuits and cheese. In the middle of Monday night, as we head for Baltasound pier, Barry prepares the main meal, huge pots of soup and stew.

The last two hauls have brought forty boxes, and these have still to be cleaned. Everyone lends a hand, including the skipper. They grade the fish for size as they are gutted, sorting them into different baskets which are then washed and emptied down the shoot into the hold. After all these hours of continuous labour in heavy seas the pace of work does not slacken, and the care taken over it does not diminish. 'What a life, boys,' muses Barry. 'Yeah, it's a great life, if you don't weaken!' Just as he is serving up the meal, Willie comes up from the hold to announce the total number of boxes for the day. One hundred and forty-six. A good start. Barry's banquet is eaten in a relaxed and quietly jovial mood. Tommy, soon to be married, is teased about dieting. James John, shortly to become a father-in-law, is encouraged to reconcile himself to a sedate middle age. The banter is gentle, and indicates collegiality rather than intimacy. The meal is finished by 3.15 a.m., and the crew retire to sleep.

Six hours later, James John and Tommy, taking the day's first watch, and the skipper rise and immediately cast off from the pier. The rest of the men stay below, asleep, until making the first shot at ten o'clock. They then go down again and sleep until the first haul is made, after a very long tow, some four hours later. Then they are all on deck once more, and fish continuously until 1.30 on Wednesday morning. 'A short day,' says Barry, but it has been poor fishing. The wind has not eased at all, and the sheer physical effort of maintaining one's balance on deck over a long period, though instinctive to the men, is nevertheless tiring. The prolonged, sparse tows are frustrating and boring. The day's work has netted only fifty boxes. The contentment of the previous night has disappeared. Tonight there is an edge to the conversation. One of the men mocks a Whalsay skipper for his navigation, recalling an occasion, now long past, when, making his first *trip* to a Scottish market port, he found himself in another harbour altogether. The skipper's brother, himself a skipper, has to take his boat to Scandinavia for repair in three weeks' time. 'He mebbe better start now!'

A Fraserburgh boat has tied up alongside us. Two of the *Langdale* men remark caustically on the slowness with which her crew gut the catch: 'One aald bugger does twartree sneuklins at it afore he gets his knife in. They'll still be here *da morn's mornin'* [tomorrow].' They are more respectful about the Norwegian shark fisher, also berthed near by. Arthur comments wistfully that it does not have radar. Willie, casting his craftsman's eye over her dory, says admiringly, 'Yon's a bonny boat fer only six boards.'

The skipper occupies an ambiguous niche in Whalsay ideology. Financially his stake in the boat is exactly equal to that of each of the other owners, so that his authoritative position in the crew is not vested in property rights. Politically his ascendancy over his crew is not based on any communal orthodoxy about 'skipper behaviour'. Rather, it is a matter of personality and personal relations. Skippers differ widely from each other in the ways in which they exercise authority (see Cohen, 1977). However, there is no doubt that they are expected to be authoritative. Their position is complicated by a host of factors: financial parity with other owners; the presence in the crew of at least one other, and generally more, 'ticketed' men (with Board of Trade skipper's qualifications); the extra-crew relationships among the men, many of whom are close kin, affines or neighbours; the overarching ethos of egalitarianism, and so forth. The most generally applicable description which could be offered of the position of the Whalsay skipper is that he is *primus inter pares*. (cf. Byron, 1986, ch. 4.)

Nevertheless the skipper is as close to the status of 'culture hero' as is any figure in Whalsay ideology. He embodies key values: diligence, seamanship, canniness, responsibility, resourcefulness. But this idealisation was the product of a different economic and technological era. Today the skipper is cruelly exposed to forces which he cannot control, however brilliant or ingenious he may be. International politics has transformed the exploitation of Shetland waters during the last twenty years. The Icelandic cod wars, and the subsequent extension of Iceland's territorial waters to 200 miles, excluded the British distant-water fleet from important traditional hunting grounds. One consequence was that the fleet underwent a drastic contraction, leaving the ports of Hull, Grimsby, Fleetwood and Aberdeen a mere shadow of their former selves. Another was that some of the remaining companies transferred their attention to Shetland, bringing larger vessels into competition with the Shetland seiners than they had ever had to confront within territorial waters.

With Britain's accession to the EEC, and the introduction of the Common Fisheries Policy, a new slate of foreign competitors entered the arena. Foreign competition was nothing new to Shetland men. For decades they had been fishing among Faroese, Danish, Icelandic, Norwegian, Russian, Dutch and Japanese fleets. But now they had also to confront French and German boats, as shortly they will have to take on the massive Spanish fleet. It is not just the volume of competition which has changed, but its regulation. Previously the British fleet was policed by British government regulations. These generally favoured the large trawler companies which formed the only fishing lobby acknowledged by successive governments (see Tunstall, 1962). But at least the Shetland men knew the enemy, and had some access to him through the county council and the Member of Parliament.

Suddenly the entire scenario changed. The centre of affairs shifted to Brussels. The regulations which emanated from Commission headquarters in an incessant, lunatic flow appeared to them to have little to do with any fishery logic at all but reflected the current state of play in the arcane political manoeuvres at the Council of Ministers. With justification, Shetlanders had always regarded the central formulation and implementation of fishing regulations as placing them at a distinct disadvantage with respect to the powerful distant-water interests. But they understood that: it was one of the many symptoms of Shetland's peripherality. The new regime, however, was more dangerous. It threatened the very survival of Shetland's fishing communities. It required new and unfamiliar forms of political organisation to represent local interests. Perhaps most pernicious of all, its ridiculous lurching from one position to another – with respect to quotas, subsidies, bans, open and closed seasons, finance, and so on – made any strategic planning well nigh impossible. As we shall see later, a huge reinvestment in the Whalsay fleet in the late 1970s was undertaken in the context of assurances about pelagic fishing policy. By the time the new boats were delivered the policy had changed, threatening the heavily mortgaged owners – indeed, the entire community – with ruinous bankruptcy.

Shetland fishermen are as well informed as any. Almost every fishing household takes the authoritative weekly *Fishing News*, and their genuine interest has maintained a high level of sophisticated monitoring of international fishery developments. But how could they cope with the new, perverse, unfathomable antics of politicians and bureaucrats whose judgement appeared to those in the remote north to be based more on slapstick mental acrobatics than on any serious consideration? *Da gruelli*, the fisheries protection vessel, had become the devil incarnate. Earlier there had been a relationship of resigned, sometimes amused tolerance between fishermen and official. But now the attitude of the Shetland fishermen was becoming increasingly bitter, not least because they could not discern any evenhandedness in the regulations. Within the last few years the struggle has become still more bitter. There was genuine delight in 1982 when a Whalsay skipper was acquitted in court of illegal fishing by successfully revealing the young arresting naval officer as unable to distinguish between a herring and a pilchard.[12] We shall have occasion to return to the fraught issue of the fishery in greater detail later (see chapter five).

Let us note for now that the burden of these new, imponderable problems rests unrelentingly on the shoulders of the skipper. Financially equal though he may be, it is his responsibility to find the fish, to organise the men to catch it, to decide which is likely to be the most beneficial market, and to get there at the most opportune moment. The days are long gone when his success could be simply measured in terms of his seamanship and 'fishiness'. He is now all that stands between his crew and their families and financial ruin, for most households and their wider families are heavily mortgaged by the new investments in boats and gear. The scale of these investments has already been mentioned. But their enduring burden must be emphasised. The *Langdale* was bought second-hand in Bridlington in 1975 for £150,000. In 1985 the same amount was again spent on fitting her with a shelter deck and other odd items of equipment. Costs are prodigious. Reinvestment is not now just a beneficial strategy with respect to taxation. It is an expression of the constantly felt pressure to do everything possible to remain competitive.

Exacerbating this pressure has been the inexorable diminution of the North Sea fish stocks through overfishing and by the development of ever more destructive catching power. 'Fishiness' is no longer a matter of knowing where the fish should be at given times of the year. The skipper has to keep in mind also the more recent aberrations. He has continually to weigh the possibilities of searching elsewhere against the cost in fuel and time of doing so. He has similarly to calculate the costs and benefits of tripping. Skippers avoid talking about the stresses of their position. Nevertheless, they do experience them. That they make so light of them is a tribute to their resilience, but should not be mistaken for complacency or insensitivity. Always figuratively a man apart, the skipper is now increasingly isolated from his crew physically as well. The modern wheelhouse has become a cockpit of electronic devices – radars, navigators, sonars, echo-sounders, fish lupes, transponders, as well as a battery of radios, intercoms, consoles for all the hydraulic deck machinery, and so forth. Skippers of modern boats complain that they can hardly even see the deck any more and have to rely on the 'talk-back' or walkie-talkie and closed-circuit television to know what is going on. On the new purse-seiners the skipper is provided with his own cabin, although when these boats first came to Whalsay some skippers were reticent about accepting the privilege. This physical separation complicates the skipper's problem of social relationships: he must exercise authority without flouting the supreme value of egalitarianism, and without risking a reputation for gratuitous bossiness. Like everyone else, he is trapped by public knowledge of him. If he appears to attempt to flee his persona he will swiftly be brought down.

Small wonder, then, that Arthur looks so wistfully at the Norwegian shark-fishing boat and comments on its lack of radar. It evokes a different, simpler era of fishing, one he would remember from his own apprenticeship. No wonder, either, that he is so cautious about committing himself to our destination when asked, first by the ethnographer and later by the mate. How could he express certainty when everyone else on the box was claiming doubt? If no one else were to steer for the same place, would he risk the accusation of 'being different' or so strongheaded as to ignore the judgements of all his fellow skippers? He must continuously face up to his crew's hopes and disappointments, and cannot do so if he has not made a proper show of weighing the situation in all its complexity. Perhaps Arthur is also sensitive to the recent merger of his crew with James John's. Not only has he to prove the wisdom of the merger, but he also has to establish his personal position, for James John is himself a qualified skipper and highly experienced fisherman, a remorselessly hard worker with a strong local reputation. We shall meet skippers and their dilemmas again. Let us just conclude this introduction to them by observing that, though they occupy a customarily honoured place in the Whalsay scheme of things, they may feel that they now have more to lose than was previously the case.

Commercial fishing in the northern North Atlantic is renowned for the severity of the competition. There is little indication that local loyalties mitigate its intensity or soften its tactics.[13] Shetlanders would seem to be exceptional in their rejection of such behaviour. In Whalsay there is a spirit of competition, a consciousness of competitive evaluation, and a mild jousting for reputation and prestige. But the competition is never destructive, never entails a deliberate attempt to place others at a disadvantage (cf. Andersen, 1972, 1973) and never wantony courts danger, either to one's own or to others' crews (cf. van den Hoonaard, 1977). The origins of their more civilised approach to fishing may lie in their shared subjection to the tyrannies, first of the laird, and later of the fishing companies. Whatever its historical pedigree, it is significant that it has survived into the modern circumstances of cut-throat fishing economics. Indeed, despite all their pronouncements in favour of independence, Whalsay fishermen frequently fish in close proximity to, and in some degree of collaboration with, each other. In the old days of the drift-net herring fishery the fleet tended to fish *en masse*, calling forth exceptional seamanship to avoid collisions and the entanglement of the long fleets of nets. One skipper would report by radio each morning to the community the whole fleet's overnight catch. Sometimes a skipper might achieve an exceptional shot by going off on his own, well away from the other boats. But the norm was, and remains, to fish in proximity. In the present strange days of quotas a purse-seiner which has already caught up to the permitted limit may give fish to a boat which still has to fill its quota. Moreover, as the purse-seining fleet began to develop in Whalsay its experienced skippers would often *go off* with the crews of the new vessels, their own competitors, to advise and instruct them in techniques and procedures.

We can therefore read into the radio exchanges among the boats this locally idiosyncratic form of competition. Every skipper is anxious to know the others' intentions, and avidly gleans whatever information may be available: about the presence or absence of fish, about the weather, the markets, the location of the Protection vessel. Some skippers have been known to practise mild deceptions in the information they purvey, generally understating the size of their catch. But this is not common, and, by comparison with the cases cited above, is insignificant. Shared locality tempers competition. Among the Whalsay boats there are definite alliances and factions. The association of the *Langdale* with the *Ardsheean* is an instance; the asperity of the supper-time comments about two other skipper-brothers indicates an opposition. This segmentation is apparent also in frequent talk in the community about 'good' skippers. During the 1980s the fleet seems to have become increasingly polarised between the pelagic purse-seiners and the smaller white-fishing boats, and these interests have somewhat complicated the previous pattern of alliances. Nevertheless, at the time of the trip described here the instinctive solidarity of locality is noticeable in the tone with which the *Langdale* men commented about the Fraserburgh crew, clearly implying the inferiority of the latter, not just to themselves but to the generality of Whalsay fishermen.

The fishing boat is physically a self-contained unit, sometimes isolated. Financially the crew have the characteristics of a corporate group, with a defined sphere of interest. No fishermen holds shares in more than one vessel. The boat is both working and living space, with its own routines, its own hierarchy, none of them replicated ashore. These kinds of consideration have enticed writers into categorising the crew-at-sea as a Goffmanesque 'total institution' (e.g. Aubert, 1965). Whatever the merits of Goffman's concept, it is an inaccurate categorisation of the Whalsay boat. The boat may be discrete space, but socially and culturally it is the community-at-sea. The crew are associated through links other than those of their co-membership; shipboard behaviour owes at least as much (and probably more) to the prevailing values of Whalsay society as to the technical logic of the working environment (cf. Knipe, 1984). The same kinds of structural linkage, and the same commitment to Whalsay culture, go far towards decreasing the distance and muting the competition among crews. Close ties of kinship, including siblingship, of friendship and of neighbouring cut across crews, and in many cases are more important than those of crew membership. The animosity which divides agnates with discrete fishing interests in the Newfoundland community of Cat Harbour (Faris, 1972) would be unthinkable in Whalsay. Whalsaymen may well have a strong commitment to 'their' boat, as we saw earlier. But it does not subvert their greater commitment to those entities – kin, friends and neighbours – which bind them to the community itself.

Notes

1   See, e.g., *Shetland in Statistics* (1980), p. 35, and *Mareel* (1980/81), p. 17.
2   The Estate is the remnant of the original holdings by the lairds, the Bruces of Symbister, after the continuing sale of crofts and other land to tenants following its insolvency early this century. It is administered by Edinburgh solicitors and a local agent.
3   Sweaters and cardigans knitted from Shetland yarn are stretched, after washing, on a board, adjustable for size, which replicates the shape of the torso with outstretched arms. These are placed outside while the garment dries in its proper shape. The long skeins of yarn are wound into manageable quantities around two wheels arranged vertically on a stand, approximately 3 ft high. Although commonplace, both items are highly valued if well made.
4   A *foureen* is the generic name for a small clinker-built boat, usually between 16 ft and 20 ft in length. These are all of the 'Shetland model' design, pointed at both ends in the manner of the Viking yoals. Like the larger versions, the *six'erns*, which were the mainstay of the *haaf* fleet, *foureens* were built for sail as well as for oars. Nowadays most are fitted with small inboard or outboard engines. Until the mid-1970s they were also raced as yachts, but, in common with other sailing communities in Shetland, the Whalsay racing fleet is now composed almost exclusively of purpose-built ballastless boats.
5   For much of the time since the estate was broken up, and crofters began to purchase their crofts, boundaries were assumed as publicly recognised and often given by folk topographical references. Attempts in recent years by solicitors and others locally concerned to put land holdings on objective and legal bases have occasionally thrown up anomalies which have caused disputes among neighbours and kinsfolk.
6   In 1980 the first island policeman, a Devonian by origin, began a Pentecostal meeting in Whalsay. Its popularity was short-lived. A chapel has been founded in

an old cottage, but all its members are outsiders.

7　Crozier (1985) notes a similar self-belittling of achievement in her study of domestic hospitality in Ballintully, Northern Ireland, a community which she describes as strongly egalitarian (pp. 299 ff.).

8　In Whalsay *hofsa* refers to a plain sweet cake, with perhaps a little dried fruit. It is often spoken of depreciatingly by its bakers as something 'just thrown together'. The word does not appear at all in Graham's *Shetland Dictionary* (1979). However, in Jakobsen's authoritative dictionary (1928) we find entries for *hofs*, 'to hurry along, hasten . . .' and *hofs*, 'to cause anything to swell, e.g. applied to bread. . . .' Further, he gives *hofsek* as 'a big, clumsy, unwieldy person. . . .' Any of these might have been etymologically significant in this instance of Whalsay's verbal creativity.

9　Often they are identified with people and incidents in the past. T.'s repeated references to Aald Davie are an instance of this kind of association. The original croft cottage which W.'s new house was to replace was still known as 'Davie's hoose'.

10　I owe special thanks to this crew, not only for their hospitality and for their tolerance of my intrusion but also for their sympathetic and considerate care of a chronically seasick ethnographer – who always seemed to recover in time to share their food, and whose washing-up was poor return for their generosity and kindness.

11　The word does not appear either in Jakobsen (1928) or in Graham (1979). However, the latter lists 'gruelly-bag (n.): nickname given to a person from the district of Whiteness' (p. 31), which suggests the possibility of an intriguing etymology in the folklore of inter-community relations.

12　See *Shetland Times*, 26th February 1982. For an only slightly less successful outcome to the prosecution of another Whalsay crew see the *Shetland Times*, 26th November and 3rd December 1982.

13　See, e.g., Tunstall (1962), Andersen and Wadel, eds. (1972), *passim*, Zulaika (1981), Thompson *et al.* (1983) and Warner (1984).

Chapter 3

Making some sense of it all

Parts and wholes, forms and meanings

A number of themes recur through the sketches presented in the previous chapter: the boundedness of the community *vis-à-vis* the 'outside world'; its egalitarian discipline, which inhibits assertive or disruptive behaviour; the sense of place, and of the past; the dialectic of communality and segmentation, and so forth. These issues will surface again later in the book; they are primary colours on Whalsay's canvas, too complex in themselves to be reducible to any overarching cultural logic. They should not be thought of as *determining* people's behaviour, but as intruding certain constraints which have to be acknowledged if behaviour is to be mutually interpretable. Whalsay people do not respond to these constraints in a uniform manner; they are negotiable. But they use them to render behaviour and events intelligible. We can imagine the community as a field of raw data, of stimuli, which have to be processed to become recognisable as knowledge and information on the basis of which people can interact with each other in an orderly manner. They comprise the basic vocabulary of social life. But a knowledge of vocabulary does not determine what shall be said: it only gives to its bearer a means of expression, and a partial means of rendering intelligible other people's statements. So it is with these themes: they do not compel Whalsay people to behave in given ways about which we can usefully generalise; they are elementary cognitive forms through which meaning is expressed in and imputed to behaviour. The forms are not *inherently* meaningful: like all symbols, they are the vehicles of meaning.

Therefore, when reference is made to kinship, or crew membership, or neighbouring, the salient topic is not their configuration as elements of social structure. It is, rather, their efficacy as idioms which encapsulate the foundations of social knowlege. They are 'carrier concepts', or devices through which people make the world meaningful. In her seminal study of the village of Elmdon, and in various publications since, Strathern (e.g. 1981) has shown that ideas which Elmdoners held of their kinship were more than genealogical models. They were also statements about 'village', 'class', about 'insiders' as opposed to 'outsiders', about rootedness. Earlier Schneider (1980) had shown that the terminology of kinship used by urban Americans expressed far more than the structural nature of the relationships to which it referred: it embraced also ideas, sentiments, and theories of kinship which differed widely among those who used the *same* terminology. Structure does not entail meaning. Further, as Strathern has so fruitfully demonstrated, kinship, as a vehicle of meaning, goes far beyond the lexical, legal and anthropological notions of it as a discrete component of social organisation. The formal elements of Whalsay society, such as those mentioned above, have precisely this character.

Indeed, social life in Whalsay could be viewed as a struggle among its members to render these forms meaningful in particular ways – as a struggle to *inform* them with character. The 'form' is the apparently harmonious, placid, timeless veneer. But its bland appearance only masks the competition for evaluation and meaning which simmers under the surface. This contrast is apparent in the most fundamental of all social juxtapositions, that of individual to society; and is replicated in the nature of relations among the groups into which individuals coalesce.

These are enduring topics in social theory, and their introduction here does not call for yet another detailed rehearsal of the anthropological tradition, examining the influential statements of M. G. Smith, Evans-Pritchard and, earlier, Durkheim, and so on back through the classical and ancient social philosophers. The notion of the segmentary lineage has been extensively and critically reappraised (e.g. Peters, 1967; Sahlins, 1961) and I do not wish to enter that debate. My own interest is less in the structural bases of segmentation than in its cognitive implications, and in the ways in which people's orientations to segmentary boundaries affect their view of the whole. Influential organisational analysis has suggested that sectional interests may become so predominant as to obscure the wider organisational context altogether.[1] My view of Whalsay is that this is not the case: that, rather, the community as a whole, and its constituent segments, coexist in a dialectical relationship, but one in which each enriches and informs ideas of the other.

One of the powerful criticisms of the tradition of community studies was that they were based on, and perpetuated, an unjustifiable reification of the concept of 'community'. Writers were criticised for giving the community 'arms and legs'. It will not have escaped readers' notice that this tendency is apparent also in the present book. I argue that, in the case of Whalsay at least, the tendency is defensible. People *do* speak of the community as an entity: it has character imputed to it and, in this way, is given life. It is even implied that it has some kind of independent existence: that, like 'public opinion', it is 'out there', confronting its individual members. But to speak of it thus is to give the quality of authority and objectivity to a partial idea. People's ideas of the community are actually generated through their experience of *sectional* interest and *segmentary* membership. 'The community' may be a generalisation from these partial views; or it may be a way of emphasising their discreteness. In either case 'the community' is seen through the medium of its parts. Just as Strathern's Elmdoners conflated their views of the village as a whole and of their place in British social structure with their own kinship histories, so Whalsay folk construct 'the community' from the perspective of their idiosyncratic experiences as members of particular bilateral kinship groups, crofting townships and fishing crews. It is in this respect that the community has the character of a symbol: its form is shared among its members, but its meaning is constructed differently by them.

But the commonality of form does have some importance, for without it the sense of community would be insubstantial; it would lack all authenticity. Whatever the degree of variation in their constructions of it, Whalsay people do attribute integrity to their invocation of community. It distils for them not only their sense of similarity to each other, or their mutual belonging, but also their sense of the ways in which they differ from non-Whalsay people. Whilst the very term 'the community' may be an ichoate condensation of history, convention, personalities, life itself, it is especially eloquent, and most frequently invoked, as an expression of *boundary*. There are, then, these complementary themes in the relation of parts to whole in Whalsay: that Whalsay people recognise their essential likeness to each other in contrast to people elsewhere, a likeness they express symbolically and in their solidarity. At the same time they are deeply committed to those factors which distinguish them from each other, both as individuals and as members of segmentary factions. Moreover, these complementary themes become inextricably joined. The *commonality* of Whalsay is perceived through, and enriched by, its competitive *particularities*, which, in turn, are rendered intelligible by their assimilation to the shared, basic vocabulary of form and theme.

The public allocation of identity[2]

Byron (1986) quotes a frequently repeated assertion by Burra people about themselves: 'We're aa' da same here'. In one of my first publications on Whalsay I cited a revealingly different comment by a Whalsay informant: '. . . We're aa' da same here – but different too' (1978a, p. 449).

In both cases the statement 'We're all the same' can be regarded as normative rather than as a description of reality or a statement of belief. It derives from the dominant imperative to egalitarian conduct, and is really tantamount to the view that 'we all ought to behave *as if* we were the same as each other'. Both Byron (1986) and I (1977) have noted that this egalitarianism as a style of conduct extends even to the command structure of the fishing boat, in which skippers take some trouble to reduce to a minimum the explicit giving of orders, seek to minimise the distance between themselves and their crew, and go through the motions of consultation in order to contrive a consensus on strategic decisions. However, it would be absurd and naive to suppose that people *believe* they are indistinguishable from each other. First, to hold such a belief would remove any means of discriminating among a universe of potential associates. Second, it would fly in the face of the continuous competition waged among factions for the recognition of their members as the best skippers, sailors, footballers, shepherds, knitters, filleters or whatever. Questions therefore arise: How can public egalitarianism be maintained in the face of its continual private subversion? How can the egalitarian suppression of distinctiveness nevertheless accommodate the celebration of individuality, such as we have seen in the previous chapter?

Earlier in this book I referred to a public treasury of personal knowledge. This treasury contains the public identities of Whalsay people: the characters attributed to them in public discourse, and formulated on the bases of the stereotypical qualities of their kinsfolk or their township of origin; the anecdotal knowledge of incidents in which they were participants; supposed personal idiosyncracies, and so forth. The individuals thus identified have little, if any, control over the construction and dissemination of their public identities. The manner of their origination, especially of nicknames, may no longer even be widely remembered. Yet these frequently fictitious personae are accorded the quality of reality. Their unfortunate and frustrated bearers are stuck with them and are virtually powerless to alter them. Public identity is not easily negotiable.

Such labelling might be regarded as an instance of the despotism of the small community, but the truth is more prosaic. Public identities provide some of the signposts through the fields of unprocessed data to which I referred above. They are like compass bearings. If they were mutable, people would lose a fundamental means of social orientation. In such circumstances the authenticity of the community would be severely jeopardised. It is precisely such a deleterious condition which Byron diagnoses in the Burra of 1979, when people had ceased to cultivate the illusion of being 'da same'. Moreover, in circumstances of intensive social change, these personae, formulated largely in terms of the timeless structural character of the community, serve as means of anchoring the community. They relate its present generations to their lineal predecessors; to place; to historical incidents – one of the many ways in which time is telescoped.

The public allocation of identity also helps to maintain the discipline of egalitarianism by setting limits within which difference can be acknowledged and, thus, by setting the terms for much of the community's public discourse. The terms emphasise the qualities being celebrated, and diminish the significance attached to individuals who display them. Thus for X. to be known as a good skipper may draw attention more to the indigenous theory

of 'skipperhood' than to the personal attributes of X. In this respect it has the
competence which Comaroff (1975) attributes to the 'formal' as opposed to
the 'evaluative' code of oratory among the Barolong boo Ratshidi, used, he
says, '. . . for the purposes of stating shared values and ideals. . . .' (p. 150). By
the same token, allocated identity in Whalsay marks the person, but *as a
member of the community*, whose repertoire of ostensibly shared values is
thereby substantiated. For example, in noting an individual's skills, reference
may be made (by way of explanation) to the geography and genealogy of his
personal history. D. was born near Sodom, which lies between Symbister and
Huxter on the road which joins east and west coasts at the southern end of the
island. He now lives in his wife's natal home in Sandwick, at the extreme
south-west of the island. He is especially skilled in improvising with
oddments of materials to produce all kinds of devices. As observed earlier,
this kind of resourcefulness has a central place in the ethos of 'being Whalsa'.
D.'s skill must be accorded recognition, but in a way which would not portray
him as inherently superior to others. So some people explain his ingenuity by
pointing to his 'Skaw blood'. Skaw is a settlement in the extreme north of the
island from which, by turning through 150°, one faces the Mainland of
Shetland to the west, the island of Yell to the north-west, the islands of Fetlar
and Unst to the north, and the isles of the Out Skerries to the north-east. Thus
surrounded by inhabited land and jutting in to the confluence of various tidal
streams, the beaches of Skaw have long been a rich source of flotsam,
particularly of timber, a fact which is cited locally to explain why Skaw has
produced a substantial number of noted carpenters over the centuries.[3]
Associated with their skills as joiners is their creative imagination and
appreciation of the potentialities of materials: 'If een o' dey Ska' men comes
on a fish box on da beach, he disnae see a fish box; he sees a table or a chair, or
some deckin' fer his model yacht.' D. was born and lived all his life in the
south of the island, but his mother's mother was born in Skaw of a Skaw
father. Moreover, to substantiate the association between Skaw and such
skills, and to 'depersonalise' D.'s achievements, it is also pointed out that the
most accomplished carpenters in Whalsay tradition have belonged to what
used to be the major cognatic kin group in Skaw, the 'Ska' Bruces', of which
D. is a member through his mother. Therefore, to acknowledge his mechanical resourcefulness, he counts as 'een o' dey Ska' men'.

But when considering and commenting on his hand-line fishing, different
associations become pertinent. The *eela* fishing exploits the shores of holms
and skerries in the nearshore waters around Whalsay and in various small
rocky niches on the sea bottom. It requires a very exact knowledge of the sea
bed and considerable navigational expertise. (See chapter four.) Each species
is caught in particular spots, in different tidal conditions and with different
kinds of gear. So, despite its leisurely appearance, the *eela*, properly prosecuted, is a precise art. Its practitioners tend to specialise in particular areas of

the coastline. J. always works the waters along the west coast of Whalsay and through the sounds among the islets between the west coast and Mainland. Indeed, throughout his fifty-odd years he has hardly ever fished elsewhere. D. is one of his closest friends and was his protege in crofting and other skills. Until D. married they were close neighbours and D. still works the croft immediately adjacent to J.'s. But D. fishes only the south coast of the island, where J. does not venture, from Sandwick (where he now lives) west to Clett. In general conversation, J. attributes D.'s practice and performance to the fact that he is a 'Sandwick man'. This does not really mean very much, since some Sandwick men fish the same waters as J. to the west of Whalsay, and some fish farther to the east. But identity thus allocated 'excuses' D. for differing from his close friends and suggests that he does so not because he believes his opinions are more worthy or his places better, but because he properly conforms to the practices of the neighbours and affines among whom he now resides. We noted in the previous chapter a tendency to mute the expression and assertion of self; paradoxically, it clearly extends also into the area of personal identity.

In this example D.'s skills 'place' him by descent and marriage – two entirely separate principles which can be invoked simultaneously to explain his behaviour without making either it or the explanation appear contradictory. Place often figures in accounts of working practice. It has to be borne in mind that association with place is also usually underpinned by kinship, so that idioms of place and blood may often imply each other. The residents of one particular township may be collectively denigrated for their incompetence in clipping sheep, or for their incorrigible annual haste in cutting their grass for hay and for beginning to cast their peats before the weather is suitable. Even in such mundane and ubiquitous matters there seems to be a concern to depersonalise difference. At the Burns, on the west of the isle, there originated the practice of 'singling' swede seedlings very early to maximise growth in the short Shetland season. Yet the very contrary view is attributed, again collectively, to 'Sandwick', that the seedlings should be left dense in order to trap moisture. Collectivity is also used to impute personal characteristics. In the past Skaw was known not only for the inventiveness of its folk but also for their propensity to practical joking, and for the naivety and gullibility of some of its old people, now long dead. By contrast, 'da Sandwick men, du kens, dey're jus' rather quiet. Dey like a yarn aroon' da fire – not a lok o' on-carry.'

Kinship stereotypes are used in much the same way: the X.'s will be spoken of as 'guid wi' deir haands', whilst the Y.'s are said to be 'handless' (manually inept) or to have a particularly quirky sense of humour. Differences of opinion will be attributed to the vested interests of kin groups, or to the dynamics of kin factionalism. In all these respects, the individual is regarded largely as the product of his social associations, with individuality legitimated only within strict limits and generally explained by a person's structural connections with the community. Local personalities may be celebrated as colourful, but the colours fall within a finite spectrum of recognisability and permissibility (Cohen, 1982a, p. 24). The consequences are sometimes odd. An individual may be 'known' for a particular skill – say, as a shepherd or a joiner – not only when there are others more skilful but when the person in question has more obvious skills. It may be that the ways in which people become known are not random but (*a*) recognise the claims of other sections or factions to similar skills, and (*b*) maximise the range of characteristics within the constraints of the community's coherence. I suggest that such strategic logics are implausible. These would be better regarded as consequences, rather than as motivations, of identity formulation.

The eccentricity of the practice may be attributed more accurately to the value which is placed on privacy. Thus far we have been talking about *publicly* allocated identity. But Whalsay people are no more compliant than any in the suppression of their selves. The tension of community life may be partly attributable to the continuous scrutiny of and by other people. But part of it is also due to the possible contradictions between public persona and private self-image. The commonality of knowledge is often more apparent than real. Whalsay people are reticent in the expression of their deep convictions. By and large, they tend not to display emotion, nor to divulge personal feelings which may set them at odds with others. Much of the discipline of community life consists in precisely this kind of self-containment, relaxed only in the company of one's close family or closest friends. The public persona is a burden, but it is outwith the control of individuals, rather like the *joik*, the 'signature tune', given to Saami at birth. Yet its imposition, and its disparity with the private sense of self, would not seem to culminate in any unusual frequency of neuroses. One must conclude that people tacitly accept the burden as part of the cost of belonging to the community. There is a sense that the persona is acknowledged as providing only the terms for public discussion of the individual, and it is not confused with the deeper reality beneath. To examine the reality any more intrusively, and to comment on it publicly, *would* be disruptive. Therefore it is simply excluded from public dialogue. The community satisfies itself with the actors on stage, and avoids public speculation about what lies beneath the make-up and behind the script.

There is evident in this restraint people's awareness of the need for self-control which became apparent in the ethnographic sketches above. It limits both the intrusiveness with which the public observes individuals, and the aggressiveness or persistence with which individuals publicly pursue their own selfhood. The community is too small, too isolated, and socially too compact to withstand the unfettered battle of egos. The competition is thus limited and codified to produce an exemplary harmony of collectivity and individuality which recognises the identity needs of each.

The 'dialectics' of identity can be represented on several levels. They are present in the relationship of community and individual; of community and its constituent segments; of segments and their individual members. These segments – kin, *folk* (see below), neighbourhood and crew – are the media through which individuals belong to the community. Like those of individuals, their identities can be divided between the disparate forms of public and private discourse. Thus they have stereotypical character allocated to them, and, through the private discussion of their individual members, no doubt have a different self-consciousness. Clearly, we can not generalise about the content of these self-images except to note that they can be grounded easily in their own appropriate symbolism – of croft, neighbourhood, boat, antecedents, and so forth. Thus, however widely their individual members may differ in the meanings they impute to these intermediary groups, they will share substantial common ground in the terms of their expression. The vocabulary of *community* identity is scarcer, less subtle, enabling only grosser expression. Its common referents relate less intimately to individuals' lives. For this reason, it does not conflict with the terms of individual or segmentary identities. Relative to them it is vacuous and can be constituted by the experiences and interests of its members. In turn it provides them with the tempo and the key for the construction of their own score. The relationship of whole to part is not one of simple determinism, but of mutual reinforcement. Nor is it one in which individuals assimilate their own selves to a *conscience collective*. It is almost the other way round: the collectivity provides its members with the vocabulary they need in order to make their statements of identity. It does not determine the *content* of these statements. Rather, it just requires its members to make statements in terms which will be intelligible to their fellows. Finally, the articulation of these statements, and their common currency, validates the community's language, and continuously regenerates it. (Fig. 2.)

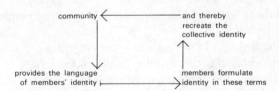

Fig. 2 The public allocation of identity

When the collective terms are inadequate for the individual's expression of self, she departs from the score (in the privacy of the rehearsal room, so to speak), improvising, or speaking *sotto voce* – but stopping short of tearing up the score or publicly impugning its integrity. So the whole and parts rehearse theme and counterpoint in an elegant, complex cycle. There is no composer, no conductor. But the players are well practised, the instruments finely tuned, and, through long familiarity, they manage to play more or less in time, in reasonable harmony. More jazz than symphony.

Kinship, and 'people we know'

In our attempt to locate some of the themes of the last chapter's sketches within a more analytic view of social organisation in Whalsay we have to deal early with the thorny issue of kinship. Unfortunately, a simple account of local genealogical conventions and kinship theory would not begin to comprehend the meaning and use of kinship in Whalsay. As in most societies, it is more than a morphology of social relationships, although it is possible to abstract a general logic of relations. In part, it is also a rhetoric of legitimation which is used to justify contraventions of its own logic.

There is a high degree of local endogamy. Marriages involving a partner from outside the isle are exceptions to the general rule. A slight majority of such marriages involve women marrying out of the island. In the past the herring stations provided the meeting ground for partners who eventually married. Fishermen from other Shetland communities may have landed herring at the station in Whalsay, where local women were employed to gut and pack the fish. Similarly, Whalsay women may well have worked at stations elsewhere in Shetland. Nowadays it is still more common for single women than single men to work elsewhere in Shetland, for the simple reason that there are fewer employment opportunities for them on the island. Since the high school in Lerwick became fully comprehensive in 1978, Whalsay girls have been more inclined than boys to transfer there for the two final years of their compulsory schooling. They may also train and work as nurses in the Gilbert Bain Hospital in Lerwick. However, the general practice is for girls to remain on the island, and the substantial expansion of the casual labour force at the fish factory has made available to them employment which was previously lacking.

Because of the historical incidence of local endogamy the members of the population are linked to each other by blood and marriage in complex and plural ways. During the mid-nineteenth century the Church would not sanction first-cousin marriage. Later ministers took a more liberal attitude and, though they are not common, there are regular instances of first-cousin marriage since civil registration began in 1855. Perhaps because of the dubious light cast on genealogical enquiry by those earlier clerics, people in Whalsay still occasionally refer to genealogical history as 'dirt' (rubbish). It is inevitable that marriages between local people will relate affinally people who have blood ties within a minimum of four generations. I cite one here as an example, with no claim that it is typical, but no reason to suppose that it is unusual. X. in Fig. 3 asked me to compute for her the number of ways in which she was related to her husband. They both knew, of course, that they were second cousins, but had only heard 'rumours' that they were connected in other ways. They are, in fact, linked consaguineally in six ways within four generations. For reasons which I shall shortly make clear, I have excluded from the diagram four of these links of which X.'s father was unaware or had forgotten. By the same token I include an affinal tie which he and his wife recalled when I pointed it out. If one was to add the affinal links among the generations of X. and her husband, and of her parents and parents-in-law, the picture would become impenetrable in its complexity. The dimensions of the problem may be rapidly appreciated. X.'s husband is one of ten siblings. Her father is one of seven; her mother's father was one of six. It is reasonable to assume that one could therefore trace a relationship between them and almost every indigenous household on the island.

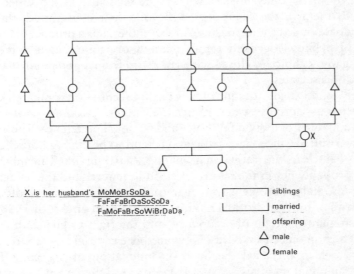

X is her husband's MoMoBrSoDa
                   FaFaFaBrDaSoSoDa
                   FaMoFaBrSoWiBrDaDa

siblings
married
offspring
△ male
○ female

Fig.3   A consequence of local endogamy.

As a term in ordinary use in Whalsay 'kin' does not discriminate between consanguines and affines. This lack of bias mirrors also the unbiased nature of bilaterality and cognatic descent. It would be difficult to substantiate a claim to any noticeable patrilineal bias, such as Byron (1986) makes for Burra and Mewett (1982b), among others, notes in Lewis.

The structural features of Whalsay kinship can therefore be summarised as the prevalence of local endogamy; bilateral kinship; and cognatic descent. The logical conclusion to the application of these principles would be the redundancy of kinship as a means of social discrimination within the island, simply because everybody is related in some manner to everybody else, and, beyond a certain degree, modes of relationship are not clearly ranked in importance. In practice the principles are not applied in a uniform manner. Rather, they are used pragmatically to justify the maintenance of particular relations – although, interestingly, *not* to justify the absence of relationship. Thus somebody's invitation to a wedding might be explained on the grounds that 'he's kin, like', although the lack of invitation does not elicit the explanation 'he's not kin'. Firstly, it would probably be technically incorrect; and secondly, by explicitly privileging kinship over other forms of association, it would dent the egalitarian imperative. Nevertheless, kinship has, or is said to have, empirical supremacy over other social ties, even though its conformity to biological and affinal linkages is somewhat haphazard. In collateral terms, first cousinhood would be reckoned as kinship. But beyond this there is no general rule. People may invoke associations with second or third cousins as entailed by their family links, but may not recognise as kin other people related to them in the same degree. Beyond first cousinhood, therefore, kinship does not determine social relations; rather, it is a product of them as a matter of acknowledgement rather than of obligation. It is a means of justifying one's choice of close social associates from a potentially unlimited universe of associates.

This, then, raises the question of why certain sections of a potential kindred are selected as close associates rather than others, assuming that it is not entirely a manner of individual choice and personal preference. The assumption is warranted, since these associations tend to be among households, or groups of nuclear kin, rather than among their individual members. The answer probably lies in the nature of crofting tenure, and the tendency for households related in some way to aggregate around the family crofts.

The laws of modern crofting tenure originate with an Act of 1886 which gave the tenant the right of occupancy, and the right to bequeath tenancy. There is a pronounced similarity between this early right of tenure and the udal law which preceded the Scottish annexation of Shetland. Further reforms, culminating in an Act of 1976, increased the tenant's security, the latter Act giving crofters the statutory right to purchase their crofts. It has been powerfully argued that the origin of crofting in Scotland lay in the lairds' requirement for a captive labour force. They thus allocated to their tenants portions of land too small to yield their entire subsistence needs, rendering them dependent upon local employment at wage levels so low as to require, in turn, supplementation from the croft to generate together a basic subsistence (Hunter, 1976). The Bruces of Symbister, lairds of Whalsay, certainly exploited the feudal advantages of their power over their local tenantry, conscripting them into fishing, and exemplifying what was known as 'the Zetland method'. (See, e.g., Wills, 1984.) It is generally agreed that the croft was always envisaged as a part-time undertaking to complement other local employment (cf. Collier, 1953; Mewett, 1977), and as a basic resource to stem the outflow of labour and to retain a small population in place. This latter point is still applied as a principle by the Crofters' Commission when considering applications by outsiders, or by people with other sources of income, to take over croft land in circumstances where a local person in need of it might thereby be deprived.

Crofting law renders the croft impartible, a provision whose enlightened intention was to prevent the parcelisation of land seen so commonly in other parts of Europe, culminating in its redundancy; and, thus, to limit tenants' dependence on the exploitative employment offered by their landlords. The impartible inheritance of land in Whalsay did not have the consequence, again widely noticed elsewhere (e.g. Brox, 1964; more generally, Macfarlane, 1978) of forcing the non-inheriting sons into emigration, since it seems to have been tacitly agreed that, although only one son or daughter could legally inherit, the others could have access to the croft. It has thus always been worked collaboratively, and its produce shared. Access may be available to affines as well as to consanguines. There are occasional instances of dispute over access and boundaries, but these are so exceptional as not to call the general rule into question.

The croft, therefore, is less exclusive property than a core around which related households aggregate. As a consequence, crofting *townships*[4] (or neighbourhoods) are frequently strongly associated with particular kin groups, the association often extending back to the earliest available records.[5] The crofting life was characterised by a high degree of informal collaboration. Cultivation, the cutting and curing of peat, *rooing* sheep, and so forth, were all activities in which the members of neighbouring households and crofts would help each other. (See below and, e.g., Jamieson, 1949, pp. 188 ff.) Townships thus acquired and maintained a solidary character, coming to be seen as quite distinctive sections within the population, as we noted earlier. Their members shared ties with place, with work, and were frequently associated by blood and/or marriage as well. But to describe this complex association as one of 'kinship' is to put an overly simple gloss on it. It is from among the people who share, or whose predecessors shared, these complex associations than the span of acknowledged kinsfolk is to be found. In this respect 'kinship', as it is operationalised in social interaction, refers to a sharing of experience as well as to a sharing of blood. These old solidary groups, now glossed as 'kin' or 'wir folk', may well still be maintained even when their successor members have moved away from the township of origin, and are recalled in spreeing companies, and on other major social occasions (see below, and Cohen, 1985b). As a general rule relatives who are not readily acknowledged as kinsfolk may be assumed not to have shared, in this or preceding generations, in the same solidary, neighbouring groups.

The distinction is between 'kinship in theory' and 'kinship in practice'. The strength of the distinction is such that in practice affines may share considerably closer associations with each other than with their own consanguines, an observation which perhaps applies especially to men who go to live in their wife's natal township. The openness of kinship is evident also in the absence of any biased rule of residence. The decision of a newly married couple whether to reside with the husband's or the wife's kin is generally a matter of convenience: which household can most easily accommodate them; on whose croft can they most easily obtain a site for a house.

Yet Whalsay kinship also has this practical means of closure in the *conventional* acknowledgement of who is kin to whom. There is rarely dispute about this. The appeal is not to genealogical theory, although many people are knowledgeable genealogists, *redd'n da kin* having been a frequent and popular fireside activity until quite recently. It is, rather, to the folk logic of 'da people we know'.

Wir folk, yon folk

'Knowing', in this usage, obviously means more than acquaintanceship. Where people in urban society may be inclined to use the term 'know' to indicate that they have 'met' a person, in the small-scale milieu of Whalsay, even of Shetland generally, it has to indicate more than that. Virtually all islanders are known to each other at the level of acquaintanceship. Indeed, there may even be some familiarity among people who, nevertheless, would not claim to 'know' each other. Those who are completely unacquainted are *unken folk* – though, interestingly, this term seems to be reserved almost exclusively to outsiders, 'folk frae da sooth'. At the other extreme, the 'people we know' are habitual associates, usually of a household or family, possibly through the association of earlier generations.

To acknowledge some individual, or group of people, as 'known', *ken't*, invokes the same senses of relatedness and opposition as the notion of boundary outlined earlier. Membership of a group implies opposition to, or exclusion from, some other. Despite all its real commonality, and all the rhetoric of community, similarity, equality and so forth, which characterises social life in Whalsay, intra-communal relations are founded upon this plurality of segmentary or factional associations. People 'belong' to Whalsay. But their pre-eminent belonging is to more intimate groups, often glossed as 'kin', which are composites of kinship, neighbourhood, crew membership – people who are *ken't* and who are often referred to colloquially simply as '*wir* [our] folk'.

As noted already, the attempt to identify in general terms who might qualify for inclusion in the category 'wir folk' would be misleading. It would be absurdly general; would, of necessity, deploy such analytic categories as kinship in a rather more rigid sense than is appropriate; and would, in any case, emphasise the *structural* implications of such a category, whereas its real significance is cognitive and ideal: it is a means of discriminating, and of locating, one's close associates within a field of potential associates limited only by the geographical bounds of the community. Moreover, its structural imprecision allows it to be modulated in such a way that it can, for some purposes and on some occasions, be muted; in other circumstances, emphasised. But, because it conflicts with the expressed ideals of commonality and homogeneity, it has to be expressed in such a way that it avoids the explicit suggestion of permanent, faction-like sub-community groupings. The problem of definition is that the groups to which we refer here are bounded, but by practice rather than by rule or ideology. Hence they do not have the closed exclusivity of the *clique*, but, empirically, conduce to the association of people who are already associated by some means or other.

The anglers' meeting, described in the previous chapter, gives some indication of the nature of the beast. As may be seen from Fig. 4, all those attending can be seen to share close association, either through kinship, neighbourhood, customary friendship (extending back through previous generations) or a combination of these. No. 1 is 2's uncle by marriage, 2's wife being still closely associated with 1's neighbourhood, although she has not resided in it since her marriage. Nos. 2 and 3 are first cousins, as are 10 and 11. The brothers 5 and 6 are brothers-in-law to 7. Moreover 3, 5, 6, 7, 8 (7's son), 9 and 10 all live within a quarter of a mile of each other. Nos. 5 and 7 (8) are co-resident and jointly work 7's croft. Nos. 5, 6 and 7's wife grew up on 3's croft. Nos. 3, 10 and 11 form an *eela* fishing crew, and 5 and 9 were crew mates. The friendship of 3, 10 and 11 extends back to and beyond 3's now deceased parents, 10 and 11 being related by both blood and marriage to

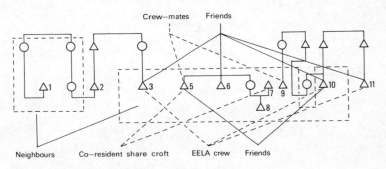

Fig. 4 The Anglers

3's mother. Again, if one were to add all the consanguineal and affinal links between the central figures, the picture would become impossibly complex and probably no more instructive.

Membership of the angling club was not restrictive, other than by payment of a small annual subscription. It did not require election, and could not reasonably be described as oligarchic. There were more members than those who attended this meeting. Yet these participants were clearly the active membership of the club. They are manifestly associated by things other than their enjoyment of fly fishing. These men do not go fishing because they like each other, or because they have long-standing relationships. They go because they enjoy fishing. But their enjoyment of each other's company is not merely incidental. They feel comfortable with each other; they are *ken't*, and that, as we have seen, is an important consideration in Whalsay. More to the point is that their associations with each other may be so well known as to have created an impression of the club as belonging peculiarly to 'yon folk' and, therefore, as being an inappropriate or uncomfortable activity for others. It so happens that, in 1986, the club is in very different, younger hands: a generation of activists, again with notable links of kinship, friendship, and so forth. It is now so closely identified with 'yon folk' that, though others would not be actively dissuaded from participation, it may not occur to them to regard it as practically accessible. The boundary notion of 'wir folk, yon folk' is a means by which members of communal segments recognise familiar and alien social territory. The latter is not forbidden to them – quite the contrary. But it does not tempt them.

By contrast, the football team *was* regarded as a self-recruiting and perpetuating clique, firmly in the hands of one of the most extensive and celebrated descent groupings in the community (chapter six). The regular team in 1975 is shown in Fig. 5. Nos. 3 and 4, the two eldest of the four brothers shown, were widely spoken of as 'too old' for the team. Ten years later, 4 was still a regular player. No. 7 had retired, though family representation was main-

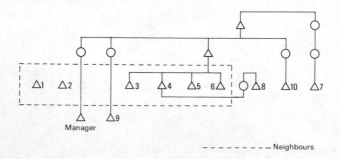

Fig.5   Whalsay football team, 1975

tained by the accession to the team of his brother's son. All the rest are still members of the team, though other, younger players, some of them linked with the core descent group, now play frequently.

I have no reason at all to suppose that the team was selected on anything other than merit. But my judgement is irrelevant. Some people *outside* the group clearly did identify it as an exclusive clique to which others, however deserving, could not gain access. In defence of this view they would point to the relation between the team manager and the rest of the team. In separate conversations three women referred to the team as '—— United'. It seems to me unlikely that factional considerations operated any more in the selection of the team than they do in other activity. Nevertheless, in the public view there was a qualitative difference, the judgement of sectional interest being too strong, to definite, to be encompassed by so intangible a category as 'yon folk'. This was clearly seen as a case of the paramount solidarity of family.[6]

Close kin relations involve inescapable obligations and, as we have seen, they compromise individuality. 'Wir folk', by contrast, implies a greater degree of pliability and voluntarism. Within it relationships are reproduced as an expression of choice rather than of ascription. It is not entirely separable from kinship but is a dimension of it, as of other close associations. It really describes close relationships *in practice* rather than principle.

Sprees and funerals[7]

The preceding discussions amplify some of the dialectic of Whalsay social life apparent to us from the earlier sketches. For example, we have dwelt at some length on the juxtaposition of the ideals of community, egalitarianism and homogeneity, to their empirical realities of segmentation, differentiation and individuality. But just as these overarching principles of the Whalsay ethos can be seen to be qualified by empirical practice, so also the terms of these qualifications need to be unpacked to reveal, in their turn, disjunctions and complexities. As we have seen, segmentation goes beyond the plurality of kinship groups, townships and fishing crews – the 'official' collective components of the community – and extends to more nebulous and subtle nexus of association which people know about by experience, but which have no name other than 'yon folk', 'dat crowd' and so forth. These associations are the products of people's excavations of the bland surface of communality to provide themselves with secure toeholds of mutual support, friendship and the intimate security of belonging.

As suggested above, these associations are based on the collaborative groups of neighbours, relatives and friends which, in the days before the occupational specialisation of the post-war fishery, made it possible to gain a livelihood from a variety of indigenous resources. People built each other's cottages, giving their labour freely, all working under the supervision of the joiner, who was the only paid hand. They worked each other's hay, helped each other at *hairst* (harvest), helped to cure, carry and *bigg* (stack) each other's peat. Even when collaboration was not required, people now recollect their labour as having been synchronised so that it became a sociable activity. Crofters *dellin'* (cultivating) adjacent *rigs* might pause and rest together on their spades to pass the time of day. Men casting peats on their respective banks would walk together to and from the hill, and would share their *faerdamaet* (snack). One of the most emphatic contrasts drawn by people between present-day and 'traditional' work is its pace. The past is recollected as onerous, as entailing extraordinarily arduous labour, which was nevertheless paced in such a manner that people could always find time for the important things in life, pre-eminent among which was sociability. The present is seen as frenetic, tawdry and asocial. Modern work takes people away from 'their folk', and these associations have therefore to be maintained outside the normal circumstances of everyday life. They are reasserted now on notable occasions. Where previously they rested on the informal reciprocity of mutual support, they are now expressed symbolically in such specialised forms as the composition and geographical orientation of a *spree*, and the allocation of special roles in funerary rites.

The spree is a peripatetic party, moving from house to house, collecting the occupants of one to proceed to the next. Its membership may alter as people branch off in different directions. Husband and wife often spree separately, each reverting ultimately to a township to whose 'folk' they belong or with which they have a close association.

Until quite recently sprees were held on several fixed festive occasions such as Christmas night, the 'second night' of Christmas, Hogmanay, New Year's Day, the 'second night' of New Year, Old Christmas, and Regatta – the final night of the annual three-day sailing competition held in August. They would also be held on the second night of a wedding, and when crews *settled* on one of the three customary accounting days in the fishing year. In 1975 a round-the-isle sailing race was instituted, and this too now provides a regular occasion for a spree. So does any major social event which is open to the whole community – the annual dances held by the football club (such as the one described in chapter two) and the local branch of the Scottish Rural Women's Institute, for example – when the spree follows the end of festivities in the Public Hall. These major sprees are island-wide affairs, involving all age groups and all localities. More specialised sprees are held throughout the year by young people, generally those still unmarried. By 1985 it was clear that the recently opened licensed premises, 'Da Club', had changed the incidence of the latter sprees, and may have changed the nature of the major sprees. These always originated in private houses, as in the two cases represented below. There is now a tendency for many of the younger people to spend the early part of the night in the club before the sprees become mobile. The institution of 'the party', based on specific invitations, already apparent in Burra Isle in the early 1970s, has still not secured a foothold in Whalsay. The principle remains that on a spree a house, if open at all, is open to any caller.

The examples given in Figs. 6 and 7 are sprees on Christmas night, 1974, and regatta night, 1980. They are cited here not as necessarily representative in form but because these occasions are almost universal in Whalsay. The Christmas Day spree begins in the late afternoon, when neighbours and close family gathered for tea turn to the whisky bottle once the teapot has been emptied. If the weather is suitable the men will already have spent a sociably alcoholic morning at the Loch of Houll, sailing or watching the 'Yule Dee' model yacht race. With Christmas dinner eaten, the bonfire is kindled and fireworks are lighted for the children, after which unbidden visiting may begin. In the case of Regatta, the final day may include children's land sports, refreshments sold in the Public Hall, a ladies' rowing race; and, following the end of competition, a dance in the Public Hall or the club which will last until after midnight.

The usual catalyst for the start of the spree is the arrival of a visitor bearing a bottle of whisky. He offers his whisky to the company in the same manner which we saw at the anglers' meeting, and this form will be observed throughout the spree, well into the early hours of the following day. Obtaining a small tumbler from the hostess, the visitor fills it to the brim and offers it to the first drinker, usually the host or hostess. A brief toast is exchanged between donor and drinker, a sip is taken, and the glass returned to the donor. Again it is filled to the brim and offered to the next drinker, and so the procedure is repeated until everyone has taken a drink. Finally the donor quietly offers a toast to the entire company, takes a sip, and returns the whisky remaining in the glass to his bottle. As the night goes on the sips may become a little less restrained, but the generosity of the donor is not abused. Unwilling drinkers will not be pressured to participate but may just *lay a lip in*. When the glass has circulated around the company, the conversation resumes until the next person produces a bottle and starts all over again. As noted earlier, a person should not offer whisky again until everyone else present has had a chance to offer his, the order of offering should not be broken, and there should be no prompting to offer.

The company will remain in this initial house for an hour or two until someone suggests moving on. The core members of a spree usually have some ultimate destination in mind, and the spree visits certain houses *en route*, remaining in each long enough for each of the callers to offer their drink at least once, for conversation and, as the evening progresses, for food. The traditional fare is *reestit* (dried and salted) mutton, usually boiled, and

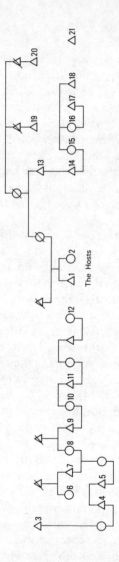

Fig. 6 The participants in a spree on Christmas night, 1974. The spree was held in the house of unmarried siblings 1 and 2. Nos. 14 (their MBS, from whose house the spree originated earlier in the afternoon), 15, 16, 17 and 18 are all close neighbours of 1 and 2. No. 18 is also an age mate of 1 (they are in their mid-fifties) and, though not associated by occupation, they trace their association back to their childhood neighbouring, friendship at school, and frequent journeys together to and from leave on National Service. Nos. 19 and 20 are long-standing friends of the family of 1 and 2: they are sons of their MMBs, and are regular members of 1's *eela* fishing crew (small-boat recreational fishing). The affines 11 and 12 are close neighbours of 1 and 2, and 12 is one of their closest friends. Nos. 8 and 9 are the children of a now deceased close neighbour of 1 and 2 who was also a crew mate of their father. Nos. 6 and 7 are the children of a now deceased crew mate of 1 and 2's father, who was also a frequent visitor and close friend of their parents. No. 5 (7's DH) is a close neighbour to 1 and 2, and 4 (5's B) is DH of 3, a neighbour of 1 and 2 and a close friend of their parents. No. 21 is the ethnographer, 1 and 2's closest neighbour and crew mate of 1.

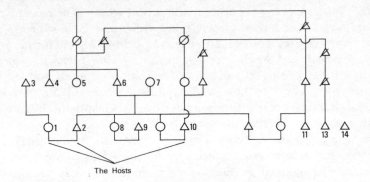

The Hosts

Fig. 7 A regatta spree in 1980. The spree was held in the house of 1 and 2. No. 1's F is an outsider, born and resident in Lerwick. No. 7 (2's M) was born on and spent her childhood on the croft on which 1 and 2, and 10 (2's ZH) now live. No. 8 (2's other Z) lives away from her parents and siblings with her husband's family. No. 11 is 2's BWB, and is also his second cousin. No. 13 is 10's closest friend (2 and 10 being co-resident on the same croft almost always begin their sprees together, so that in this context 10 is a co-host), although they are not associated in day-to-day affairs, and is, incidentally, his second cousin. No. 14 is the ethnographer, a close neighbour of 1, 2 and 10.

bannocks. Any one visiting group is likely to meet up with others, and people may leave one to join the other, or eventually head off independently. When the company reaches the principal destination of the spree, usually between 11.00 p.m. and midnight, they rest from their travels for a couple of hours. Whisky will now be circulating continuously; there may be dancing to Scottish and 'country and western' music, and, if people have already *got'n a bit dram in,* singing as well. Women are active participants, offering as well as receiving whisky, though they generally carry only half-bottles, whereas men invariably carry full-size ones.

The company assembled at this central point of the spree is composed substantially of the hosts' close associates, its members representing important marks on the social map which locates the host and hostess in the community. The spree is now one of very few occasions when people cross the everyday boundaries of kinship, neighbourhood and occupational association, to reassert their previous connections to the community. It thus revives these old relationships, some dating from childhood, or even those of preceding generations.

This reversion to earlier associations is even more marked at a further stage of the spree to which those still ambulant may proceed. After leaving the 'central' house they tend to disperse into smaller groups, each going its own way. A married son or daughter might walk the couple of miles back to the township in which he or she grew up and lived before marriage. They may call on the cousins or friends or crew mates with whom they had earlier been especially closely associated. These are the people who will be recognised as their 'folk', even though their present relationship may be less intense than those they now have with others. These 'folk' are those who, in former years, would have constituted the co-operative group, a memory now sustained by reciprocal gifting, visiting, the occasional exchange of goods and services, and by the spree. They are those who would still be regarded as providing one's social character because they provided one's social origins. It is now left to sociable occasions such as the spree to evoke the relational sense of the category 'wir folk', the category which provides the fundamental mode through which people *experience* their membership of the community.

The successive nights of spreeing on the main festive occasions allow the spreeers to revisit numerous landmarks of their social lives so that they are not forced into arbitrary or invidious choices of destination. The importance of the spree used to be recognised by the ready willingness of a host or hostess to rise from their bed and admit late callers. During the last few years the regular Saturday night spreeing of the younger people has come to be regarded as something of a nuisance, and so the simple signal of leaving the outside light on informs callers whether or not they will be welcome. However, on major occasions most people are anxious to have visitors. As we saw in the last chapter, there may often be some competition at the end of a dance about the house to which the company should return.

The social reciprocity of the spree can be seen as an echo of the strategic and material reciprocity of social life in the past. Perhaps it is significant that, as the occasions for such reciprocity have decreased in frequency as a consequence of economic change, so the frequency of large-scale sprees has increased. The old attachments are thus maintained symbolically. The spree is one item among several in a repertoire of symbolic devices through which Whalsay people are enabled to experience a continuity between the cultures of past and present. It evokes a collaboration of a kind quite different from that of the modern corporate partnership of the fishing crew. Because of its dependence on outside financial agencies, management and financial advice and political support, the latter is at odds with principles of self-sufficiency and mutual interdependence which were implicit in traditional co-operation. The spree has no economic value for its participants. Its significance is symbolic, and is present both in the egalitarian and reciprocal process of the spree, and in its composition.[8] It expresses the essentially segmentary nature of people's social membership on which is predicated the broader notion of the community.

Funerals   The organisation of funerals provides an instructive snapshot of part—whole relationships in Whalsay, revealing the tension between, and the reconciliation of, the categories of 'wir folk' and the community.

When a death occurs in Whalsay there follows a suspension of normality (marked symbolically by the stopping of the clocks in the deceased's home), gradually spreading outwards with a ripple effect in a series of concentric circles from the bereaved household. If the death has been expected as a result of debilitating illness, the sick person will already have been accorded a designation reserved to the dying: *a puir (aald) body*. People enquire of each other for news of the illness just as, when the death eventually occurs, they will repeat all they know of its circumstances. Sometimes this discussion focuses upon the conduct of the doctor, often with a hint of criticism. Might he not have done more? Should he have said what he did say? Such criticism is hardly a uniquely local phenomenon. One may suppose that, whatever the doctor's professional conduct, it has something to do with his detachment: he is a central participant in the drama of death, but is not bereaved (cf. Warner, 1959, pp. 310–13). Like a priest or a minister, he stands on the other side of the boundary (cf. Jorion, 1982). But in Whalsay his distance from those bereaved has an added dimension, for he is an outsider, a *soothmoother*. In commenting about him, then, other islanders are identifying themselves with the bereaved family *vis-à-vis* him: they are *all* bereaved, whereas he is not.

The core circle of close mourners is composed of the deceased's 'folk', the same nexus of close kin, neighbours, co-owners of or selected crew mates in fishing boats with which he or she may have been especially associated, as is expressed in the composition of the spree. Immediately following the death, the men of this group suspend their normal work. If fishermen, they remain ashore. The women reorder their normal daily routines to focus on the home of the bereaved widow, mother or daughter. They keep company with her from the time of death until the end of the funeral day itself and, sometimes, for several evenings after.

Two men from this core circle may be allocated the task of *bidding* selected people to the pre-funeral gathering in the home. This mirrors the practice of bidding guests to a wedding. Those invited to this phase of the funeral are segmentary affiliates of the deceased, though not having the intimate associations of his or her 'folk'. They could be regarded as belonging to the secondary circle. They are acknowledged kin, neighbours and other associates. Apart from attending domestic prayers and offering condolence to the bereaved, they are also invited to view the body. The bidders are also responsible for posting funeral notices in the local shops.

Men from the core circle of mourners will have been responsible for digging the grave. On the day of the funeral the ripples reach out beyond close associates to the further reaches of the community. Fishing boats owned and crewed by people connected with the deceased or with the bereaved remain ashore for the day. If the deceased was a prominent fisherman, or a member of a prominent fishing family, most of the boats in the fleet will remain ashore or will return to Whalsay to enable the men to attend the funeral. Upon the death of a young fisherman in 1975 the entire fleet returned home.

The funeral begins with a short service at the home, attended by members of the core and secondary circles. They proceed to the church hall at Saltness, in the south-west of Whalsay. The service may be attended by mourners further removed from the inner concentric circles. The main item in the service is an eulogy. This is the last phase of the funeral which women attend. They are not present at the burial itself. Before the construction of a road around the island, funeral processions went on foot to the kirk at Brough, the coffin being borne on a wooden stretcher by relays of bearers, and followed by mourners joining along the route (cf. Vallee, 1955, p. 124). Today the delivery van belonging to one of the local shops is used as a hearse, and other mourners follow in their cars, driving very slowly with headlights switched on. Most mourners who are not 'members' of the two inner circles will be waiting at the kirkyard for the arrival of the cortege. Everyday clothes of overalls, jeans and Fair Isle 'garnseys' give way to dark suits, black ties and high-crowned black caps. Those awaiting the arrival of the procession may be visiting the graves of relatives, or musing on stories, recollections and genealogies of others interred there. When the hearse arrives, two or three of the core men carry the wreaths into the kirkyard. Then a further six or eight of them carry the coffin to the graveside. These pallbearers are prominent members of the deceased's folk, representing each of the three bases of close association: kin, neighbourhood, and crew. They are followed to the graveside by other members of the core group and, sometimes, by a few self-selected members of the secondary circle.

There is, then, a clear spatial distinction, for the rest of the mourners stand in an adjoining section of the kirkyard, at some remove from the gravesite itself.[9] They do not participate in the burial service, but observe it, or merely occupy the kirkyard. They talk quietly among themselves about matters which may or may not ostensibly be connected with their reasons for being there (cf. O'Neill, 1983, p. 49). The spatial arrangement of mourners in the kirkyard expresses clearly the distinction between the community as a whole, and its partial, segmentary structures of belonging. But the conversation of the 'peripheral' mourners expresses a further relational distinction, between the community as a whole and the outside world. A common denominator in their talk of the dead, of the war, of the previous week's fishing, of people, places and boats is its communal introspection. It is conversation which is predicated on Whalsay and, implicitly, on a sense of boundary.[10] This localism was also apparent in what I discerned as embarrassment at the presence there of outsiders – not just the intrusive ethnographer but even relatives from other parts of Shetland, well known in the community. They seemed to be unacknowledged, commented on but ignored until and unless the conventions of politeness were pressed.

For all those other than the inner circle folk the interment marks the end of abnormality. The men are swiftly back at the pier, changed into working clothes, busily getting their boats ready again for sea. The usual clamour of life, whistling, singing, shouting, swearing – until then silenced – again fills the air. Immediately also critical comments about the deceased, suspended until he or she has been safely despatched, may once more be heard. Life has reasserted itself.

There are, then, a variety of respects in which the funeral refracts the nature of local life and, in particular, its internal segmentation and external solidarity. We have noted already the local and introspective character of cemetery conversation and demeanour; the criticism of the doctor, reflecting his outsiderhood; the obvious demarcations between the circles of mourners as statements of the deceased's social relationships. Those who occupy the core circle do not have the simply ascriptive character of kinship. Some first cousins, or nieces and nephews, may be included; some excluded. Some affines may be preferred to some consanguines. An intimate friendship based on long association in neighbourhood or fishing crew may take precedence over kinship. In this respect Whalsay funerals appear to be unusual in so far as they map actual rather than ideal or normative relationships, and thus differ notably from funerary rituals elsewhere (e.g. Douglass, 1969, pp. 202 ff.; Mandelbaum, 1976; Vallee, 1955, p. 129). This acknowledgement of social reality, as opposed to its theory, is an emphatic statement of the distinction drawn in Whalsay between actual and ascriptive relationships, a distinction which is an integral element in kinship ideology and which resolves the tensions that might otherwise be generated by the arbitrary definition of kin. It is a sophisticated qualification to kinship which Whalsay people regard self-consciously as distinguishing them from people elsewhere.

There is also a conscious claim to distinctiveness in the fishermen's practice of remaining ashore to attend funerals. The practice may have originated in the days when the opportunity to stay at home was a welcome relief from the toil of the *haaf* fishery and the unceasing demands of the laird and his bailiff, a rare opportunity to see wives and children and to sleep at home instead of in the spartan fishing lodges. Even after the demise of the haaf fishing attendance would not have involved much financial sacrifice, since relatively few men fished full-time, and those who did returned home on most days. During the lean fishing years between the wars, and for years after the second war, the price of fish was so low that the cost to the household budget of taking a day off would have been fairly inconspicuous. But that is not the case now, when, as we have noted earlier, boats have to gross thousands of pounds weekly just to meet their expenses.[11] The potential cost of lost fishing time is now enormous. Moreover the Whalsay crews are fishing well away from home waters, in the south-west of England or off the Western Isles, so that the costs incurred in just getting home can be prodigious. Their attendance at funerals is not simply a matter of personal sentiment. When the funeral is of one who was not himself a close associate it is seen and explained as an obligation imposed by the fact of community membership, yet willingly born, for it signals the community's distinctive character. It is thus an expression of the external solidarity of Whalsay *vis-à-vis* elsewhere. Failure to honour the obligation would thus diminish the very *raison d'être* of the community and, indeed, might well signify its demise, as suggested in comments made on the occasions of different funerals.

The first was offered by a skipper who had brought his boat all the way back from the Minch, arriving an hour before the funeral, and leaving again with the tide some three hours later. He uses the idiosyncrasy of segmentation to emphasise the distinctive locality: 'Well, we had to try an' wen hame. I mean, Aald G. [the deceased], he wisnae kin, like, but he an' me faither were together for years, du kens. Ach, it's a bloody nuisance, I ken, but if du willna' try an' do dese tings, du moit as well bide in comfort in Aberdeen or Fraserburgh.'

Following the death of an old lady, three fishermen reflected ironically on the financial perversity of their attendance at her funeral:

'Man, it's a funny ting dat we're aa' sittin' here ashore, an' dere's fish i' da sea. I never even likéd dat aald wife avaa' . . .'

'Du's roit, enyoch. Man, she could be sic' a witch. But, du kens, du's nae a' funeral fer to honour da dead. But da wye I look at yon, it's to honour da livin'.'

'Ach, it's dis bloody place! If we was Aberdeeny men, instead o' fra Whalsa', we'd likely be at sea.'

Being Whalsa'

As we see above, apparently conflicting claims of part and whole are reconciliable, and both inform Whalsay people's sense of the distinctiveness of their community. Indeed, their consciousness of the community and of its distinctiveness is so sensitised that it intrudes on their total experience of social life and, therefore, affects the meanings they attach to their symbolic constructs. It leads them continually, in Boon's phrase, to 'play the *vis-à-vis*'. 'Every discourse,' he says, 'like every culture, inclines toward what it is not: toward an implicit negativity' (1982, p. 232; see also Strathern, 1984, p. 186). The sense of community membership, however it may vary among its members, and Whalsay's difference from elsewhere, seem to pervade almost all aspects of local social life. The diversity of local attributes and the oppositional nature of local groups are themselves seen as tribute to the community – testimony both to its wealth of character, and to its sophisticated accommodation of such variety and the absence of overt strife and conflict. Thus, whatever may be used as emblematic of Whalsay – skills, humour, dialect, social organisation – people use *both* sides of it, without contradiction, to emphasise the integrity of local identity: its difference from forms manifest elsewhere, and its variability within the island.

The Whalsa' ethos is thus much less constraining than might otherwise appear. To the outsider it might seem to be expressed in a rigid ideology, to demand proficiency in a range of specified skills; to be represented in distinctive dialect; to be reproduced through a limited number of kin groups; to be sustained by a single, specialised occupation. The reality is different. The ethos provides *categories* of notable and legitimate performance. Social life exercises people's ingenuity and resourcefulness in developing variations within these categories which do not impugn the essential integrity of the categories themselves. Thus Whalsay people might pride themselves on being skilled fishermen, fine carpenters and ingenious mechanics. But this does not require agreement on how these virtues might be tested, nor on who might be credited with them. The competition for definition and attribution provides much of the dynamic of social process, but is kept within bounds such that the *lack* of consensus need not surface publicly. It mirrors the mediation of community and kinship by the more subtle, segmentary nexus of 'wir folk'.

Because of the inescapably competitive nature of scrutiny and evaluation, the ethos itself is always subject to reappraisal. It cannot stagnate, for people are always finding new ways of doing things, new standards of performance, and the ethos has to be adjusted accordingly. This elasticity in core ideas has been a necessary complement of Whalsay's unusually vigorous development. 'Being Whalsa'', an ethos which masquerades as orthodoxy, is itself always a matter of competitive definition. So intense is this discourse that it addresses the most mundane of activities, and is not specialised into rarified ritual. We could take, as an example, the construction of the 'block barrow', made for carting peats down the rough-hewn paths across *da hill* from the banks to home. It is a flat, open barrow, with an angled board at the front. Ideally the barrow would be made to fit the user, for he walks between its elongated shafts the easier to control it going up and down slopes, and manoeuvring down the high step and ditch between bank and moor. It is built of wood, except that the wheel, also usually home-made, would be rimmed with iron. The rim would be made slightly smaller than the wheel, then expanded by heat and doused in cold water after fitting, to shrink it on tight. A simple job for the wheelwright or smith. But it is one of countless infrequently used skills which the crofter had to master. On his mastery depended not only the successful pursuit of his livelihood but also his local reputation. Men would come to inspect and try out a new barrow, commenting on every aspect of its workmanship. There would be animated debate about how to position the wheel in order to achieve an optimal distribution of weight and make it easier to control a load while going downhill. Some argued that the wheel should be slightly recessed under the front, others that it should be set further forward. Such a debate was no more capable of resolution than the disagreement we encountered earlier about whether and when to single swede seedlings, or about how to tack a course across the Sound, or the latest date by which it was feasible to cut and cure peats. The influence of engineering, horticultural, navigational or meteorological logics on the outcomes of these discussions was limited. More important considerations were who was engaged in the debate, and who it was about. It is also instructive that these everyday, unremarkable topics remained matters for argument, belying the impression of orthodoxy. People would thus assent to the platitude that there were 'Whalsa' wyes' of doing all of these things – but would be hard-pressed to reach any substantial consensus on them. Although some of the topics for dispute may now have changed, there remains a similarly vigorous denial of orthodoxy in routine matters, still providing an invaluable source of vitality.

We can therefore identify the kinds of category of skill and attribute on which the ethos of 'being Whalsa" may be based; but they do not contain inherently criteria for judgement. The latter are not subjects for orthodoxy and vary according to who is making the judgement of whom and in whose company. The ethos requires self-sufficiency in manual skills. In fact, however, this self-sufficiency is being rapidly attenuated by the shortage of time men can now spend away from the fishing, and by the easier availability of services from the Mainland of Shetland. As late as our arrival in the early 1970s most men would have mastered most of the basic skills required to build and maintain a house. They might have called on local specialists for assistance with plumbing and wiring – mains water and electricity being relatively recent amenities. But the ability to carry out the concreting, joinery and plastering was general. Women, as now, were responsible for the internal decoration. During the 1970s a building boom began. Islanders were no longer reconstructing and enlarging old croft houses, but were preferring to import prefabricated kits of Scandinavian-type bungalows, generally for erection by specialist builders. One such firm was formed by two Whalsay men, and is still in business. Other local partnerships have surfaced briefly and then dissolved. Most men would still be able to undertake routine repairs, but would certainly not be capable of more specialised jobs, such as making windows, or roofing. In part, of course, this is due to the general change in the kinds of materials used. Again, in 1973 quite a number of roofs were still covered with tarred felt, requiring annual maintenance. They were gradually replaced by various bituminised coverings and, finally, by slates. Similarly, the standard hardwood sash windows were superseded first by metal frames and then by double-glazed sealed windows.

Whalsay men were also accomplished practical mechanics. Their engineering may have lacked a theoretical basis, yet they were able to adapt and maintain their boats with extraordinary ingenuity and resourcefulness. The technology of the modern fishing boat obviously now requires specialist attention. But this practical bent served local men well when car ownership spread. The ability to maintain a vehicle was general, although two men worked part-time as mechanics, sorting out problems that others were unwilling or unable to take on. Once the ferry service began, however, local people had easy access to Lerwick garages. At the same time the nature of car ownership changed – from hardy, unglamorous, second-hand vehicles suitable only for transport around the island, to brand-new, frequently exchanged family saloons, used regularly on the roads of Mainland, themselves vastly improved to cope with the oil-construction heavy traffic.

Interestingly, whilst both these areas of skill have decreased in necessity, and in consequence have become rarer, they have resurfaced in specialised revivals. Stonemasonry has become something of a local art form, with painstakingly constructed boundary walls, peat houses, and so forth, now adorning several households. Further, time and effort previously spent in keeping an old banger on the road may now be devoted to the rehabilitation of old, and sometimes the fashioning of new, agricultural machinery. The demise of arable cultivation on the crofts, again usually explained by shortage of time and lack of necessity, is matched by a recent interest in gardening. A few Whalsay households had long boasted spectacular conservatories, but many now also display ingeniously designed and meticulously tended gardens, based on rockeries, alpine plants and low shrubs.

In the past, household self-sufficiency extended also to clothing. Women spun wool from the fleeces of the croft's own sheep, from which they knitted 'garnseys', socks, undergarments and shirts. When a cow was slaughtered locally, men would obtain pieces of its cured hide to make *rivlins* – moccasins – and to patch and otherwise repair boots. A customary hearthside scene is recalled as comprising women spinning and knitting, with men *jannin'* – putting new pieces of cloth into oilskins or jackets – or bent over a cobbler's last. The lines used for fishing would be home-made, as were the flies and *fleets* of hooks used with hand line or rod. Many of the tools and implements required for work would be home-made: the rope 'parceller', the twine needles for repairing nets, the *kavv'lin tree* for extracting the hook from a large fish, the *clip* for hauling aboard halibut or skate, chisels, *gurneys* and *joktalegs* (knives), spades, *tushkers* (the all-purpose peat-cutting tool), *kishies* (baskets for carrying peat), *kjils* (kilns) for smoking fish, the specially shaped boxes for long lines, furniture, toys, traps and snares and so forth.

Women were spared little of the labour involved in working a croft. Apart from the hours spent in baiting long-lines, a woman might also have to tend *da kye* (cows), the pig and the poultry. She would be an active participant in *dellin'* (digging, cultivating) the vegetable plots, would help to turn and *bigg* the hay, bore the main responsibility for curing the peat and for carrying much of it home. There is an archetypal image of the 'aald wife' coming home from the hill with a kishie full of peats on her back, and knitting as she plodded across rigs and clambered over ditches.

But knitting was and is the skill most obviously associated with women. In complexity, speed and design it differs markedly from the art elsewhere in Britain. The origins of the traditional Fair Isle motifs have long been the subject of speculation, one popular (but unlikely) theory being that they came northwards from southern Europe via shipwrecked seamen. Apart from the shape and intricacy of the patterns, the distinctive features of the art are the subtle blending of several colours, the use of naturally hued and naturally dyed wools, and the knitting of garments in a single piece 'in the round', using three needles. The knitter wears a belt with a perforated pad at the front into which the third needle is secured. The women knit so fast that the staccato clicking of *da wires* is almost resolved into a steady hum. Patterns are 'dotted out' on exercise paper, and handed on through families.

Apart from outfitting her family, a woman's knitting was an important source of cash. Although ill paid, knitting money provided at least a minimal hedge against poor fish prices or the outright failure of the season's fishery. Indeed, the poor pay which knitters, like other home workers, received was a spur to speed, for they were paid (as they still are) on piece rate. Women are recalled as knitting whenever their hands were not otherwise engaged. In the 1970s it was still the case that a middle-aged women would not go visiting without her *sock* (knitting). But, again, the nature of the enterprise has changed considerably. Women no longer spin and dye their own wool. It was long the practice to exchange fleeces with Highland mills for half their weight in spun yarn. Moreover the advent of knitting machines divided labour and created a type of product made almost exclusively for export. Machines would be used, often by men, to knit up plain 'basks' – front, back and sleeves – and the women would graft on Fair Isle patterned yokes across the chest and round the neck. A woman could finish dozens of such garments every week, whereas an *all-over* Fair Isle sweater might involve upwards of seventy or eighty hours' work. Moreover the recent development of electronic programmable machines has made the production of more complex garments, in quantity, a yet more economic undertaking.

In the wake of these developments hand knitting, though far from dead, is becoming a more specialised activity. The 'garnsey' is still standard daily wear, but the machine-knitted garment is more in evidence than it was. It remains to be seen whether the traditional skill will be generally maintained as an 'ordinary' aspect of women's work and leisure, or whether it will be transformed into an atavistic art form.

In all these areas, as in the matter of boatbuilding mentioned earlier, there has unquestionably been a loss of skills. Nowhere is this more evident than in fishing itself, where seamanship and the rich lore of tides, weather, navigation and fish behaviour are all regarded as having been depleted by reliance on new technology. Yet the value attached to skill and to all-round competence remains, albeit in respect of skills transformed by 'modernisation'. A long-time resident of Whalsay who originates from a neighbouring island still speaks admiringly of the 'cool competence' of Whalsay men. 'They can do things – no bother at all. They can just do anything.'

The competence involved in being Whalsa' obviously extends beyond technical skill to more profound, characteristic modes of behaviour. These cannot be catalogued. Some of the important traits have already surfaced in the ethnography: the reserve, the self-effacement, the control and egalitarianism. There is a certain quietness in people's conduct. Indeed, they often comment on the 'noise' which typifies outsiders: 'Dey're *aye* [always] *claakin*'[12] and carryin' on.' Lengthy silences are a frequent feature of Whalsay conversation, since the pause does not cause any discomfiture: it can be as sociable as the transaction of words. A talkative person at the *eela* or the loch strikes a discordant note. Like all other resources, words are used with interest and care, and are not wasted. One seems not to hear the ubiquitous small talk or gratuitous exchanges of the south. Intrusive questions are frowned on; pointless talk is wearisome and foolish. Uninvited comment, or the passing of critical remarks about third parties among people who are not 'thy folk' is embarrassing.

One summer's day in 1975 an elderly man was helping four others (including myself) to launch a *foureen*. Two crew men from a dredger working in the harbour asked for directions to the pub. Our elderly helper replied, 'Dere's nae pub. Na, nae pub. But dat isn't to say dere's nae drink ta'en.' Where could they buy drink? He saw his brother-in-law approaching, a man locally renowned for his drinking, and said to them, 'Aks-you dis man comin'. He's bocht as much drink as anyone here.' This remark was received in silence by my companions, who, though all familiar with and near contemporaries of the speaker, were not of his folk. To thus comment on an affine, in however jocular or innocuous a manner, was clearly rather shocking. Even to remark critically on public *performance* is suspect. A player having a poor football match is spared from public comment. Such comment is probably superfluous: if he is obviously playing badly there is no point in saying so repeatedly. But, furthermore, it suggests a presumption on the speaker's part that he has more right to comment than his hearers. But, essentially, criticism is embarrassing because it offends the necessary discipline of the isolated, small community.

Another aspect of the discipline of self-control which we have noted in the ethnography is manifest in the concern to minimise the possibility of future conflict. This concern has consistently frustrated the establishment of co-operative enterprise in fishing, and even in the infinitely less capital-intensive crofting. It was repeatedly observed to me that, although co-operation might make economic sense, people would not do it, 'not unless things get really desperate'. Why the reluctance? 'Well, they think one might not work so hard as another – and this is a lot of it. They don't want to have to feel this.' A striking instance of this sensitivity is to be found in the district of Isbister, the most northerly settlement on the east coast of the island. Isbister displays a number of distinctive features within the island. It was the last district to observe Old Christmas instead of the calendrically 'new' version, and it maintained other customary practices such as the ceremonial burning of tar barrels for longer than other Whalsay townships. Demographically it has a higher proportion of elderly people among its population. It is also the last area to maintain a 'run rig' distribution of croft land. Under run rig all grazing land is treated as common, divided by fences and gates, the sheep being moved from section to section as appropriate. The 'opening' and 'closing' of the specific gates is regulated by date. Moreover the cultivable land is divided into small, narrow strips, entailing the dispersal of a crofter's land over the entire township. The rationale of such parcelisation was that each crofter should get roughly equal access to the same kinds of land: everyone would get some access to well drained, fertile soil; likewise, everyone would have to suffer wet and shallow topsoil. At various times the Crofters' Commission has suggested sending in a surveyor to rationalise the boundaries. The Isbister crofters always refused. Other people surmised that it was because the Isbister folk would be unable to agree on a reallocation. Each might feel, or would imagine that others felt, disadvantaged and aggrieved, and they feared the arguments and bitterness that might ensue.

Such is the grapevine of local information that people rapidly discover who might be annoyed or offended by some contemplated course of action, and they avoid it. In 1979 the football club decided to construct a new pitch, after years spent fruitlessly trying to improve the existing one. They raised funds, found a site and marked it out. It was then rumoured that a local crofter objected, or might object, or was concerned about possible interference. The imprecision is instructive, for he could not be tackled direct about his fears: that would put him on the spot, and would reveal him as obstructive, or might simply cause him to feel unduly pressured. So the whole enterprise was scrapped. If, as in 1985, a croft is offered for sale, and the vendors refuse a bid from someone locally felt to have a legitimate interest in it, nobody else will bid.

It might be concluded that such highly developed sensitivity might, at worst, stultify social life, inhibiting development and progressive change, as in the resistance to co-operative organisation; or, at the very least, make it tiresomely anodyne. It is certainly sometimes experienced as frustration; it also clearly requires deliberation and effort. Yet there is a sense in which people take pride in it, however perverse its effects may be on their material well-being. It is regarded as a condition of their life in Whalsay and, as such, something they must cope with. The more obstacles which may be placed in their paths, both by nature and by culture, the harder they have to strive to overcome them. It may be this very sensibility which therefore accounts for the community's success, untypical in Shetland, in retaining its population during the last 130 years, and in developing its economic base. It is certainly a characteristic which distinguishes them in their own eyes from people and communities elsewhere.

This sense of difference, and fluency in the symbolic means of its communication, constitutes the essence of 'being Whalsa''. Most of what follows in this book attempts to capture it in descriptions and vignettes. But, to conclude the present chapter, we must turn briefly to the amorphous entity from which Whalsay people see themselves as differentiated, and, again, to symbolism as the vehicle of this sentiment.

Da sooth

As we have observed already, the presence of the outside world looms large on Whalsay. It is what sociologists refer to as a Significant Other, although what it signifies follows almost entirely from the collective self-image of Whalsay itself: the rest of the non-Shetland world is everything Whalsay is not. This omnipresent shadow is generally referred to simply as 'da sooth'. But this general category needs some unpacking.

The relationship of Shetlanders to Scotland has frequently been a matter of detailed historical investigation (see especially B. J. Cohen, 1983; Withrington, ed., 1983, *passim*). Its analysis is, properly, inconclusive. Quite apart from the distortion which inevitably accompanies its generalisation, the tenor of the relationship is also continuously modified by contemporary political circumstances. This was well demonstrated by the response of Shetlanders to the campaign for Scottish devolution which culminated in a referendum in March 1979. Under the terms of the government's Bill, a Scottish Assembly was to be established in Edinburgh, with review powers relating to certain aspects of domestic legislation. The Shetland Islands Council, with the support of an amendment to the Bill proposed by the local Member of Parliament, advocated self-exclusion from the Scottish Assembly, and asked instead for the creation of a commission to enquire into Shetland's constitutional status within the United Kingdom. After the exertion of considerable pressure by the government, and on the MP's advice, the Council voted narrowly to accept representation in the Assembly. The Secretary of State undertook to amend the Bill to give himself powers to override decisions of the Assembly 'if it endangered the special interest of the islands. . . .'[13] In the subsequent referendum Shetlanders, in a 50% poll, voted against the devolution proposals by a majority of more than two to one.[14] The reasons must remain a matter of speculation. However, the ambivalence of Shetlanders to

Scotland has been such as to suggest that many felt no more affinity to
Edinburgh than to Westminster and, indeed, may have felt that their distinctiveness *within* Scotland would have been blurred or even ignored in the
nationalist euphoria of a Scottish Assembly. Their essential loyalties are local.
Indeed, Shetland had already successfully defeated the recommendation
made in 1969 by the Wheatley Commission to amalgamate its own county
council into a new hybrid Highland regional authority. In the aftermath of
the devolution debate a variety of investigations into Shetland's status have
been conducted, but appear to have excited little interest other than among
the activists of the Shetland Movement, an organisation created in 1978 to
campaign for increased autonomy.[15]

People from the south are inclined to treat the Scottish islands as an
undifferentiated category. In this they are, of course, grossly mistaken. The
many islands of the Hebridean groups are themselves starkly different from
each other in social complexion. As Gaels, their populations are also eth-
nically and linguistically distinct from those of the Northern Isles – Orkney
and Shetland – which have hardly any Gaelic influence. Moreover, although
the social connections between Orkney and Shetland have been strengthened
through years of intermarriage, and notwithstanding the regular reciprocal
visits made by representative groups from each, the two island groups share
few interests. Their economies are substantially different, Orkney's resting
primarily on agriculture, Shetland's on fishing. Their dialects, though subject
to the same influences as a consequence of their historical subjection to the
same processes of colonisation, have diverged considerably. The two groups
have markedly distinct literary traditions, and in recent years Orkney has
been more subject to an intellectual colonisation from the south than has
Shetland. Politically Shetland has been rather more inclined to radicalism
than has Conservative Orkney. Nevertheless, in so far as Shetlanders would
make qualitative distinctions within the gross entity 'Scotland', they would
identify with Orkney rather than, say, with the Western Isles.

By extension, they would also recognise and acknowledge a greater affinity
to the north-east-coast mainland ports than to west-coast ports and Highland
towns. Many Whalsay fishermen have served brief periods in Aberdeen
trawlers; many have regularly landed their catch at the Aberdeen, Fraserburgh and Peterhead markets and have associations with shipyards on the
north-east coast. Although they, and especially the herring men, are familiar
with west-coast ports such as Stornoway, Mallaig and Ullapool, they do not
seem to figure so prominently on the local map, possibly because the latter are
less important as the home bases of comparable local fishermen. Shetlanders
have stronger associations with the east coast of the British mainland generally than with the west. During the season the East Anglian herring drifters
were regularly based in Shetland during the heyday of drift-netting. There are
still many among the present senior Whalsay fishermen whose early career

included experience of fishing for herring out of Lowestoft. Indeed, the principal local firm of fish salesmen and managing agents originated in Lowestoft. Moreover the majority of Shetlanders who went into the merchant service sailed out of Leith and the Tyne ports, and many families settled in those areas as a result. Some were based in Glasgow or Liverpool but these, again, seem less prominent in local consciousness.

Whalsay fishermen express some affinity with other Scottish owner-operator fishermen who prosecute a similar fishery with comparable vessels. In effect, this tends to mean the men of Peterhead. For various reasons, foremost among them, perhaps, the obligatory use of *lumpers* (shore porters) at Aberdeen, they used to prefer to sell at the Peterhead market if possible. The larger vessels in the Aberdeen fleet were mainly owned by processors; the smaller vessels, notably shabby by comparison with Shetland boats, reflect what is regarded as a lesser commitment to fishing. Ports farther south on the Scottish east coast – Montrose, Arbroath, Pittenween, Anstruther, Cockenzie and so forth – seem to be quite absent from the Whalsaymen's world.

Although they may favour other ports, Aberdeen is nevertheless the primary point of contact and experience on the Scottish mainland for most Shetlanders. It is the home port for 'da steamer', the passenger and cargo vessel which plies three times weekly in each direction, and is also the principal air link. Shetlanders who require any medical attention not available in Lerwick are taken to Aberdeen hospitals, and Aberdeen consultants make periodic visits to Lerwick. Whalsay people may well spend time in Aberdeen to shop for special items, or may make it their base for a summer holiday.

In short, it may be said that Aberdeen is not alien territory in the way that Glasgow or Edinburgh might be; and Edinburgh, as an east-coast city, may be favoured over Glasgow, which has stronger associations with the Western Isles. So, just as local relationships are layered or segmented, so too are those which the locality has cognitively with Scotland.

Such qualitative discriminations may be made in specific instances. But when the general reference is 'oppositional' or self-reflexive they are inapposite and blur anonymously into the undiscriminating 'sooth'. The self-conscious, if sometimes contrived, nature of Shetland's differentiation from the rest of the United Kingdom, including Scotland, obviously owes much to the historical relationship with Scandinavia. Politically this relationship was severed more than 500 years ago. Yet it remains a residual and fruitful resource of identity management. During the late nineteenth century substantial research was conducted by indigenous and foreign scholars in order to locate Shetlandic within Scandinavian linguistic and mythological traditions.[16] Philological and other ethnological research has continued ever since.[17] At the same time dialect literature, much of it evoking the Norse past, became a prominent genre, and was associated later still with the emergence of socialist political organisation in Shetland. The nineteenth-century cod fishery brought Shetland fishermen into close contact with the Faroe Islands, the Danish dependency which lies only 200 miles from Shetland. As an island group they provided an instructive contrast to Shetland experience (cf. Manson, 1978). After the second war the Faroese, similarly insistent on their linguistic and cultural distinctiveness from their colonial master, achieved substantial autonomy in their internal affairs. The formidable economic development they subsequently generated contrasted markedly with Shetland's long post-war depression, and since then they have been regarded by many Shetland 'nationalists' as a model of the kind of autonomy to which Shetland should aspire.[18]

The historic association with Norway was revived, and considerably revitalised, during the second world war. Shetland provided the base for the 'Shetland bus', a continuous maritime link operated by Norwegians to bring refugees out of occupied Norway and to support the Resistance (see Howarth, 1957). Shetland men were recruited by Norwegian companies and skippers for the South Georgia whale fishery. Lerwick is twinned with a Norwegian town, Maaloy. Norwegian fishing fleets have long used Lerwick as a base, and a Norwegian fishermen's mission is still maintained in the town. Recent innovations have included the initiation of a direct summertime air service to Bergen, and a number of excursion holidays are organised locally each year. There is a long tradition of reciprocal visits by Norwegian and Shetland yachtsmen. More significantly, nearly all the present generation of purser-seiners in Shetland (most of them belonging to Whalsay crews) were built in Norwegian yards, some with the benefit of loans from the Norwegian government. The proprietor of the Flekkefjord yard was a regular guest at Whalsay weddings during the 1980s. Many of the purser crews landed herring regularly at Danish ports during 1984 and 1985, and will probably continue to do so.

It is clear, then, that Shetland's 'use' of its Scandinavian associations as a means of distinguishing itself from the UK is not merely a romantic exercise in atavistic rhetoric and mythology but reflects the modernisation and intensification of those links (Smith, 1978). The process was itself partly motivated by the well grounded feeling that, prior to the North Sea oil era, Shetland was neglected, misunderstood and poorly served by those in power in mainland Britain, who remained wilfully ignorant of local circumstances. This sentiment was further reinforced by the hostility of the British government to the efforts made in 1972–74 by the then Zetland County Council to exercise some control over the development of oil-related facilities, and to secure a financial interest in them as well as financial compensation for the disruption they created. The council had eventually to negotiate the tortuous passage of private legislation through Parliament. Further alienation from the political mainstream has been fuelled by the United Kingdom's accession to the

Common Fisheries Policy, with its paraphernalia of lobby politics and special pleading; and, complementary to this, the apparently greater success of the Norwegian fleets, Norway having declined membership of the E.E.C.[19]

Thus the enticing models of Norway and the Faroes make Scandinavia a persuasive, if politically inaccessible, alternative to the British association in which Shetland can be plausibly presented as a grossly unequal, exploited and misunderstood member. There is no evidence to suggest that many Shetlanders are enthusiastic about political autonomy. The Shetland Movement itself has little popular support in Whalsay. Similarly, the Scottish National Party did not arouse much sympathy on the island during the 1970s, when it attracted a substantial following elsewhere in Scotland. The only issue on which Whalsay people do support the SNP and which galvanises them into the sustained assertion of special interest, is the fishery and the need to protect Shetland waters and the local fleet through the locally advantageous application of policies on quotas, limits and marketing. In pursuit of this campaign the Shetland men effectively seceded from the Scottish Fishermen's Association in 1985.

Shetlanders' attachment to an alternative, non-British history and their commitment to a view of themselves as different from the rest of a Britain largely antagonistic to their interests is, then, more a matter of identity than of politics. It is a predicate of the essential integrity of a culture, buttressing it against a history of isolation, depopulation, exploitation and impoverishment. It also provides a model for their internal distinctions, community from community, and within communities.

Symbolism and identity

All the issues raised in this chapter relate to aspects of social identity. Their discussion here makes explicit concerns which, in the ordinary course of life in Whalsay, would rarely surface explicitly and, if they did, would probably be expressed quite differently. This is an admission not of falsification but of interpretation. In so far as anthropology purports to explain behaviour which is taken for granted by its perpetrators it is bound thus to alter the terms of discourse. But perhaps in this respect anthropology only mirrors what happens whenever we make things explicit which people are not conscious of in themselves. We all attribute motive or rationale to people on the basis of the sense *we* make of *their* behaviour, rather than the sense they make of it themselves. We cannot know and comprehend the latter, other than by assimilating it to the former. For much of the time we are speculating on what lies 'behind' the actions we observe in other people, but we then conflate our speculations with their actions so that we cannot tell them apart. That is how we make sense of other people's behaviour.

In chapter one I suggested that we think of symbols as 'the ideas behind the words'. As in his explanation of people's actions, the observer 'claims' symbolism behind their behaviour, interprets it through the sense *he* makes of it, and then attributes that sense to *them*. Symbols are vehicles of expression which have meanings imputed to them by user (speaker) and observer (listener) without any inherent power to make those meanings coincide. This presumptuous examination of Whalsay is thus an outsider's interpretation of the symbols by which he believes Whalsay people make their world meaningful to themselves, and through which they express these meanings. It is also *his* interpretation of what he believes those meanings to be. As was admitted at the outset, it is no more than version: but, hopefully, it is more than *mere* version. In other words, I have attributed various kinds of segmentary affiliation to Whalsay people; have suggested contexts in which these are expressed; have argued that they inform the sentiments people have about their community, and about the outside world. But, in truth, they are the ways in which *I* make sense of them.

The only defence of an interpretation can be its plausibility, and this in turn must rest on the observer's sensitivity to the concurrence of consistent themes in the plethora of contexts in which he observes local life. Thus, rather than plucking symbols out of the air, or inventing meanings and motivations for other people's behaviour, the anthropologist is essentially compiling a symbolic vocabulary from rigorous observation of and analytical reflection on the same few people engaged in different aspects of their lives. What he calls 'symbols' are the constructs of meaning which he sees surfacing repeatedly, and which are thus commended as significant to the analysis. While this apparent consistency may itself be a figment of the analysis, it is the only basis on which interpretation can proceed. It entails the assumption not that people's behaviour is a reflex of some ingrained cultural logic but that to achieve an understanding of any aspect of a person's behaviour we have to refer to other of its aspects as well. We have, in the jargon, to 'situate' it: to treat any one item of behaviour as text, and then to *con*textualise it in order to render it intelligible to ourselves. The symbolic vocabulary to which reference is made above is, essentially, context, through which the components of people's behaviour can be identified and interpreted. To invalidate the interpretation the critic must do more than point to its methodological circularity: he must also go on to provide another interpretation of similar or greater plausibility.

Thus a serious objection to the suggestions above that the spree, the construction of a wheelbarrow, the design of a sweater, or the spatial distribution of mourners at a funeral, are (*a*) symbolically instructive, and (*b*) signify certain features of Whalsay thought and process, must not merely chortle at such a far-fetched notion: it must *argue* that such an approach is unjustified and that an alternative explanation is more warranted by what is known about the society. On that polemical note let us briefly recapitulate the claims made here about the symbolism of events which have been described.

All the forms of behaviour discussed in this chapter have undergone considerable change over the years. The segmentary groups of 'wir folk' and kin no longer make the kind of material contribution to economic life which they did previously. They are no longer so discrete geographically as they were before roads were built, nor so obviously reflected in the composition of fishing crews. The practical skills of husbandry, joinery, knitting and general self-sufficiency are no longer requisites of island life. Sprees have become more intoxicated, more mobile, probably more frequent and, perhaps, more frenetic than once they were. Funerals no longer command universal attendance. Further, they are now motorised, and therefore privatised, whereas they were previously pedestrian and sociable. Because access to hospital is now so much easier, death occurs more frequently away from the island and, because of advances in medical skill and technology, is somehow more remarkable. Even at home outsiders, in the persons of the doctor and the district nurse, intrude upon the scenario of death, formerly a wholly indigenous affair.

Despite all such change, people do not think of their modern behaviour as making them 'less Whalsa''. But neither do they invoke customary practice in a traditionalistic manner. Rather, they adapt it to the new circumstances. They make it carry new messages. Its symbolic potency is still such that people can read into it whatever messages may be relevant to themselves. Whether or not such behaviour is actually different in form from that which is observable elsewhere is irrelevant. Whalsay people think of it as different. That is what matters, for it is the sense of difference which motivates the meanings they contrive for, or find in, the symbolism of their various activities. It constitutes their 'tacit', taken-for-granted, not-requiring-to-be-expressed, knowledge. Not only do they believe their behaviour to be different; they also see in their tenacious adherence to its difference the cause of the demeaned status of peripherality which they believe is imputed to them in 'da sooth', and, certainly, by those in da sooth who hold power over them. I discern in their attitude a resigned, sometimes frustrated but also amused resignation to such labelling: they can do little about it except have the last laugh, for they also suppose that such labelling indicates the ignorance of those at the 'centre'. It is as if, like other negatively categorised groups, they find a wry, if perverse, satisfaction in being misread: it keeps the boundary intact, thus preserving their culture from further encroachment, and gives them the space to develop their own symbolic means of coping with changed circumstances. That such symbolism may be expressed in more prosaic forms than anthropologists are used to encountering elsewhere should not blind us to its significance.

The argument is, then, that the retention and modernisation of customary modes of social organisation, of skills, ideas and beliefs, in circumstances which have diminished their material relevance, express more than mere traditionalism. These forms may properly be regarded as symbolic and their expression now is a new phenomenon, a response to the influence of social change. The forms are now invested with a significance which they may have lacked in their earlier incarnations. It is figuratively as if people stand at the boundary and witness its blurring, its fading, feel themselves being tugged across the line. So they reach into their symbolic and cultural reserves to reformulate their sense of distinctiveness from those on the other side. They contrive new meanings for apparently old forms. Indeed, they use the very symbolic devices in virtue of which they imagine themselves to be regarded as anachronistic, parochial and peripheral. By using them, they neutralise the perceived implications, at least to their own satisfaction. Through such counterpunching the seeming homogeneity of the 'modern' society supposedly creeping out from the centre and insinuating itself into the nooks and crannies of the margin is revealed as a superficial veneer and as largely illusory. Ironically, it is an illusion which protects the vitality of the margin and enables it to nurture, relatively free from outside interference, its new distinguishing features.

We pursue this theme in the next chapter, turning ethnographically to means by which Whalsay people manage social change, preserving a sense of cultural continuity whilst nevertheless instituting substantial changes in their individual and collective modes of life.

Notes

1   See, *inter alia*, Merton (1957); Gouldner (1955); also Mouzelis (1967); Pugh *et al.* (1967).

2   Some parts of this section are taken from Cohen (1978a).

3   Since there are no natural growths of trees in Shetland, timber was a scarce and highly valued resource. Even today people comb the beaches for wreckwood. They gather it into piles near the shore above the high-water mark, and it is then regarded as their private property. Even though they may leave it lying there indefinitely, such property is regarded by others as sacrosanct.

4   *tún* (Old Norse): fenced plot or field. Whalsay people still refer to inbye grazing land, or to cultivated plots, as *da toon*.

5   Such long-standing associations are evident from records for 1715 and 1804, kindly made available by the late R. W. J. Irvine of Linthouse, a dedicated local genealogist. Earlier records are less informative on this matter because of the common use of patronymics until the early eighteenth century and, in some cases, for a considerable period thereafter. Thus another list compiled by Mr Irvine of landowners ('*peerie* [small] lairds') in 1576 gives no indication of how their descendants might be identified. (See appendix A.) Civil registration did not commence in Scotland until 1855, and the Church's early parish registers pertaining to Whalsay were destroyed by fire. Further documents which might have been informative were inadvertently destroyed by builders converting the laird's

Haa' into a school during the late 1950s. The remaining papers of the Symbister Estate are now held in the Shetland County Archive.

6   Indeed, it was even occasionally suggested that the four brothers favoured each other with the ball during matches.

7   Parts of this section are taken from Cohen (1985b).

8   The Whalsay spree must therefore be distinguished in both form and apparent significance from the alcoholic transactions in the Faroe Islands which Blehr (1974) calls 'token prestations'. He suggests that the offering of drink is a means of sustaining long-term economic relations. Social drinking in Whalsay clearly lacks the materially pragmatic character which Blehr attributes to Faroese drinking.

9   All burials during the last twenty years have had to be accommodated in an extension to the kirkyard, space in the kirkyard proper having become exhausted. This clearly emphasises the spatial distinctions among the mourners, but the fact that such a distinction is made remains instructive.

10 Vallee similarly notes the presence of the mundane in Barra funerals. He explains it in terms of their 'normalcy', but also remarks that frequent funeral attendance '. . . intensifies the awareness of belonging to the community' (1955, p. 128).

11 Estimates of these costs during the 1970s are given for Burra, and for Shetland generally, by, respectively, Byron (1986) and Coull, Goodlad and Sheves (1979). During the 1980s costs have increased substantially over these figures following the inflation in the price of fuel. Moreover, costs in Whalsay would be greater because of the larger boats.

12 *Claakin'*: talking loudly about nothing much. The word is usually applied to hens cackling.

13 *Shetland Times*, 16th June 1978.

14 The figures were: 5,466 against; 2,020 for. (*Shetland Times*, 9th March 1979.)

15 See, *inter alia*, Underhill (1977), Kolinsky (1978).

16 For a detailed examination of Shetland studies in the context of northern scholarship generally see B. J. Cohen (1983). Also Grønneberg, (1981, 1984).

17 See P. S. Andersen (1984); also Melchers (1980, 1983).

18 During the last twenty-five years Shetland organisations such as the Shetland Islands Council, the Shetland Council of Social Service and the Shetland Movement have undertaken a number of studies comparing Faroe and Shetland.

19 Like the Norwegians, Shetlanders also voted against membership of the EEC in the 1975 referendum. The Western Isles were the only other British region to do so.

Chapter 4

Managing change: the past in the present

The main body of this chapter examines ethnographically four aspects of customary behaviour. All originated in historical circumstances very different from those which now obtain; all have changed substantially from their supposed traditional forms, and are anomalous in the context of the intensive change which Whalsay has undergone since the last war. For each the question is raised of how and why Whalsay people maintain such a strong commitment to them. In the final section we turn to other aspects of Whalsay's folk history, and attempt to reach some conclusions about how people's perceptions of the cultural past influence their adaptability to the rapidly changing present, and their attitudes to contemporary relations between Whalsay and the wider society.

The croft[1]

'Ideas,' writes Sperber, 'cannot be observed, but only intuitively understood; they cannot be described but only interpreted' (1985, p. 9). A description of the activities involved in Whalsay crofting would most certainly fail to grasp the meanings which Whalsay people attach to the idea of crofting. A croft is an agricultural holding so designated by the Crofters' Commission, whose statutory jurisdiction extends through the seven Scottish crofting counties. Most Whalsay crofts are small, even by crofting standards, few extending to more – usually less – than ten acres, or are composites of such units. They might be thought of as agricultural smallholdings, though it should be noted that crofts elsewhere in Shetland, and especially in poor grazing areas, may be much more extensive, some exceeding a hundred acres, even though only a fraction of this land would be suitable for cultivation. Yet its description as a smallholding should not evoke the impression of farming on a small scale. In the British Isles farming is a business, regardless of the geographical scale on which it is prosecuted. Whalsay crofting is *not* a business. Although crofters

The crofting township of West Hamister, with Sudheim in the foreground. Note the proliferation of fences, a phenomenon of the post-war years.   [Picture by Gordon Craig]

have to keep rudimentary profit-and-loss accounts for taxation purposes, the logic of balancing income and expenditure is frustrated by, rather than reflected in, the activity of crofting. There are approximately 130 crofts on Whalsay. Few, if any, of their proprietors or tenants would claim that the actual or potential income represents what might be regarded as an economic return. If one were to attach a monetary value to the labour expended, they would maintain that their crofts would be revealed as so uneconomic that the very notion of 'economy' would appear inappropriate.

How else are we to make sense of it? There is no help to be gained from falling back on some such cliche as 'way of life'. To be sure, until a certain moment in the past crofting *was* a way of life, regulating much of the time, routine, work and habitation of the crofting family. But it no longer exercises such sway. To most Whalsay crofters the croft is incidental, not only to their annual income but also to their allocation of time and labour. It commands substantial resources in neither capital nor labour; nor does it contribute more than marginally to the household income. Nevertheless, many Whalsay people identify themselves closely with an idealised crofting 'way of life', and enthuse about crofting even though the demands of fishing prevent them from devoting much time or effort to it. They hanker for retirement in order to devote themselves to 'crofting', although the crofting in which they then engage bears only slight resemblance to that of the pre-war community.

It is clear, then, that crofting occupies a prominent place in the Whalsay ideology. It has more salience as an idea than as an economic activity. Its continued salience must be treated as parodoxical in the context of contemporary economic life. Therefore, we have first to disclose the nature of the idea; and, secondly, to resolve the parodox.

In 1974 the rationale of co-operative organisation in buying, producing and marketing, so extensively applied to marginal enterprises throughout the peripheral regions of northern Europe and the northern North Atlantic, had largely passed Whalsay by. Elsewhere in the Scottish Highlands and Islands the rationale was to take root and flower during the 1970s, having been nurtured by the Highlands and Islands Development Board, effectively rescuing some tenuous communities from the kind of remorseless decline so trenchantly described for the west of Ireland by Brody [1973]. (See Grassie, 1983, pp. 49 ff.) But the idea left Whalsay people cold. In the case of the fishery, it was regarded as rational, but as compromising the independence of the individual crews. In the context of the community ethos, we saw in the last chapter that it was regarded as potentially prejudicial to harmonious social relations. In the specific case of crofting, a man sympathetic to the idea gave me another reason why it would continue to be rejected. Yes, he said, people would have an instinctive prejudice against co-operation because they were too 'conservative', too independent. But there is more than that to their resistance. Co-operation *could* make crofting economically viable. But that would be to apply an entirely inappropriate philosophy to people's view of crofting. They do not regard the croft as a business, and for that reason would not be prepared to invest in it. They would not contemplate borrowing money to capitalise it. They were reluctant even to take full advantage of the grants available from the Crofters' Commission, since these entailed obligations. Debt was always a terrible source of anxiety and people were desperate to 'die clear'. Even though they had reconciled themselves to massive indebtedness in respect of the fishery, they would find it unthinkable to incur any debt in relation to the croft. The ideas of debt and crofting were incongruent.

It is a discrimination which results in what would otherwise appear to be contradictory modes of behaviour. Men who are shareholders in the most modern fishing boats, costing in excess of £1½ million, stuffed with the very latest electronic wizardry and labour-saving devices, who could easily afford to buy a second-hand diesel tractor in good condition, would instead labour over, and be frustrated by, an ancient petrol-paraffin machine which had already seen thirty or more years of service on a succession of farms. If they put it into working order, they would worry about using it too much lest it break down.

Moreover, some of the people most interested in crofting were not themselves crofters, but would happily look after other people's livestock for the sheer enjoyment of it. Why would they not take on crofts themselves? Because they knew they would have to invest to bring the land up to the standard with which they would be content.

Four years later, in 1978, this man had not changed his estimation of people's attitudes. They were still disinclined to see the croft as productive of income. As a consequence, their view of the croft as financially non-viable became self-fulfilling. 'These folk,' he says, 'they're living on the idea of the hill.' He means that people are relying on the unimproved common grazings, the *scattald*, to sustain their sheep. They feed lambs expensively through their first winter, then put them to the hill, and after two or three years 'they're useless.' People keep too much stock. They would be better advised to reduce the quantity drastically to the point where they could feed their lambs properly in order to offer them for sale as 'stores' (i.e. for fattening) or for killing. They should keep only enough ewes to reproduce the flock and to stock their own deep freezers.

When he puts this argument, people always volunteer the example of Magnie (see chapter two) in its support. 'We aye ken dat Magnie'll hae da best lambs on da pier' (i.e. at the annual sale). In 1975 Magnie had the use of about twenty acres, and ran no more than a sheep per acre. He fed sheep from the ground he previously cultivated for his cows. 'Even if dere was nae profit in it, Magnie'd do it. He likes to hae someting guid, something really bonny to look at.' So crofting embraces both an aesthetic ideal which motivates Magnie to feed his stock in what may be an uneconomic manner to produce fine animals in insufficient quantity; and a wholly contrary view which leads people to overstock, underfeed, and produce an excess of poor animals.

Magnie is not the only example of great effort eventuating in a perverse result. 'Look at yon —— boys, aye strugglin' awa', working really hard. But, man, dey've naathin' avaa' ta sell.' 'Take 'George'. He never has anything to sell. I don't believe he had the pleasure o' eatin' an early tattie las' year. He was so pleased wi' himself for da wye his aald tatties kept, by the time he finished them the early eens were aald!'

'Aye, man, an' look at 'Lowry'. He does all dis work wi' da sheep, growing crops fer dem, re-seeding, an' den he puts dem to da hill an' dey come back "gangly-wye" an' useless. All dat effort, fer nae return.'

The conclusion: 'These men, they won't look at the croft as something that can produce cash for them.'

So, whatever the aspirations for the croft, they do not include financial reward; and, in pursuing them, people put themselves increasingly at odds with financial rationality. Even when, as in Magnie's case, the sale of produce recoups the cash paid out for feed supplements, fertiliser and medicines, the return is not commensurate with the time and effort. In 1983 Danny, with the top prices and the most sheep in the annual sale, realised just under a thousand pounds. For that, he devoted to the croft most of his weekly days off from his full-time employment; most of every weekend throughout spring and summer; most of his summer holiday, and at least part of most weekends throughout the winter. He inspected his flock twice every day throughout the year. He built machinery for the work, renewed fences, cleaned ditches, dipped and drenched the sheep, and so forth. He knows that, despite his expertise and dedication, he could not make a living from the croft. 'Not unless you had eight hundred sheep. Two men, wi' da whole isle, an' eight hundred sheep. You might jus' make it.'

So it is clear that although the language of economics may be used when people discuss crofting, the ideas which motivate them in their crofting behaviour are quite different.

The crofters' dismissal of the economic potentialities of crofting should not be regarded as defeatism. The possibilities of exporting any surplus which they might manage to produce is severely limited by distance and freight costs, factors which also make the purchase of bulk items extremely expensive. This, together with the decreasing availability of time and labour, has fundamentally altered the nature of the croft from a basic subsistence resource into a hobby. In no single aspect of crofting is this more evident than the demise of dairying. It is not possible now to retrieve accurate information on the number of crofters who used to keep cows. But the popular recollection is that, until the second war, it was unusual for a croft *not* to have *kye*. The Whalsay cow was popular throughout Shetland, as a relatively small beast, weighing approximately 3½ cwt, with a plentiful and predictable milk yield. Some people claim that the stock began to deteriorate following the importation of shorthorn bulls. However, in 1975 the invariable reason advanced for the virtual disappearance of dairying, other than from one specialised unit, was freight charges. For example, costs on feed and supplements were then estimated at 75p per hundredweight. In effect, freight exhausted the money which might otherwise have been used to employ labour for the intensive cultivation of feedstuff for the cattle.

The financial costs of their isolation have been a persistent post-war theme of Shetlanders' views of their relation to mainland Britain. Successive governments have been repeatedly urged to subsidise seaborne freight on the same principle applied to mainland trunk roads, and have resisted such a commitment. There can be no doubt that in Shetland, as in other areas remote from major markets, the costs of transport are a major obstacle to economic development. Whalsay is further disadvantaged by its distance from the mainland of Shetland. In 1973 the local fish factory purchased an old fishing boat, the *Swift Wing*, to carry the fish bought for processing at the Lerwick and Scalloway markets, and to take some processed fish to Mainland for onward shipping. Later the Shetland Islands Council agreed to subsidise the cost of carrying the factory's lorries on the ferry. But in 1985, when the continuation of this subsidy appeared to be in jeopardy, it was estimated that the additional annual cost to the factory might be as much as £6,000. It is a problem which stymies enterprise. In 1975 the manufacturer of a pesticide which destroys 'leatherjackets'[2] announced a freight charge of £4 on orders under £20, and of £2 on purchases worth between £20 and £40. In addition to paying freight charges, Magnie was burdened by a £2.50 'administration charge' on every purchase and return of the gas cylinders he used for welding. In 1977 crofters had to pay £3 freight on every sheep sent south for sale. Such financial penalties were sufficient to make the most enthusiastic crofter opt for cheaper, if less productive, avenues.

Crofters kept cows when their own family could supply the necessary labour. They required vast quantities (up to two thousand) of cabbages and kale, potatoes, corn, oats, swedes, hay and straw. They needed labour for daily milking, for *kirning* the butter, and for mucking out the byre. Children were often made responsible for *haad'n da coo*, bringing the cow back from the hill, grazing it along the ditches on the way home. They might then be sent out to collect baskets full of kale leaves. It was in the early 1950s that they began to give up cows. Until then 'folk tocht du couldna' do wi'oot kye – for *blaand* [buttermilk] an' kirn milk, an' fresh milk an' so on – but I tink dey began to be fairly relieved when dey stopped it.'

'Yeah, man, it's jus' a lok o' rubbish fer da aald people ta complain dat folk nooadays canna be ta da bodder o' keepin' kye. Dey don't hae da time! Can du see a wife gaain' oot o' da hoose a' six a' mornin' ta milk da kye, an' den see ta da crops an' dat? Dey'd be aff ta Glasgow, fast.'

When keeping kye was the norm, considerations of the diseconomies of the required labour input were inappropriate. As we were repeatedly told, it was simply 'the way of life'. Its diseconomies were not conceptualised separately from those of the rest of the 'way of life' in which it was embedded. But, as the whole occupational basis of life changed, so its specific activities could be considered separately and the option became available of discarding them.

When the kye went, intensive cultivation became unnecessary. People grew only their own staple household vegetables. They also began to keep sheep as their main stock – sheep having long been the principal stock elsewhere in Shetland. The chief object of cultivation, therefore, was hay, requiring intensive effort over a much briefer and more concentrated period. This late accession of serious sheep husbandry accounts for what some regard as the relative incompetence of Whalsay crofters as shepherds, an incompetence or lack of experience which adds a further dimension to the puzzle of modern crofting – an activity which is costly in time and labour, which is not very productive, and at which until very recently they did not feel altogether confident or competent. The sheep which were kept when kye still prevailed were treated largely as scavengers. The specially produced feed was restricted to the cows. Since people did not think of selling lambs, there was no need to fatten them.

The pure-bred Shetland sheep are hardy, and need little more to survive than the hill can provide. But they are small compared to mainland breeds. Their principal value to the crofter was in the fleece. This would be *roo'ed* (plucked) and spun into wool at home. Most of the spun yarn was used at home too. If there was a surplus, it could be exchanged with a Scottish mill for spun yarn. The wool of the Shetland fleece is so fine that it could not be mill-spun alone on normal machinery. The Scottish mills blended it with coarser wools and it was only in 1985 that a commercially viable means of spinning unblended yarn was finally perfected in Shetland, and a mill opened at Sandness. When Whalsay crofters began to keep sheep more seriously the Shetland sheep was manifestly unpractical, for its meat yield was simply too low, and Shetland's exclusion from the Wool Marketing Board helped to depress the value of the fleeces. They had to turn to suffolks and cheviots, and had to learn from scratch how to breed and rear them, patterns of feeding, of diagnosis and care and, since these sheep could not be roo'ed, of shearing and preparing the fleeces for sale.

Few local crofters had any depth of experience with these sheep, and those who did looked slightly askance at the uncertain performance of their neighbours. If sheep 'were nae i' deir blood' how could they expect to be able to work successfully with them? They had to learn how to recognise and cure the diseases which were common: *braxi* (inflammation of the stomach), 'pulpy' kidney, meningitis, *warbiska* and flukes, foot rot, and so forth. The last two were gradually eradicated as people became increasingly expert, and were more assiduous about drenching their flocks systematically. Many sheep diseases are easily cured through the use of 'folk', as well as of veterinary, remedies. But such skills are built on long experience, which was in short supply on Whalsay. One man in particular, James Arthur, continued right through the 1970s to bear a heavy demand for his assistance at lambing time[3] and when crofters were worried about their stock. He never failed to answer a call, and would never accept payment. Unlike his 'clients', he treated these crises matter-of-factly. 'They were all there watching! Then one would stick something under me knees; another would come and haul up me sleeve. Lot of silly fuss!' He persistently urged on crofters the need for more selective breeding and for reducing the numbers of sheep being grazed on the land available. Eventually, in 1977, he managed to persuade some forty of the more active crofters to form a group for the co-operative purchase of drugs, fertilisers and so forth. This group later built permanent pens for the annual sale, and, with the North of Scotland College of Agriculture representatives in Lerwick, sponsored specialised local courses on such skills as electric shearing, welding and high-tensile fencing. Through their efforts, and with increasing awareness of the desirability of improving grazing through reseeding, the quality of the stock has gradually improved, and now bears comparison with that of other Shetland districts.

Significant changes of attitude had to be accomplished for this transformation to be effected. First, the Shetland sheep had to be virtually discarded in favour of breeds which, as suggested earlier, required more intensive care. The common choices were the suffolk, a favourite with buyers of store lambs, since they continue to fatten throughout the winter; and cheviots or crossed cheviots which, although they do not grow during the winter, will maintain their weight. These breeds required feeding and, thus, the production of good quality hay. Hay-making can be a frustrating task in Shetland because of the frequency of rain or of drenching sea-frets. Ideally, once cut, the grass should be cured rapidly in order to retain its nutrients. If it is repeatedly dampened and dried it loses quality. The lack of machinery exacerbated the problem, for the grass was cut and turned by hand. Therefore it could be done only when labour was available. Uncertain of when they might next be ashore, men might be tempted to cut the grass before it was quite ready; or to cut grass which might have to lie in the ground until people were again available to work with it. The attempt to beat the natural calendar, or to rush into jobs, is absolutely contrary to people's recollection of traditional crofting, in which the work was done systematically, at the *proper* time, and with due regard to the weather.

Further, the very nature of land-occupancy had to change. The classic pattern, outlined above, was the dual system of *inbye* or enclosed croft land, and *da hill*, *scattald*, or common grazings. (Also, see Knox, 1985.) The island

is divided into three grazings areas, each administered by a clerk and committee. The great majority of the island's 134 crofts belong to the North
grazings (ninety-two shareholders in 1977), which run northwards from
Hamister in the west-south-west to Skaw in the extreme north and to Isbister
in the east; the Buwater grazings (twenty-five shareholders) covering the
island's south-west; and the Clett grazings (ten shareholders) on the south
coast. The remainder are not registered crofts and, therefore, do not carry
rights to grazings. Each committee is responsible for maintaining fences and
dips, and for any other routine work such as occasional drainage and burning
off heather. Their disproportionate sizes are largely the result of historical
accident. The North grazings are composed of the original crofts and
common grazings, formed before the dissolution of the Estate's farms in
1903. These farms became the crofts incorporated into the Buwater grazings.[4] Without extensive improvement, which, quite apart from substantial
costs, would require collaboration, the hill could not be more than poor
grazing. Indeed, its availability arguably impeded the development of the
stock, but perpetuated the commonality and 'democracy' of crofting, without
subjecting it to the rigours of active co-operation.

Under the 1886 crofting Act crofters were able to apply for 'apportionments' of the hill land. If these were granted, they had the right to enclose
a given area of land, nominally their share of the *scattald*, the right entailing
an obligation to improve a specified proportion of the land by draining and
reseeding it. Until the 1970s, however, few Whalsay crofters applied for
apportionments. The apportionment is a right to exclusive grazing rather
than to ownership and thus does not provide the opportunity to create a new
croft. However, under the 1976 Act, if the apportionment is contiguous with
a crofter's inbye land she does have the right to purchase it and it thereby
gains the same status as croft land. Once deeds to the land have been thus
obtained the crofter is entitled to apply for permission to 'decroft' portions of
the land in order to dispose of them, by gift or sale, as house sites. Sites have
become increasingly scarce, and their value has risen sharply. In 1984 crofts
could command upwards of £5,000, mainly because of their value as
potential building sites.

A glance at the landscape indicates the avidity with which the right to
apportionments has been exploited. Stretches of heathery or dull, green hill
are punctuated by regularly patterned plots of the vivid green new grass. The
sudden sprouting of boundary fences has made the hill something of an
obstacle course. The topographical division of the land has social consequences. With the acquisition of increasing quantities of machinery, however
unsophisticated by modern agricultural standards, making less necessary the
availability of voluntary labour for hay-making, the whole activity of crofting
has become less communal, and increasingly privatised. The common grazings, though not yet redundant, are coming to be regarded as anachronistic,

the conversation and banter of folk turning the hay increasingly replaced by the splutter of the tractor engine and the clanking of wuffler and baler. Indeed, the precedents of 1984 and 1985 portend the end of hay-making as increasing numbers of crofters are buying in hay from Orkney and the Scottish mainland, shipped north in bulk and delivered direct to the island.

In the recent past, then, crofting has been stripped of its traditional guise. Formerly vital economically, it is now marginal, and a pastime; formerly labour-intensive and communal, it is now increasingly mechanised and privatised. Sheep have replaced cows; on most crofts grass has replaced crops, other than those required for household consumption. Shetland oats, previously a staple, are cultivated by only a handful of crofters. Poultry-keeping is no longer general; the pig is a rarity. People are aware of the transformation and, without indulging in bucolic nostalgia, regret it.

'Man, I mind me oot i' da toon, among da *corn* [oats], an' da docken sparrows an' corncrakes were in deir hundreds! Now dere's nane avaa'.'

'An' you'd feel da smell o' bannocks bakin' frae up i' da hoose. Yeah, tings surely has changed.'

'Dose days when we *delled* [dug, cultivated] da rigs, oh, dey were happy. I really likéd yon.'

The scene is easy to visualise. The *dellin'* would be done by two *paets*[5] (teams), each composed of three or four people, men and women, one *afore* and one *ahint*, with, if possible, one or two between them. They worked from one side of the rig to the other, in one movement lifting the turf (*braakin' it*), turning and chopping it, all in unison without a word needing to be spoken. They used narrow and short-bladed home-made 'Shetland spades'. Having finished a row, they walked back to the other side (*fetched deir paet*) to begin again. They dug continuously for half an hour, and might then stop to straighten their backs, perhaps to have a smoke. A young child might be put in the middle of a *paet* to 'learn him foo ta do it'. A boy of twelve or thirteen was already 'worth giving a spade to'. People who did not have their own land might dell for others. In return they would 'get a dellin'' on the croft for their own vegetables, or the women might be given a *head* of yarn. The payment was always in kind. All those dellin' ate a big meal together in the middle of the day. Whoever was cooking would signal to those 'doon da toon' by some prearranged means, perhaps hanging out a white cloth, to let them know 'when da tatties wis boiled'. A good day might see half an acre delled; the croft might have three or four acres altogether under cultivation.

A chore? 'Nah! Folk were fit then,' and because it was sociable work it was enjoyable. There might be a pleasurably competitive element in it too. 'Remarks' would be made if the dellers on the adjacent croft were resting too much; and the dellers of one might try to outpace those on the other.

It bears little resemblance to contemporary crofting – an essentially solitary activity now, crammed into a hectic weekly routine for the working fisherman; pursued more intensively only by those enjoying retirement. Why, then, do they continue to croft?

When the question is posed in Whalsay it often elicits the reply, 'a man likes to have some land to walk over' – a response which merely begs the question. Sometimes it will be suggested that, for the older men, it is something to which they can 'come ashore' when they retire; for the younger men it is a passage to stability, marking a break from the freedom of youthfulness, of sprees, from the absence of responsibilities. Perhaps its appeal is in its very creativity, contrasting with the destructiveness of fishing; or that it requires ingenuity and a subjection to nature now lost from the fishing.

No doubt all these have some significance among the crofting population. But none would command general assent. It may be that to find a plausible rationale we have to turn back to the notion of 'bein' Whalsa''. The prosaic version of this might be that the question does not really arise: Whalsay people have 'always' been crofters and cannot conceive of themselves apart from crofting. This may be true, but it is inadequate. It ignores the passion for crofting among families who have *not* previously had crofts, and also fails to take account of the fundamental change in the nature of the activity. It is an explanation 'from inertia': if people croft now merely because they always have done, how can we simultaneously account for fundamental differences between past and present styles of crofting?

The fanciful anthropologist prefers a more elaborate resolution to the paradox, one which may lie behind the consciousness of Whalsay people (which is to say that they have not been over-excited by his theory). The croft is an anchor: spatially, it keeps people *in situ*, on the same small patch of land which has been occupied by generations of their antecedents; symbolically and ideologically it provides a sense of cultural continuity amidst the flux of modern economic and technological life. I referred above sceptically to the suggestion that men like to 'have some land'. But why do they? Perhaps what is compelling about the croft is not just that it is land, but that it is a particular piece of land. As indicated in the previous chapter, Whalsay families show a remarkable stability in their domiciliary histories. For many people, 'home' is not just where one resides at present, nor even where one was born: it is 'lineage' territory, the tiny, finite space in which much of one's history is located. As such, it is a fundamental referent of personal identity. Through nicknaming, it often becomes a feature of *social* identity. As argued earlier, the croft provides a focus for the aggregation of kin in residential clusters which, in turn, historically became the cores of fishing crews. The croft *qua* place is therefore fundamental to forms of social association; it seems to be permanently identified with people even though they may move residentially to other parts of the island. The historical ambiance of the croft is obvious in the personalisation of its various features. Rocks, *knowes* (knolls), wells, burns, and so forth, may all be known by personal names: 'Eppie's Crubh',

'Geordie's dyke', Maggie's knowe, 'Aald Kirstie's hoose', Peter's noost, Polson's Kirn, etc. Almost every topographical feature bears a name, although the provenance of many of the names is now unknown. Many such features also appear prominently in yarns: the rig where 'Aald Kitty' felled her dog with a dead sheep's jawbone; or the *toon* where 'da aald women ran ahint da sheep flappin' deir skirts, an' caa'd dem into da crü'. Some croft houses are built upon or around the foundations of earlier dwellings; and everywhere there stand the crumbling remains of cottages, byres and *crubhs*, even whole crofting townships,[6] now empty and abandoned, evoking in stone the earlier generations which preceded the present occupants of their crofts. Of all Whalsay *milieux* apart from the kirkyard, the croft is the supreme repository of the past, and the instrument which connects past and present most tangibly. To borrow Geertz's term (1971, p. 27), it provides Whalsay people with a 'sentimental education' into the meanings of 'being Whalsa''. Ironically, it is more effective in this respect than fishing, for the scale of the transformations in the economics, technology and routine of fishing is so immense as to render tenuous the cognitive identification of present practice with that of the past.

The croft, then, condenses the past through the landscape itself, and through its associations with the natural calendar; with community; with an earlier mode of subsistence and the ideal of self-sufficiency. It evokes the astonishing breadth of skill, the ingenuity and the stamina necessary for physical survival in 'da aald days'. It may even be that it suggests an orientation to values somehow more substantial, more genuine, than those of the materialistic, debt-burdened, tax benefit-maximising present.

If this reading is plausible, it leads to a view of crofting, however changed it may be, as an essential counterweight to, if not rejection of, the modern, market-oriented life to which Whalsay has become increasingly subjected since the war. In this respect it is the very *ir*rationality of crofting in economic terms which provides its attraction. It provides relief from the pressure associated with modern fishing not because it is *un*economic, but because it is *non*-economic: it belongs to a quite different realm of discourse. People are conscious of and articulate about the anachronistic nature of life in the small, remote community. They talk about its physical discomforts, the unceasing labour, the powerlessness of the periphery. They only hint at its compensations, since most people have only a cursory experience of life on the mainland. But the croft is an inherent feature of what they suggest is their perversity in clinging on to island life. In this version, to croft is to make a statement of commitment to the community and to the life it represents. If it could be subject to 'rational' and mensurable criteria, it would immediately lose its efficacy in this regard, and would probably die forthwith.

This is not to suggest that people confuse fat lambs and bountiful crops with their symbolic virtuosity as Whalsay folk. But they are conscious, in their labour, of its cultural context too. The Whalsay crofter cultivates his vegetables and rears his lambs because these are proper things for Whalsay men and women to do. The *manner* in which the tasks are accomplished will be evaluated not in relation to scientific standards of agriculture but as what Bateson (1936) calls 'cultural acts', and for the evidence they reveal of commitment to established factional practice. Croft work is one of the most potent ways in which Whalsay people make themselves recognisable – to themselves and to others – *as* Whalsay folk and as belonging to a particular group within the community. The croft models both the culture and the transformations which it has undergone.

Peat

> Oh Mallie's aye to da mür has gone,
> In a t'ree-paet bank you will find him,
> His spade and ripper he has girded on
> And his tushkar hung behind him!
>
> Land of floss and burra toog,
> My ripper sharp shall slay thee,
> An' wi' a croil a' ta my back
> My faithful blade will flay thee.[7]   [Hunter, 1937, p. 32]

Apart from crofting, there is no work task in Shetland so suffused with lore and tradition as the cutting and curing of peat. Peat is the most powerfully evocative emblem of domesticity, 'da peat reek' instantly conjuring the impression of a company gathered together, engaged in the timeless sociable activity of the hearth. The fire is the very symbolic centre of the home, serving, until the accession of kitchen ranges during the last fifty years, as primary means of cooking, as well as of heat, and as the focus of household inter-action.

That peat itself should occupy so prominently valued a place in Shetland's material culture is not surprising. It is, after all, one of the primary sources of physical survival, and represents the triumph of social adjustment to the ravages of a severe northern climate. But the importance attached to the process and method of reclaiming the peat as fuel requires rather more thought. It might, in part, be seen as a celebration of this social achievement, but that would not account for the distinctive character of the activity in Shetland, nor for its retention in Whalsay long after it has become technologi-cally anachronistic and less crucial economically than it was even twenty years ago.

Peat is thought to have developed on the hillsides up to 7,000 years ago. A worsening climate caused the deterioration of the soil, preventing the complete decay of organic matter in humus which accumulated over a thin layer of grey soil which covered the impervious 'iron pan'. This 'blanket bog' peat covers Whalsay, much of Yell and the north Mainland of Shetland to a depth of several metres (see Spence, 1979, pp. 17–21; Berry and Johnston, 1980, *passim*). The estimated reserves are so huge as to be virtually inexhaustible under present circumstances (Nicolson, 1972, p. 156).

Peat is exploited as fuel in Ireland, the Western Isles and parts of the Highlands as well as in Shetland, but the Shetland method differs in almost every respect. In technology and terminology it clearly reveals the Norse influence, resembling some of the techniques employed in the Faroes (Williamson, 1948, pp. 62 ff.) but differing from those of Norwegian coastal Saami (Paine, 1957, pp. 127–9). Elsewhere in the British Isles, peat (or 'turf', Faroese *torv*) is cut by at least two men working together (e.g. MacDiarmid, 1939, p. 22), often by co-operative work groups (Mewett, 1980; Breen, 1980) and using ordinary spades. One man lifts the turf in a lump with his spade, and his partner chops it up. The broken turf may be carried either in barrows or by women in their aprons to wherever it is to be laid to dry. The Shetland method, by contrast, uses specialised tools for different stages of the cutting, but all the cutting and stacking of the peat to be cured is done by one man working alone. The process of extracting the peat also incorporates an element of land reclamation, as will be evident from what follows.

For purposes of ownership, peat banks are treated as an extension of the house rather than as the property of its occupants. The peat *leave* is now an integral part of the title deed. The bank is not legally exclusive to any householder but, by convention in Whalsay, is treated as such. In theory, once a person has 'ta'en his tushker home', i.e. finished cutting peats for the year, anyone may dig the same bank without seeking the owner's permission. In practice, it does not happen. Subject to the approval of the Grazings Committee, a person may open up a new bank, but not 'too close' to a neighbouring bank. What constitutes 'too close' is, again, not a matter of legal definition. A practical criterion, however, is that it should be at least as far from a currently worked bank as the distance which a person could throw a *tushker* backwards over his head.

The *tushker* (Faroese *torvskeri*) is a long-handled knife. The wooden handle varies in length according to the height of its owner, but the entire implement, including the blade, would be at least five and a half feet in length, usually more. The upper half of the handle is rounded, to be easily gripped; the top of the handle itself is rounded to fit comfortably the palm which pushes it down into the peat. The rounded upper part broadens into a slightly concave shaft, four to six inches in width, and on to the end of it is wedged the steel blade, which broadens a little more and ends in a sharp, straight edge. Protruding at right angles from this edge is another thin blade, *da feather*. Once cut, the peat is lifted on the blade, kept in place by the feather and the concavity of the lower shaft, and raised to the *mjür* (moor), where it is laid to dry. The *tushker*, therefore, functions both as cutting and building tool

(Fig. 8). The feather may also be used to *rip* the bank, although some men use a separate tool, a *ripper*, specially for this purpose. This, again, is a long-shafted implement with a blade extending at a right angle to the bottom.

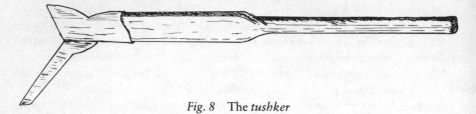

Fig. 8   The *tushker*

Ripping da bank is making an incision in the turf at a width of five or six peats from the edge of the bank. This marks the width of bank to be cut that year. It is done quickly but precisely: the bank should be the same width along its entire length. The cutter then *flays* the bank, or *dells da fjils*. The *fjil* is the sod of turf on top of the bank. Having ripped the bank, the man works along its length, making lateral cuts from the rip line to the edge of the bank, cutting the turf into even sods convenient for his spade. These are turned over and left to dry for a week or so. The previous year's cutting will have left a ditch, *da graaf*, between the foot of the bank and the lower moor. It is filled in with the new year's *fjils*, 'laid dün i' da graaf' (see Fig. 9). The man then goes along the newly uncovered top of the bank, using his spade to 'clean' the surface of bits of turf and to level it ready for cutting. If the surface is very coarse and full of roots (*möld*) he must *pohn* it, that is, cut off another layer, throwing it down on to the lower moor beside the graaf.

All is now ready for the cutting proper to commence. The outer peat, *da skjumpik*, is coarse, dry and mossy, having been exposed throughout the

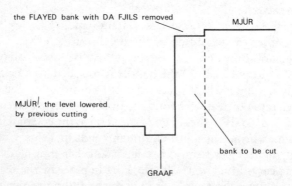

Fig. 9   The peat bank

previous year. As it is cut, it is thrown by the tushker *überd* (overboard) down to the moor below. These *skjumpik* are kept separate from the rest of the cut peat. As they dry to a thatch or a spongy consistency, they make an ideal covering for the peat stack which will eventually be built at home or in the hill, and are also useful as kindling. The cutter then *casts* (cuts) five peats across the width of the cleaned bank, using the tushker to lay them in ranks on the moor. It is because of the desirability to those who must later turn and raise them of having regular, even ranks of drying peats that the bank must be of consistent width so that the cutter takes the same number of peats off each width. He works along the full length of the bank in this way, cutting peats from twelve to eighteen inches in length. The first layer, 'da first peat', is often more brown than the blacker ('blue') peat lower down. The blue peats are preferred in the belief that they exude more heat when burned.

The tushker is held in the right hand, whilst the *löf* (palm) of the left is used to push it down, at a slight angle, into the peat. If it is pushed in too straight the peat tends to fall off the tushker. Some people put a *heel* on the shaft of the tushker so they can use a foot to ease it into hard peat. The peat is cut, removed and raised to the moor in one smooth movement, a skilled cutter casting perhaps as much as fifty bags' worth in a good day. Once finished on 'da first peat', the cutter goes back to his starting point to cut the 'blue' second peat. These are wetter and so rather trickier to control on the tushker. Once cut, rather than being laid flat on the ground in ranks, they are built into a dyke, the peats overlapping and leaving regularly spaced holes for the wind to pass through. If adequate spaces are not left, the entire dyke might be blown over into da graaf. It is a skilful operation and, to the novice observer, produces results stunning in their symmetry. In some parts of Shetland a third peat may be cut, but this is rarely done in Whalsay. Not only are the banks of insufficient height, but it entails lifting the cut peat well over a man's own height. If possible, the peats are cast with the man facing uphill in order to minimise the amount of bending.

The first part of the cycle is now accomplished. Most people start to cast peat in May, though some may already have flayed their banks in late April. Most of the cutting will be finished by early July.

Depending on the weather, the cut peat is left for a week or two, then the arduous and lengthy process of turning and *raising* begins. The first peats are gathered into little pyramids, three or four in each. After a few days, these are *turnéd oot* so that the inner face of the peat is exposed to the weather. The dyke is dismantled and its peats are raised in the same way. Although they start off wetter, these black peats tend to dry more quickly than the fibrous ones. After a further interval of days or weeks, again depending on the weather, the peats are gathered into larger heaps (*röhgs*) which may again be dismantled and rebuilt to expose any which are still wet. It is back-breaking work, for it demands continuous bending. Whilst it was usually (and is now invariably) a man's job to cast the peat, the women bore the major responsibility of turning and raising them. The children would also help. Nowadays the entire family, including the men, tend to help.

People recall 'da aald days' in the hill with some longing. The hill was 'peaceful' by contrast with the clamour of boat and township. As in most such recollection, food plays a significant part. Old peats would have been gathered to make a fire so that the workers could 'boil a kettle' and have some tea with the *faerdamaet* (snack). Some people even built rough shelters in the hill. The uneven ground, profuse in hiding places, ditches, puddles, rabbit holes, and the proximity of lochs, made it ideal and fondly remembered play territory for children.

The final stage of the process is to bag the cured peat and take it home to be stacked. Some people build a stack in the hill for the following year's use. Those who have none in reserve must get it home while the hill remains fairly dry and accessible to tractors. The peat is gathered into bags and sacks preciously hoarded for the purpose. If they have no tractor and trailer of their own, the folk contract with Magnie or Angus to transport it home. Neighbours in the township turn out to help, both to bag the peat and load the tractor, and to *bigg* the peat into a stack at home. The stacks are built up in walls, preferably with the more fibrous peats on the outside, whilst the rich, hard blue ones are thrown into the middle of the stack. The whole is topped off with the skjumpiks. Some people build sheds with regular ventilation openings to store peat, but these are not general. The ease with which the stack is built, and its strength (a necessary consideration, given the ravages of wind and wandering sheep), depend upon the regularity of the peats. Once the peats are *hame an' biggéd* a major defence against the winter has been erected. It is a moment of relief, an arduous chore finally accomplished.

When Whalsay men talk about peat-cutting they give the impression that each stage of the process is hedged around by strict orthodoxy. The reality is different: as with all skills, particularly those with deep historical roots, each segment jealously claims the superiority of its own method, denigrates the performance of others, and critical scrutiny and comment is rife, if surreptitious. This competition is itself traditional. The 'aald men' are recalled as competing strenuously about who could 'bigg da bonniest dyke'. Arguments raged over whether the peats should be thrown out with the tushker feather pointing up or down. People took great pride in the appearance of banks and dykes, not that any of this made any difference to the efficacy of the fuel – '. . . dey'll aa' dry, an' dey'll aa' burn' – but because 'It wis jus' deir way o' life.'

The peat-cutting of the present generation is disparaged by the older men. 'Man, deir peats is jus' horrible' – too long, too thick. The blame is placed on haste. The peat-cutting of the past is recalled as work done in a somewhat leisurely manner, with the men 'layin' deir haan's ipo' deir backs' as they walked slowly and companionably to and from the hill and, once there, stopped their work at frequent intervals to yarn. But the peats of '. . . modern times, dey're a' lok o' rubbish – aabody rushing to get back to da TV!'

It therefore becomes appropriate to ask why people continue to undertake the time-consuming and physically arduous labour of peat-cutting, and continue to use such labour-intensive means. A further question – 'Why burn peat at all?' – is also pertinent, and is not disposed of quite so easily as might be supposed. The obvious answer, 'Because it is free', is true but inadequate. There are people on the island who found it increasingly difficult to work with peat, both because of other demands on their time, and because of the decreasing availability of family labour. Some of the new prefabricated house kits made no provision for open fires or for solid fuel ranges. They were designed to be 'all electric', and some households expressed sentiments amounting almost to those of liberation from the peat regime. People who lived in the chimneyless Saetr council houses were less sure. During 1975 and 1976 there was a noticeable drop in the number of men cutting peats. By 1977 the trend had been reversed. New houses, including the new council houses at Tripwell, were designed to incorporate fires.

The renaissance of peat was, again, not to be wholly accounted for on financial grounds, for many of those who cut peat for the fire also retained oil-fired ranges for cooking and central heating. The critical factor was the fire as the spatial focus of domestic interaction. But this only adds to the mystery: why go to all the trouble of casting and curing peat just to keep the *ben end* (living room) fire going, when it would be so much simpler to buy in a few bags of coal? The answer seems to involve the complementarity of customary objects: the fire is inextricably associated with peat. The sight of coal burning in the grate engenders a feeling of discordance, and inevitably triggers comment about the superiority and preferability of peat. Some people seem to feel that the coal fire, though hot, is not 'quite the same', and induces the discomfort often associated with the perception of dissonance. Peat clearly touches a deep nerve in the Whalsay psyche. Middle-aged and older people who attended the old Brough and Livister schools frequently recall having to take a peat to school every day. More than a fuel, it must have become for children a fact inseparable from daily existence. It is not just familiar material but a basic material referent of local identity.

I think we must follow this line of speculation to understand the sentiment attached to cutting and curing peat. From time to time there have been people on the island who contracted with two or three households to cut peats for them. This served two purposes. It eased the pressure of work on the households concerned, and provided some occasional employment for men who were otherwise hard up for work. But the practice has never become established in Whalsay. Nor has there yet been any enthusiasm for the mechanical devices which are being developed to cut peats and which have been successfully tested in Yell. Of course, they may yet come. But thus far they appear to have elicited little more in Whalsay than the expression of scepticism, even of some distaste.

Peat cutting is treated as the very quintessence of traditional skill in Whalsay. Like the croft it provides a direct link with the past. Although people no longer cut and cure the huge quantities of fuel that used to be necessary, and may be less meticulous in the work than their predecessors are supposed to have been, they still use recognisably similar methods and the same kinds of implement. Moreover, they cut their peat from, or near to, the banks that their families have worked for generations. As they now steer the tractor along the rudimentary but improved 'peat roads' it is not difficult to imagine the men of a hundred or more years ago hacking out paths along the same route to provide easier passage for their barrows or for the pony and cart. Everywhere there are the remains of worked-out or disused banks, so that when working in the hill one is among the visible labour of one's ancestors. The activity may seem anomalous, even to those who practise it; yet, as with crofting, it may be its very anomalousness which accounts for its compelling appeal and which also helps to reconcile people to the trans-formations required of them by the circumstances of modern life. When they talk about the 'peacefulness' of the hill it may not be only the relative silence to which they refer.

Almost all the features of peat-cutting are mnemonics of the past. The physical effort recalls the nature of life which prevailed until as recently as twenty years ago. The reclamation through effort and ingenuity of valuable material from the inert bog distils the values of resourcefulness and self-suffi-ciency which lie at the very heart of Whalsay ideology. Place itself emphasises the sentiment of rootedness, not only through the inheritance of peat banks but because, like most topographical features on the island, the banks are surrounded by apocrypha. The technology is an historical document in itself, and its coincidence with the tractor rather than the *kishie* or barrow, and with plastic fertiliser bags rather than the old hessian or jute sacks, makes nice comment both on historical change and on the capacity of Whalsay folk to deal with it.

Peat takes us inexorably back into ethos, back to the ideas behind the words, into the symbolic life of Whalsay people. That also explains why competing orthodoxies of practice and performance are such potent topics of critical talk between and about different segments of the community. They appear to share the common form, yet assimilate it to their own idiosyncratic purposes and readings.

Da eela

On each side of the outer breakwater and the main pier, and inside the ferry pier, the Whalsay fishing fleet is tied up. Magnificent pursers, 180 ft or more in length; 70–80 ft steel-hulled white-fish trawlers, all packed with the most modern equipment: winches, power blocks, 'transporters', rope bins, tanks, shelter decks, and all bristling with aerials of one kind or another. But a few yards away, in the old inner dock and anchored through the South Voe, are dozens of *foureens*, dories and dinghies, a multitude of craft of twelve to twenty feet in length, mostly powered by small outboard motors; a few of the larger vessels have 8–10 h.p. inboard engines. There are new fibreglass hulls, and there are the traditional clinker-built Shetland models, some of which have been afloat throughout much of the century. Add to these the new racing yachts drawn up in neat lines on the yacht slipway and, faced with this plenitude of craft, no one could reasonably doubt that Whalsay men have a passion for the water. Some men claim to become physically disoriented if the sea is out of their sight for any length of time. However, to explain the popularity of the *eela* we have to look for more than a love of water.

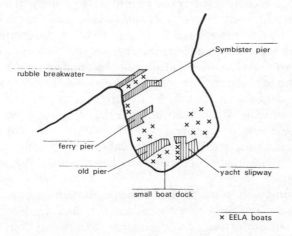

Fig. 10 The South Voe and Symbister harbour

Da eela is the term which used to be applied to sea fishing from small boats, using rods. The term is now used generically to cover all non-commercial fishing using rods and hand lines, regardless of catch species, conducted from small boats. In Whalsay it is prosecuted through the Sounds to the west of the island, and around the shore and holms to the south and east of the isle. It is one of those activities which, to the uninitiated, looks simple and straight-forward. Yet, if properly pursued, it demands a thorough knowledge of the topography of the sea bed; of the extremely complicated tidal systems; of fish behaviour, especially in respect of feeding; of traditional navigation; and of the lore relating to fish locations as they vary with tide, time of day and weather. As indicated earlier, people tend to specialise in particular stretches of water, and this itself may be taken as an indication of the expertise required if one is to depend regularly on something more than luck not only to catch fish but to do so in safety.

Until fishing became a full-time occupation for the majority of Whalsay men, most families would have depended on the eela for the year's supply of fish – and fish formed the staple basis of the diet, meat being a rare luxury. The Sounds contain many different species, small haddock, whiting, small cod, pollock, young saithe (the ubiquitous *piltocks*), young ling (*ollocks*), mackerel, occasionally skate, tusk and halibut. The abundance of each species can vary drastically over periods of time. In some years hardly a mackerel or haddock will be seen; in others they may be relatively plentiful. There is general agreement that the fish population has decreased markedly over the years as the offshore waters are fished with ever increasing intensity, and as new fishing methods destroy the immature fish and feed stock. It is worth recalling that every new technological development in the commercial fishery has been accompanied by predictions of the imminent destruction of stocks, and that this prediction was also made as long ago as the 1930s, when the seine net was first used (see Pottinger, 1952). Conservation has now become a matter of politics and bureaucracy, and the catch adjustments made over the last ten years have not had any noticeable effect on the quantities of fish to be found in the nearshore waters of the Sound. The days are long past when a crew could plan to 'go off' to catch the several boxes of fish required for winter curing with reasonable confidence that they would be able to do so. Nowadays these would be expressions of hope rather than of expectation, and to make catches of sizeable quantities calls for much effort, a willingness to try a considerable number of locations and, therefore, a wide knowledge of the eela.

Not surprisingly, the term 'fresh fish' means something rather different in Whalsay than it might elsewhere in mainland Britain. A fresh fish in Whalsay has not been out of the water for much more than twenty-four hours. After that it is said to begin to turn 'sour'.[8] Most of the fish processed as 'fresh' would be regarded locally as a little on the old side. But in the past people did not eat only fresh fish. A considerable quantity would be cured by salting and drying, and most middle-aged and older people still have a line fixed along an exterior wall of the house from which the drying fish are hung. Typically, a crew would gather the fish required for curing by giving to each man in turn an entire night's catch until everyone's needs had been met. Until the 1970s, when, through scarcity, they became a rare treat, most families would also salt down a few buckets of herring, perhaps the favourite fish among Whalsay people. Older curing techniques including sun-drying the fish on beaches, drying fish unsalted and sour in a *skjow* or *skeo* (a vented hut) and, more exceptionally, in thatch. Fish were also smoked in home-made *kils*. Traditional recipes make use of nearly all parts of the fish, including the liver, other than the gut. Even non-edible fish had their uses: the skin of the *how* (or *hoe*: dog-fish, *squalus acanthias*) was dried for use as a rudimentary sandpaper.

The *eela* of years past was therefore an integral element in the household's subsistence strategy. Before the use of small engines became common, the boats would be rowed and sailed to their fishing marks. These might be two or three miles from the harbour, and having to row a heavy foureen, with as many as three or four men in it, possibly against the tide, called for strength and stamina. The rower (*andoer*) required great skill, for when the men were 'into fish' it was his responsibility to keep the boat on the 'spot' by controlling its drift. The ability to *ando* in this way is one of the *eela* skills now generally assumed to have been lost.

Another was the extraordinarily dextrous use of the *waand* (rod). If the crew were fishing for piltocks, they might use casts with bent pins instead of barbed hooks in order that they might remove the fish more rapidly. The fishermen used a *thom* (cast) made of gut or spun horsehair, with six hooks. If the fish were not biting, they would try to make them rise by shaking the thom to disturb the surface of the water. The motion of the fly then immersed in the disturbed water was supposed to resemble feed, and would attract fish until 'da sea wis jus' boilin''. A flick of the wrist would bring up the fish on the cast, over the side of the boat, and the fisherman would use his free hand to slap it off the cast – and back went the line into the water, all in one swift movement. Huge quantities of fish could be landed in this way very quickly.

Although purists insist that the *waand* was the genuine *eela* implement, the home made devices used with the hand line have a pedigree at least as long. Their designs bear striking similarities to those used by the Vikings, and it seems likely that they were indeed introduced to Shetland by the Norse settlers. Two in particular are quite distinctive. The first, still in use, is a *dypsy*, employed for catching *ollocks* (young ling) and, in a smaller version, for haddock and other bottom fish.[9] The dypsy is made of a bent iron rod pushed through a heavy lead sinker, with a cast of two or three hooks at either end, each with a shiny tin lure (Fig. 11). The hooks are baited with mackerel belly, pork fat or piltock. The dypsy is lowered to the sea bed, then raised slightly so that the baited hooks suspend just over the bottom. The ollock dypsy is held still while the boat drifts with, and on the edge of, the tide. When a fish is felt nibbling at the bait, the fisherman must 'strike' to engage the hook. It is a fishing which demands sensitivity and patience.

A second Viking device, whose use was faintly recalled from his childhood by a fisherman born in 1905, was the *snivverik*, an oak semi-circular or semi-oval hook, with a baited thin shaft sprung with twine along its centre. When a fish took the bait, the shaft sprang and swivelled through ninety degrees, wedging itself in the fish's mouth. Its successful use required the

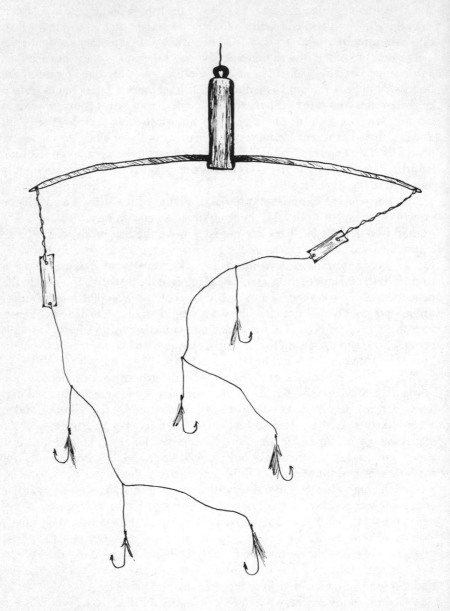

Fig. 11   A dypsy

fisherman to strike immediately he 'felt' a fish. Some local men doubted whether this elderly fisherman could actually have recalled the *snivverik* in use, but preferred to believe that he might have heard the old men of his childhood recalling stories about its use.

For mackerel and piltocks a *fleet* is used, consisting, in the former case, of up to two dozen hooks and flies. The piltock fleet is usually of about twelve flies. A lead weight is attached to the end of the cast. The line is lowered to the bottom, hauled up again some two or three metres, and then *jigged* – that is, moved gently up and down in the water. If the fisherman is 'on' a mark of mackerel he is unlikely to be able to lower the line far, for the fish bite while they are rising in the water. The line must then be hauled quickly, though still kept taut, for the mackerel continue to swim upwards when hooked and can cause the line to tangle badly. Experienced fishermen can tell from the feel of the fish's movement on the line precisely what species he has caught, and will rarely be surprised when the catch breaks the surface and is revealed. Another home-made device, occasionally used for cod, is the *murderer*, a lead weight, sometimes shaped like a fish, with two or more hooks sunk into it. This also is jigged, though, since cod often bite in mid-water, may be continuously hauled to mid-depth and then slowly released again.

The line itself is usually of a minimum fifty fathoms in length. It is regularly pitched, both to preserve it and to make it less prone to tangle in the water, and is wound on one of two types of reel. The traditional reel is V-shaped, the line wound on to it in figures of eight, leaving long slack loops (see Fenton, 1978, p. 590, and cf. Williamson, 1948, p. 79). But the second type of reel is now as common, on which the line is wound tightly around two straight axles fixed between each end of two parallel bars (Fig. 12) (Fenton, 1978, p. 589). All the tackle is home-made. Until about twenty years ago *eela* fishermen might also frequently 'set' a line, a shorter version of the traditional long line, consisting of several hundred yards of baited hooks anchored by weights and floats; and, in summer, might even set a drift net overnight for herring.[10] Both are now rare and have been superseded by the hand line, known by some people (especially from Brough, on the island's west coast) as *da shottin'*.[11] There are stories of young men deliberately irritating 'da aald eens' by setting lines where the older men were shottin' for haddock, because the fish preferred the baited hooks. Similarly, men using *waands* would be annoyed by someone using a *fleet* (hand line), for they thought this kept the fish at the bottom and dissuaded them from rising. Shottin' for ollocks, which are caught on the hard, rocky sea bottom, was a later innovation.

Navigation at the *eela* is by the use of *meyds*[12] or *marks*, a basic method of triangulation by which imaginary lines drawn from two landmarks intersect at a given point at sea. These meyds are customary, and as in Faroe (Williamson, 1948, p. 78) tend to be segment- (even household-) specific.

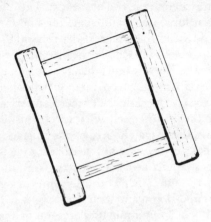

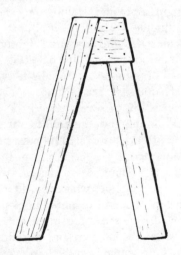

Fig. 12   Hand-line reels

Whilst particular spots of water may be known generally as *fishy* under given conditions, the meyd references for the spot will often be constructed quite differently by different fishermen. This makes the compilation of Whalsay meyds, in the manner reported by a local historian (Stewart, 1943),[13] tendentious, for it implies a uniformity of references where no such uniformity exists. (Also cf. Eunson, 1961.)[14] It may perhaps be partly because of the absence of generally accepted reference points that Whalsaymen find it extremely difficult to think about their meyds in abstract terms. One accomplished fisherman, asked for his meyds, replied after some thought, 'I doot I hae none.' Two others, the most experienced *eela* fishermen in Whalsay, found it almost impossible to specify their meyds while sitting in the living room; at sea, however, they are prolific: they have some forty meyds in regular use. One said, 'If I was on the water I could go right to it. But thinking about it – that's different.' A selection of their meyds, related to species and tidal conditions, is presented in appendix B.

Contributing to yet another incarnation of the vexed anthropological debate on 'mentalities', Frake (1985) shows that the complexity of the knowledge and cognitive models employed by medieval navigators to calculate time, direction and tidal conditions reveals them to have had a more sophisticated, more profound and far more thorough understanding than their modern successors. It is the modern navigator, who has only to look up the tide table or to read off the data from the electronic sensor without having any basic understanding and mastery of the phenomena thus described, 'who is prone to "magical thinking" . . .' (p. 268). Commenting on the navigational expertise of Melanesian islanders, he says that it depends not on rote learning, nor on the internalisation of immutable formulae, but, rather '. . . on a profound knowledge of the sea, the sky and the wind; on a superb understanding of the principles of boat-building and sailing; and on cognitive devices – all in the head – for recording and processing vast quantities of ever-changing information' (p. 256). Exactly the same could be said of the Whalsay islanders and other Shetlanders, whose successful prosecution of the open-boat haaf fishery from the end of the eighteenth century to the end of the nineteenth called for the very highest powers of seamanship. Although it may often have worn the guise of a 'folk knowledge' based on such things as the appearance of sky and sea, the 'smell' of the weather, and so forth, and was hedged around by taboo and superstition, such seamanship, at least in the case of the skipper, was built on a profound intellectual grasp of tidal systems, navigation and the geography of the sea bed.

The nearshore *eela*, though less taxing in the sense that landmarks are always in sight, and the physical effort involved is slighter, was built on the same intellectual skills. In Frake's terms, the modern eela fisherman could be said to move between two systems: the eela itself elicits his *cognitive* mastery of conditions; but his experience in the commercial fishery also equips him with *mechanical* ('magical') competence. If the older Whalsaymen are to be believed, the loss of customary skills has tilted this intellectual balance in their juniors towards the latter. Nevertheless, through their experience of the eela, they may be assumed to retain a higher level of fundamental understanding than is common among commercial fishermen.[15]

Arguing towards a conclusion similar in spirit to Frake's, Gell (1985) takes a rather different direction. He slightly recasts the dichotomy on which Frake's argument is based, of 'understanding' and 'reflex', into a distinction between intellectual, abstract 'Cartesian' understanding and 'practical way-finding', 'ultimately linked to the activities, perceptions and bodily attitude of the subject' (p. 273), a distinction he links with Bourdieu's theory of practice. He observes correctly that the distinction is somewhat unreal. Even though a skill – say, of navigation – may be habitually exercised, it does not thereby cease to be a 'skill', which demands intellectual effort and resourcefulness (p. 275). I would add that the unreality of the contrast becomes apparent when applied beyond mere 'way finding' to 'way finding in order to solve a problem' – for example, how to remain afloat; or how to remain afloat and catch fish. The 'practical mastery' thesis would seem to assume that the same conditions are continually replicated, which, empirically, would be unlikely. Thus, while stated abstractly it seems to describe Whalsay navigation quite closely, such navigation is never done 'in the abstract', a point underlined by the difficulty my informants had in recalling their *meyds* when not at sea. The two modes must surely be regarded as empirically complementary; neither would be sufficient in itself (cf. Gell, 1985, p. 282). Indeed, Gell proceeds to a logical demonstration of the interdependence of two forms of 'knowledge' (pp. 279–80),[16] and concludes that '. . . the essential logical processes in all way-finding, from the most elementary and subliminal, to the most complex and laborious, are identical' (p. 286).

I assume that Frake would reply to this that 'logical' processes are not the same as the intellectual effort required to achieve a profound knowledge of navigation and related issues from non-technological and from technological bases. It is because of the prodigious accomplishment of the former that he draws attention to the awesome feats of medieval north European navigators, and of later Pacific islanders; and on the same grounds that one must wonder at the sophistication and achievement of 'customary' navigation in Whalsay.

As well as perpetuating some of the lore of this customary navigation, the *eela* also sustains its method. But this is not to say that it merely 'museumises' an anchronistic skill, for it is a skill which makes a profound contribution to the education of the modern fisherman. Thus many of the Whalsay boys who now graduate to the commercial fleet and learn the algorithms of navigation and how to read the Decca navigator, the radars, electronic compass and so forth, have substantial experience of basic, non-technological navigation and seamanship from years of going to the *eela* with their fathers, grandfathers and friends. They have learned to 'read' tides, respond to the weather, tie knots, move in a boat, until these skills are second nature. They have ingested the wisdom of caution and the discipline of observation.

The *eela* thus maintains historical skills, although they have been attenuated and, in some cases, transformed, whilst others, such as *andoing* and the use of *waands*, may have been virtually lost. It educates, supplements the pantry, and gives a great deal of pleasure. Allowing men to rehearse skills ingrained from childhood, it provides a direct link with the past as well as a relaxing contrast with the present. It has in common with crofting and peat-cutting that it is a public activity, and performance is thus subject to public appraisal. The catch of a serious eela fisherman is locally monitored as avidly as the crews of the commercial fleet watch each other. Reports of who has 'seen' fish, and where, are retailed and will be considered by a skipper when he ponders over where to try for fish.

There is no mystique about the *eela*, but there are certain conventions which most men seem to observe. It is, essentially, a quiet activity, and to have a talkative person aboard clearly causes some discomfort. Like all Whalsay activities, the fishing should be done with deliberation, and without undue haste. One should not count a catch while still fishing. But what gives the eela its special ambience is its very contrast with the professional fishery. It is peace, relief from the immediate environment of the community – 'Oot yonder, ipo da Soond, wi' jus' da birds an da *neesiks* [porpoises] an' da seals watchin', it does you mair guid as a holiday!' – and, like crofting, its very anomalousness provides much of its rationale. A barren trip may be frustrating, but it does not matter in the way that a poor day 'at sea' would. Like the angling we looked at in chapter two, the contrast for a professional fisherman between the electronic wheelhouse and the 800 h.p. Kelvin on the one hand, and the haddock dypsy and 4 h.p. Suzuki on the other, may be a kind of reconstitution of the spirit, a reminder perhaps of the cultural and technological distances which have been so rapidly traversed, and of their points of origin. As a subject of communal interest and discourse it is a self-reminder of another reality beneath the huge investments and debts, and the fraught nature of fishery politics and economics. Like the other 'customary' activities we have examined, it is an historical anchor, now immersed in volatile water, whose line is attached to the past.

'Is du gaain' ta sea, boys?' 'Yeah, we're jus' haa'in' a run.'

'I'm been awaar o' a fish.' 'Well, he's cam' ta see me noo. Ah! Here he is!' 'Oh, dat's a beauty! Yeah, dat'll be guid: stewed wi' onions.'

'Is du felt ony?' 'Nah, naathin' avaa'. I'm not been awaar o' a bloody thing.' 'Shall we try at Lunning Head, then?'[17] 'Suit dysel'.' 'All right, haul up den! We'll be on wir road.'

'Man, I mind a noit here wi' Aald Hughie. It mus' be thirty five year *fae syne* (ago). We had twa lines an' a waand. I doot we haed twel' score in a quarter hoor.' 'Yeah, dat's roit. Dat wis a fine noit.'

'What's du mad' dose lures frae?' 'Dese? Yon's an aald can opener. Yeah, I don' suppose da man wha invented yon ever tocht 'at we'd sit here oot on da Soond drawin' ollocks on his can opener!' 'Man, I mind me makkin' da first lures I wrocht wi' fae an aald Mansion Polish tin. Dat mus' hae been i' da first days o' da Waar.'

'Does du tink we've got enyoch noo boys?' 'Aye. We surely hae.' 'Foo [how] mony is dere?' 'I dinna ken – five score, mebbe.' 'Dat's no bad fer an hour's fishin'.' 'Nah, it's no bad. It's a pickin'. But years ago, da aald eens'd be nae sae blide.'

In the modern practice of these pursuits the past is never far away.

Speakin' Whalsa'

> We're a people here in Shetland
>   An we had a speech aince, too;
> Noo hit's splintered an fragmentit
>   Laek da shoormil-brokken droo.
> An der comin fae da suddert
>   Swaarms an droves, wi pipes and proil;
> Can wir twartree wirds survive dis –
>   Or be smoared, at last, trow oil?
>
> Dem at loves da Shetlan culture –
>   Dem at loves da Shetlan tongue –
> Hing you in ta whit belangs here,
>   In parteeclar taech da young.
> Why sood we no pride wirsells in
>   Whit wir faeders passed ta wis?
> Why dan sood hit be abandoned?
>   Why sood we skjimp whit is wirs?[18]
>   [Peterson, 1974]

Whalsa' dialect has a competence as a mnemonic of the past similar to the other activities examined in this chapter. Of course, it has inherent purpose and practicality, but as its vocabulary becomes increasingly attentuated in breadth it is also used with a degree of self-consciousness reflecting its nature as a boundary-defensive resource. It is from this perspective that its use is briefly examined here, rather than as an exercise in historical linguistics.

As indicated earlier, there is a strong and continuing tradition of linguistic research in Shetland generally, mostly concerned with the reconstruction or retrieval of Norn and with establishing the nature and extent of Scandinavian influence on the language. The most celebrated philological work was done by the Faroese scholar Jakobsen, but he does not seem to have visited Whalsay. This is a little surprising, since, because of its geographical insularity, it might have been supposed – correctly – that Whalsay generated dialect and speech forms distinctive in the Shetland context. The peculiarities of Whalsay pronunciation were frequently (and tediously) observed to us by acquaintances elsewhere in Shetland. These include the transformation of '-ay' into '-oy', and of '-o', '-io' or '-eo' into '-ow'; the interpolation of a softened 'j' before a vowel as, above, in *skjumpik, fjil*, etc., and so forth (cf. Melchers, 1983, p. 13). Less appreciated in Shetland is the existence of a vocabulary (or the remnants of one) which, if not absolutely peculiar to Whalsay, does not now seem to be widely evident in other areas of Shetland. Many of the dialect terms already alluded to will not be found in Graham's *Shetland Dictionary* (1979); some are missing from Jakobsen's. Exhaustive research on local language and place names was done over more than fifty years by a Whalsay-born Aberdeen teacher, the late John Stewart. During his lifetime he published only fragments of the vast data he had amassed, and did not complete his life's work, a dictionary. The eventual publication of his papers would make a massive contribution to Shetland scholarship and, specifically, would enable a much more substantial judgement to be made about the distinctive character of Whalsay vocabulary.

But apart from the possible uniqueness of the word-stock there remains a lively tradition of verbal incentiveness and creativity; words are savoured for their onomatopoeic aptness rather than for their 'lexical' accuracy. Whalsay people *enjoy* language. They use it reflexively. It is in these aspects of their self-conscious use of it that its community-symbolic function is to be found.

Throughout most of the last 200 years Shetland scholars have bemoaned the demise of the 'old language', Shetland Norn. As early as 1774 Low observed that it had virtually disappeared (1774, p. 105; also Edmonston, 1809). Jakobsen recorded fragments in various of the county's geographical extremities, such as Foula, Norwick in Unst, and Dunrossness, but it seems clear that the influx of Scots following the annexation of the islands by the Scottish Crown made the transformation of the language inevitable (cf. Barnes, 1984). Of course, the matter is not so simple as one language being displaced by another, for Lowland Scots also bears substantial marks of Scandinavian influence. Indeed, Shetlanders reading Burns for the first time are often surprised to encounter such familiar language (see Bowie, 1981; also Melchers, 1983, p. 3). In the absence of a genuine saga tradition – indeed, of any substantial literate culture until the nineteenth century – the spoken language has become the primary means of the tradition of evoking Shetland's historical distinctiveness from the Scottish mainland. Place and family names are also strongly Norse in character, but are perhaps now too taken for granted to have this competence.

The boundary-marking character which 'Shetlandic' has in relation to Scotland is replicated in a more detailed way in the difference between 'Whalsa'' and 'Shetlan''. Within the island the contemporary Whalsa' vocabulary, like Shetlandic generally, is readily acknowledged to be a pale shadow of its former glory. Members of the older generation frequently proffer the view that the older generation of their own childhood were the last repository of 'real Whalsa'. No doubt this view of cultural loss is one which most generations have of their predecessors, and frequently reflects increasing contact with, and the influence of, the outside world. A Whalsay woman who returned to live on the island in 1974 after an absence of more than thirty years was widely judged to speak a much purer 'Whalsa'', and to have retained a larger vocabulary, than her island-bound peers. Today's children have travelled a greater linguistic distance from their parents than did earlier generations. One cause has been the ubiquitous scourge of television. But this has been supplemented by a curious and anachronistic educational policy which insists that dialect must not be spoken in school and most certainly must not be used in instruction. Teachers often commented on the relatively late age at which Whalsay children achieved reading competence. The reason seems obvious: they were being taught to read in a language that was essentially foreign to them (cf. Dorian, 1981, pp. 23, 27 ff.). A Scottish schoolteacher based on the island of Foula recorded his view in 1955 that, if children must speak in dialect, they should at least be forbidden from writing or reading it, lest they 'be encouraged to corrupt their English. . . .' (Mylne, 1955, p. 12). John Graham, perhaps the most influential Shetland teacher since the last war, replied that such an approach would doom Shetland dialect. Nevertheless, the Mylne caution would appear to have predominated in Shetland schools.

Of course, however far it may now have moved from Norn to Lallans, and whatever the degree of vocabulary change from one generation to the next, the everyday speech of Shetland people remains authentic dialect. It is unmistakably Shetlandic, and in enunciation, inflexion, sentence construction and vernacular idiom is barely intelligible to the outsider. Whatever shivers it may send up and down the scholar's purist spine, its authenticity to those who use it is beyond question. Since the last war, the quarterly journal *The New Shetlander* has staunchly kept alive the late nineteenth-century genre of dialect literature, and has also provided a regular forum for speculation about the origins of the language. However, these preoccupations of the intelligentsia hardly bear upon most people's experience of their everyday speech, whose medium is far more elastic, much less restrictive than the endless lists of local words would suggest.

The sensitivity of language as an index of social change is most clearly manifest in the addition or loss of words and phrases related to work tasks. Some of these became adapted to new technologies, producing an association of old and new whose incongruity is itself a source of humour. But some seem destined to be lost for want of anything new to which they might be applied. For example, Shetland oats are now cultivated on a mere handful of Whalsay crofts. Before the war they were a staple, and a mill was maintained at the Hillhead in the yard of the Laird's Hall. Milling was a co-operative endeavour, based on the segmentary groups described earlier which would mill each household's 'corn' in turn. When the grain had been threshed, the straw remaining was bent into *hallows* – figures of eight – then gathered into *windlins* (bundles) and used later for feeding or for weaving into *kishies* (baskets).[19] A *syer* (sieve) would be made to separate *da sids* (the inner husk) and the *tailins* (the grain 'hair') from the grain.[20] These terms, like the tasks with which they were associated, are now redundant. The word *buggiflay* would not be known now to many people under the age of about forty. It meant 'to skin a sheep in one piece'. Pieces of wood would be wedged into the head and leg holes, and the whole would then be filled with Alexandra tar and painted, to be used as a *bow* (buoy) before canvas and, later, plastic buoys came into general use. One might suppose that the language used to describe the finely observed and detailed signs of weather (e.g. Hunter, 1962; Jamieson, 1974–75) and of animal behaviour might also be diminished through the accession of electronic devices, dependence on broadcast weather forecasting, and the demise of livestock husbandry (cf. Robertson, 1971).

But if the diminution of distinctive vocabulary reflects the subjection of islanders to the vicissitudes of economic and technological change, the key themes evident in the conventions of social interaction, outlined earlier, remain linguistically vivid. A person who flouts the imperative of egalitarianism is *perskeet*, vain or pretentious, and is likely to make other people *tramshkit*,[21] *trootly* or *trootlywye* (offended). A person who manifestly lacks the control and reserve so noticeable among Whalsay folk has *da galbow*[22] (temper). Someone not moving or behaving purposefully is in a *dwaam* (a dream), is *ramish'd*[23] (sleepy) or may even be *ganniecrook* (staring trance-like).[24] Other than the first, these words are absent from Graham's *Shetland Dictionary*, which might entitle one to speculate that their currency in Whalsay is not matched elsewhere in Shetland, and even that the discipline of behavioural convention remains more highly developed in Whalsay than is common in other Shetland communities. Similarly, the value attached in Whalsay to ingenious improvisation in mechanical tasks extends also to verbal improvisation. An apt word suddenly tossed into the functional void may be retailed and reported around the island with delight for years. Thus a man who, at the eela, needed a spout to pour some engine oil, said that he *binkled* one from a lemonade can. An elderly man from Creediknowe described one of his infant grandchildren in a thoroughly chocolaty condition as *onyapee*. A person in a state of some confusion was said to be *kishmelt*, while a baby crawling was described as *oorgen* – a term more usually applied to a sheep 'crawling' with lice. These words all achieve a degree of currency, but are also treated as the property of their creators and are thereby incorporated into their public identities (see chapter three).[25] There is then a strong sense in which this proclivity to, and licence for, inventiveness mirrors the more general adaptability of Whalsay people.

It also reveals their capacity, already observed here in a number of contexts, to marry old and new. As suggested earlier, this sometimes has a humorously incongruous effect. An untoward noise from the huge engine of the modern fishing boat may be described as a *neester*, or *yaalkin*, words more familiarly associated with a squeeking hinge on the cottage gate. A failure of some highly sophisticated electronic device – say, a sonar or a fish lupe – may be described as having *carried awaa'*, the term which would have been used for a broken line, a drift net which had become separated from the fleet, or a wind-damaged building. A major mechanical repair might still be referred to as *smookin' a belt*, *smookin* being the word used to describe slipping the yarn on to a yarn winder, or the *tarm*, the belt drive made of sheep's gut, on a spinning wheel. An unexplained delay in some surgical procedure might be glossed as due to 'da surgeeyon haa'in ta sherpen his tools', and so forth. The humour resides in the perceived incongruity of Whalsay and the modern, a combination often spoken of with a slightly ironic incredulity. The adventures of an islander holidaying in the south will often be narrated in these terms, implicitly inviting the listener to ponder on the improbability of 'him – there!' The unlikelihood of the relationship is also inverted to produce a similar comic effect when a relationship is posited between an outsider and Whalsay, as in the stories, widely believed to be apocryphal, of conversations claimed to have taken place between a Whalsay seaman and King George V; and between two Whalsay men serving with the army in Egypt during the second war and a Greek cafe owner, in which both the King and the cafe proprietor profess an intimate knowledge of Whalsay, its dialect and its diet. The self-belittlement in this word play is a striking manifestation of boundary consciousness.

A similar reflexivity is manifest in the use of dialect in personal humour. Again, the effect is frequently one of gentle satire, of belittling those who might be inclined to pomposity or to individual assertiveness. Meaning here is often conveyed by inflexion, rather than by word. A response to an unlikely story: 'I *hear* dee,' or to a similarly incredible claim about a known person: 'S/heee?' But humour lies also in the pithiness with which dialect resources are composed with respect to the public treasury of personal knowledge. Any example from such prolific comment would be arbitrary, but some sense of the vogue might be gathered from the comment of a man about the progress his wife, known to be an unenthusiastic knitter, was making with his sweater: 'Shü'll craa' [literally, 'cross'; miss] Yule dee. I doot it'll still be ipo da wires nex' Christmas.' Every feature in the construction of this comment is idiosyncratic. It would have emerged quite differently from someone else's lips. This very lack of conventionality is prized as the essential richness of Whalsay speech. The humour thus rests on public knowledge of both the speaker and the person who is spoken of.

A further, equally arbitrary, example may underline the point. Here, through verbal interplay, Peter is both perpetrator and object of humour. He is an elderly man, long retired, who comments acerbically on the idleness of those younger than himself. His ponderous entry into a shop is greeted with 'Peter, is dü anidder een wi' nae wark to do?'

'*I* [see above]? I did me wark atween eelayven an' twel' las noit.'

'Well, du canna haed muckle wark ta doy if du did him aa' atween eelayven an' twel'.'

'Emptied aa' da paet bags!' He looks disgruntled by the hilarity this exchange has engendered. He gruffly concludes, 'I better wen aff an' see if I can git a boil o' fish. I don' see —— [his sixty-two-year-old younger brother] caamin' ta da hoose wi' fish!'

This remark is obliquely, but obviously, directed also against another man present in whose boat the brother usually fishes. The subtlety of the repartee lies in how much it manages to leave *un*spoken but nevertheless clearly understood – the humour also inhering in the speaker's idiosyncratic style. Perhaps it is for this reason that mimicry is an essential element in the art of yarning, for to paraphrase a person's speech, or render it just in the narrator's terms, immediately deprives it of its humorous referent. It is in this respect that, whatever its present linguistic influences may be, dialect captures and expresses the vitality of the community: the dynamism of speech mirrors that of community life generally.

Whalsa' dialect is regarded by those who speak it as having roots deep in the past. In a sense they are correct. Yet it is clear that, like the other activities we have reviewed in this chapter, it has changed a great deal over the years, and particularly during the last forty years. Although this change has involved a loss of vocabulary, it has not resulted in a desertion of the language. Indeed, quite the contrary is the case. It would seem that the greater self-confidence of Whalsay people has also made them less defensive about their dialect. People over fifty years of age invariably switch from dialect to English when talking to outsiders. Their juniors are much less inclined to do so. Some may profess their inability to 'spik properly', but it is instructive that they are sensitive to the difference and that, instead of abandoning Whalsa' for English, have developed the dialect to serve their modern and complex purposes. What would appear *not* to have changed is the sense of social and personal discipline required by the imperatives of communality. As remarked earlier, the self-effacement remains. Linguistically it is apparent in the device which figuratively separates the speaker from him/herself in the narration of experience, to soften the imposition of the first person singular on the audience: '. . . I mind me . . .' or 'I'm seen me . . .', 'I was riggin' me . . .' (getting dressed), as if the self is no different, no more significant as an object of the narrator's observation than anybody else. Melchers (1983) comments on the Norwegian and Scottish influences present in this kind of formulation. But the archaeology of the practice is less significant than its continuing social indexicality and saliency.

The 'aald days', and the past that never was

Crofting, peat, *eela* fishing and dialect are all evocations of the past, as indeed are other characteristic features of Whalsay life, most notably the social segmentation described earlier. But the historical consciousness of Whalsay folk does not betoken a stubborn traditionalism, nor a society stumbling through the late twentieth century looking longingly over its shoulder. Quite the opposite is the case. Whalsay people have become intensely modern, but have managed to do so without denigrating the past, or deserting it. They use history to orient themselves in the volatile present, and to give themselves a sense of stability in circumstances of manifest structural *in*stability. They also derive from it substance and precedent for their sense of boundary. The past is not expoloited in a Malinowskian manner, to provide charters of legitimation. It is evoked to express essential continuity and, thereby, to mask or mitigate the idiosyncratic consequences of flux.

Historians and anthropologists have long been aware of the dynamic relationship of past with present, though from a variety of theoretical and methodological perspectives. Indeed, one of the most fruitful meeting points between the two disciplines has been the study of processes in which societies continually 'reconstruct' their pasts in the light of present circumstances.[26] Shetland history has itself been the subject of such an analysis in a study focusing on the assertion by nineteenth-century Shetland intellectuals of the Norse element in Shetland identity. B. J. Cohen (1983) develops the notion of the 'past realtionship' in which history is treated as a perception of the past by a social agency – individual or collective – subject to the *contemporary* influences which prevail on that agency, rather than as a sequence of events which are isolated in time and space. 'History', therefore, is a complex plurality of such perceptions or relationships, some of which may converge, whilst others clearly diverge. Such relationships, she suggests, have a purposive character which may include the justification of change, the creation of 'satisfaction with a present state relative to the past', or the depiction of 'continuity or non-continuity' (p. 6).

The intellectuals with whom Cohen was concerned were writers and activists, people whose orientation to the historical and mythological pasts could properly be described as purposive. By and large, that would *not* be true of the 'past relationships' with which I have been ethnographically concerned here. Even though I may write in terms of a 'use' of the past, I should hesitate to claim an intentionality in such behaviour. Of course, on occasion the past may be contrived deliberately by Whalsay people in precisely the ways Cohen suggests: to underline contrast, to establish the legitimacy of an argument, and so on. But this management of history is a rather different topic from the one I have attempted to pursue here. My subject has rather been the pervasive presence of the past, its compulsiveness: it is the past as cultural resource rather than as ideological and rhetorical instrument, a resource which contributes to people's awareness of their difference and, thus, of the community boundary.

Historians would certainly find serious analytical problems in this approach. If people construe the past differently, and if the past is continually reconstructed as circumstances change and people's purposes alter, one is surely purveying a fiction in talking of *the* past. Rather, history as a matter of recollection, interpretation and creative imagination must be very insubstantial? My reply must be that, notwithstanding the charge of relativism, I see no difference in this respect between the past and the present: both are subject to the vagaries of perception and interpretation. Theoretically the problem of establishing 'what is really happening now' is as intractable as that of 'what happened before'. Certainly the sources for the former are more prolific: but that may merely mean that the versions and variations are more numerous. It does not suggest that they will be more authoritative.

Indeed, I should suggest that the processes by which the folk history of Whalsay has become established in the public mind mirrors those through which collective identity itself becomes formulated (see chapter one). Common terms of discourse emerge, focusing on personalities, events, 'customs', skills, places, and so forth. But this collective vocabulary only enables discourse to take place; it does not determine how it shall be used, nor does it entail any uniformity of interpretation. Thus the comment of the *eela* fisherman, '. . . years ago, da aald eens'd be nae sae blide . . .', is transactable among the crew: it is exchangeable currency. But it has no intrinsic meaning. Each member of the crew can render it intelligible to himself in terms of his own experience *without impugning its currency*. The meaning of the Whalsay past is thus as variable, as *contestable*, as every other matter of opinion in the community: its apparent objectivity and uniformity conceals a much less certain reality.

The past is used with subtlety. It creates the immediate impression of contrast with the present – but then delivers continuity as a kind of *coup de grace*. 'Does dü mind da *Joey Brun* [*Joey Brown*]? What wis it she haed? A 75 h.p. engine? What tinks du dose men would hae tocht if du'd telled dem dat in twenty year dere'd be boats i' Whalsa' wi' 800 h.p. engines? Dey' hae laached.' The transition from small to monster engine encapsulates a massive change in technology and economics, with extensive social repercussions. It is, in this respect, a statement of difference, of distinction. But '*Joey Brun*', and 'dose men', restore familiarity because everyone knows who was being referred to, and all present would almost instantly have summoned a sense of their own relationships with these people.

A similar impression is created as we look at Henry's collection of photographs of some old Whalsaymen, taken towards the end of the last century. 'Aald Couttsy', collecting box stems to be used in the manufacture of kishies. He was the weighmaster for Hay's, the Shetland merchants who had a branch in Symbister, and was responsible for weighing the catches. (See Nicolson, 1982, p. 123.) He is the source of the saying, still current, 'Haul 'em in, an' Couttsy'll weigh 'em.' 'Laachin' [laughing] Jimmy' ('yon's Heccie's grandfaider'); 'Durmy',[27] famous for wearing several pairs of *breeks* simultaneously; 'Jimmy 'Dot-an'-carry-one'; 'Aald Toilter';[28] 'Aald Pysket', recalled as an Irvine who, having been evicted by the laird, built a cottage on what is now the croft of Midfield and threatened to 'annihilate' the laird's men if they interfered with him.

Not everyone present was able to identify the people in the photographs, though the names were known, as, in varying degrees and with differing emphases, were possibly apocryphal stories associated with them. That much was common currency. But behind this common property were the unique connections each person present traced to the historical characters, through their own genealogies, their associations with parents or grandparents, stories about them peculiar to their childhood households, and so on. The same dialectic of change and continuity is there as well. Aald Couttsy evokes the old regime, successor to the Zetland method, which tied fishermen to the monopolistic merchant, a relationship worlds away from the present fierce independence of the Whalsay fishermen. Yet the bothy in which Couttsy lived still stands at Barnpark, overlooking Symbister harbour, and his name emerges to mark a plentiful catch. Aald Pysket, the rebel, is still succeeded on his Midfield croft by his lineal Irvine descendants, the present incumbent, Samuel, being celebrated as an expert on Whalsay meteorology.

Further on in the album there are photographs taken soon after the first world war of men cutting ice from the Hillhead loch (since filled in) and loading it on to Hay's cart to be used for storing fish. A page or two further and we come to pictures of the local herring station during the 1930s, with many men and women who are still alive clearly recognisable. Running through the comments and conversation is a hint of wonderment: how far we have come, so rapidly; and how much we have retained and is still familiar.

With the past so much around them, both materially and conceptually, Whalsay people have no need to fetishise it. Old objects are not valued for their age and there is little evidence of interest in the preservation of relics. The Pictish temple and settlement at Pettigers, on Whalsay's north-east coast, is rarely visited and is not maintained. Old millstones lie abandoned on the shores of Huxter loch; most home-made old furniture has long since been tipped over the cliffs of Clett; the restoration of the Hanseatic trading booth at Symbister, and its proposed conversion into a museum for the display of local artefacts, did not excite any noticeable enthusiasm. It was eventually used to record the history of the Shetland–Hanseatic trade. The departure of the *Research*, a locally owned and widely renowned old fishing 'zulu', to the fishery museum at Anstruther was greeted with something approaching relief. The Reverend Russell, a Victorian clergyman who served as minister in Whalsay, recorded for posterity the folk medical skills of one Thomas Henderson of Brough (Russell, 1887), but in 1975 the celebrated Henderson was remembered locally only for his dental forceps, which were still doing service in the engine of a boat belonging to his great-great nephew. There are two related themes in this lack of sentimentality. The first is that the past has no *inherent* value but is prized, rather, for its present usefulness; the second is a consequent disparagement of interest in anything related to the past which has no such practicality. There is a sense of a deliberate distancing from some aspects of Whalsay history which are seen as emblematic of a dark and demeaning period of servility, penury and powerlessness.

Hugh MacDiarmid, the doyen of twentieth-century Scottish poets, who lived in Whalsay for several years before and during the second world war, wrote in 1939 that the Shetlands Isles '. . . are happily very little encumbered with "memorials of the past" of any kind; they have to all intents and purposes – in the consciousness of the people – no history. . . .' (p. 51). This is a rather foolish statement which we may attribute to poetic licence, though the astonishingly patronising tone of MacDiarmid's commentary on Shetlanders makes it rather difficult to excuse him for any of his excesses. He fails to extend to their historical consciousness the general distinction he observes in Shetlanders' behaviour: the consensual exterior which thinly masks the vibrant and complex interior, the same kind of contrast which has repeatedly been drawn here with respect to symbolism, meaning and collective identity. Indeed, MacDiarmid comments on the effects of their history, and in particular of their subjection to the lairds, that it 'induced a secret radicalism and an external sycophancy' and continues, 'characteristics which survive in the Shetlanders today in the forms of a hidden preservation of their real lives and an outward accessibility to current conventions generally' (1939, p. 61). Sycophancy would be a ludicrous word to use of contemporary Whalsay people, who may, also, have been rather less radical, at least in their political views, than Shetlanders elsewhere. But certainly an exterior of equanimity is complemented by an understated determination to resist the kind of dependence evident in the past, and to reject any romanticisation of it.

People's attitudes to their history are ambivalent. Some history, like genealogy, is *dirt* (rubbish) [see chapter three], a depreciation which may also attach to people who show a particular interest in it. Some is practical: 'If it can be used, keep it!' Some is highly idealised, as in the imagery, to which allusion has already been made, of 'da aald wife' striding across the hill, kishie full of peats strapped to her back, and knitting all the while; or of the hearthside gathering of people, all engaged in purposeful activity. Such imagery clearly expresses implicitly a contrast with the present. So, too, do recollections of childhood. Down at the Houb, a nearly enclosed inlet of the sea near the kirk at Brough, a friend, then in his mid-fifties, said to me, 'Whenever I'm down here, I wish I was eleven years old again.' The children used to swim in the Houb during the 'dinner hour' in which they were released from the Brough school. 'Never missed a day in the summer' – an unlikely claim, given the Shetland climate. We saw three herons there, and he recalled that 'i' da aald days' 'everyone' would have been out shooting them. Innocently I asked why? Some people ate them. But also 'You could bring it in, measure the wing span. 'Course, in dose days, you could tak' een into da hoose. I doot du couldnae get into mony hooses wi' een noo.'

On another occasion an older man, then seventy, hinted at the same kind of contrast between the poor, but resourceful, past and the materialistic present. 'When we were young dey couldnae keep wis oot o' da waater. An' when we'd haed enyoch o' swimmin' we'd hae a peerie compiteeshon at trowing staines. We'd wark wi' six tins, an' see wha could hit da maist wi' six staines. Or wha could trow da farthest. Da Skerry o' Marrister wis a fine target. Dodie Irvine – man, he could trow a staine. I'm seen him trow een roit ower da skerry. Dat's a braaly long way ta trow a staine. Sometimes we'd split 'em, an' hollow oot da middle. Den dey'd go jus' like a kite. But nooadays, da women'd cam' *scaddin'* [hurrying] an' squaaking oot o' da hooses wi' a muckle *guster* [shout] a' da bairns: "Stap dat staine-trowing! Du mustna! An' mind du dose claithes!" What a row. Dose bairns don' hardly ken aboot bein' bairns.'

In his beautiful evocation of a Breton village between the wars Hélias (1978) recalls the trenchant contrast between the village child, able to fashion his toys from reeds, twigs and stones, and his playground from field and forest, and the bourgeois child from the city, curiously dependent on shop-bought devices, and completely lost outside the built environment. It is a similar kind of contrast which Henry and Glybie's Johnny make here, hinting at the familiar modern complaint that people are now too houseproud, this domesticity reflecting the surfeit of time women have on their hands since they no longer do croft work and have machines to do their housework for them!

Such an idealisation of the past is hardly unusual. But what is notable about it in Whalsay is its selectivity. The past there is always just 'da aald days' rather than 'the *good* old days', as it might be farther south. In denying an historical consciousness to Shetlanders, MacDiarmid was utterly, hopelessly incorrect. As we have seen, the past is always present in the most ordinary of activities. Some of its more negative aspects are kept alive in yarns known throughout the island about the exploitative and ruthless character of the laird's regime. Most of these relate to the underhand means by which land was obtained for the estate, or the harsh and absolute power exercised by the laird over his tenants. The first Bruce laird of Symbister was William, who had originally come to Shetland as clerk to his uncle, Lawrence the Bruce of Unst. William obtained two 'crofts'. Local tradition maintains that he expropriated land from Culbein Ormesoun, a 'peerie laird' and former 'lawrightman', whom he chased from the isle. (See appendix A.) Culbein is said to have leapt across a *geo* (an indentation in the cliff shore) in making his escape from Whalsay, and to have been given refuge by the Sinclair's of Nesting (on the east coast of Mainland, opposite Whalsay) to whom he gave in return the Holm of Sandwick. The Sinclair's Nesting estate was later added to the Symbister estate (see Smith, 1979, p. 12). Tradition has it that the Bruce purchased Nesting from the then laird, a widow. To complete the purchase, he went to her with his servant. He instructed her to raise her apron, and poured the cash for the purchase into it. The contract was thus sealed. But his servant, standing behind the unfortunate woman, cut her apron strings and the money spilled over the ground. Since the land now belonged to Bruce, so too did the spilled money, and Mistress Sinclair was forbidden to touch it. She subsequently threw herself from a cliff.

Early in the eighteenth century the Bruce added the estate of Lea, on the island's north-west coast, to the Symbister holding. According to legend he blackmailed the laird of 'Lie', William Leask, into forfeiting his land. Invited by Leask to dine with him after attending the kirk, the Bruce questioned his host about the provenance of the rum he was offered. Unwisely Leask confessed that he had found the casks washed up on the beach and had failed to notify the Revenue of his find. Bruce reputedly threatened to inform the Revenue himself unless Leask agreed to part with his land.

Such stories proliferate. They were retailed to us independently by at least four people, and, while the details vary slightly in each telling, the moral is the same: the fundamental injustice which informed the laird's domination over the isle. The same moral surfaces in stories about the way the regime was exercised. One of the most common is that of the punishment imposed upon the two Paton brothers, who, ignoring the laird's injunction, went to the Greenland fishery. He consequently forbade them ever to set foot on Whalsay again. In revenge their mother put a curse on the laird, the details of which vary from one narrator to another. The substance of it was that the laird's line would die out, with its final incumbent being reduced to penury – 'his *elbuks* [elbows] will cam' trow his jacket'; 'he'll be aeten' by *flechts* [fleas]' – and his Haa' (mansion) would fall into ruin: grass would grow between its flagstones, and 'birds'll flee in an' oot o' da windows'. However the narration differs, it always ends with a valediction: 'an aa' dis cam' ta pass'; 'an' so it happened, roit enyoch'.

In Shetland mythology some of the strongest execration is reserved not just to the lairds themselves but to their native bailiffs and henchmen. In Whalsay an Alexander Barclay who lived during the first half of the nineteenth century was particularly abominated not only for his treachery in helping to administer the laird's regime over his fellow islanders but also for profiting, by the grant of a large croft at the Burns, in the west of Whalsay (on land still occupied by the last surviving member of the Barclay family). But stories also preserve sweet revenge against him. The one most frequently recalled is of 'Aald Kirstey' (Christina) Peterson, who committed some misdemeanour for which the laird proposed to confiscate her two cows. She instructed her brothers to fetch in 'da kye' but, fearful of Barclay, they refused. She went herself and, leading them back to her cottage, was confronted by Barclay, who tried to take them from her. Thereupon she whipped him about the face with the tethers until he retreated, in tears. The same redoubtable lady is also reputed to have set upon a dog which had bitten her, and to have wrenched its jaws from their sockets.

Our neighbour, the late Hughie Lowry Polson, had been seasonally conscripted, at the turn of the century, to cart the laird's peats to the Haa'. The peat had been cut by the tenants, who, even at that late stage in the history of the estate and shortly before it crumbled into bankruptcy, received no payment. 'The natives,' he recalled, 'was just like slaves – well, maybe not just like slaves, but they had to do it.'

We have, then, a number of different features in Whalsay people's relationship to their history. In the practical activities of speech, of crofting, peat-cutting and eela-fishing we find a profusion of historical mnemonics which seem to orient people, to stabilise them in circumstances of pervasive change and, notwithstanding the homogenising effects of such change, to reinforce their sense of difference. We also find in the realms of apocrypha a selective idealisation which stresses the cultural loss incurred through social change, and a similarly selective stigmatisation of the past which allows the transformation to be positively valued. There is a consistency in this multifunctional view of the past, however insubstantial the view may be *qua* history. Those things which are clearly indigenous are positively valued; those which are extraneous, or appear to be beyond the control of islanders, are stigmatised. However long established the Bruces may have been in Whalsay, the basis of their power was in alien law. Moreover it was law which had displaced the rather more egalitarian udal tradition inherited from the Norse settlers. Of course, it would be grossly simplistic to regard the regime of the lairds as merely exploitative; some were less repressive than others, although none would seem to have been sufficiently enlightened as to attempt any substantial alleviation of the islanders' conditions (cf. Smith, 1979). However, the presence of the laird in the midst of Whalsay society appears to be regarded in retrospect as rather like an occupation by a foreign power, a living manifestation of the cultural and community boundary. It may have provided islanders with a cognitive model alerting them to the likelihood that most of the ills which oppress them originate outside their own society. In 1864 Hay & Co. took over the fishings and the kelp trade from the Bruces, but the change can hardly have seemed to the islanders to ease their circumstances appreciably. It simply substituted one exploitative agency for another, more efficient one. Moreover, whilst the Bruces were physically tied to the island, come what may, Hay's moved in and out of markets as economic circumstances changed, often leaving the islanders in an even worse condition. It seems likely that the despair which Whalsay people now express about external authority, and their general suspicion of 'da sooth' (chapters one, two and three), derive from these centuries of subjugation and dependence. It is ironic, but poetic justice, that, in breeding what is now a fierce and determined independence and a positive orientation to the supposedly indigenous features of their past, it should also have equipped them to deal so triumphantly with the intrusive change of these post-war years.

Notes

1 The subject of this section was previously addressed in Cohen (1979). The present discussion differs somewhat.
2 The larvae of the 'daddy long legs' (*tipula oleracea*).
3 Lambing difficulties actually increased as the stock was being improved, for the lambs were larger. Occasionally they were difficulties caused by incompetent breeding, such as, for example, putting a Suffolk ram to the much smaller Shetland ewe.
4 Clett is anomalous. It was administered separately by the Symbister Estate, which suggests that it may have been the residue of what was originally a separate estate.
5 The origins of this word in Whalsay are uncertain. It does not appear in Jakobsen (1928), or in Graham (1979). However, the Gaelic *am pàirt* is reported, and explained, by Father MacDonald as follows: '*Tha sinn am pàirt muir fhearann*, we work the croft in company' (1972, p. 192). The terms would seem to be too similar to be merely coincidental. (Also see McKay, 1967.)
6 A particularly striking example is the township of Berg, on the island's east coast. With a grim historical irony, this was deserted *after* the construction of the 'county road' around the island in the late 1940s. The road bypassed Berg, and thereby accentuated its isolation. Sufficient evidence of its habitation remains to give one a sense of what it might have been like to carry sacks of provisions, building materials, baskets of fish, kishie-loads of peats, buckets of water and so forth across the boggy and hilly moor, over burns and peat banks, a half-mile from the track to Berg's spectacular cliff top; or to set out from there on a foul, drenching winter's morning to walk a hard two miles or more to the boat.
7 *da mür*: the moor, the peat banks; a *tree-paet bank*: a bank of sufficient depth to cut peat from three layers (approximately 8 ft); *ripper*, *tushkar*: see text; *burra toog*: heathrush; a *croil*: a hump; *flay*: see text.
8 White fish are now kept fresh more effectively on the commercial boats by improved icing and storage facilities, whilst fish caught at the *eela* can be

deep-frozen. But in the case of *piltocks*, if these are to be eaten fresh (rather than dried or smoked), they will always be eaten within a day. Thus it is said that nobody would want piltocks caught on a Saturday night: everybody eats meat on Sunday, and would not wish to keep them until the Monday.

9 Fenton (1978) does not record the word *dypsy* in his description of hand-line tackle (pp. 585 ff.). But much of the terminology he attributes to Shetland generally is not in use in Whalsay.

10 There are still a handful of men, mostly retired fishermen, who set fleets of lobster creels. However, since this fishing is totally market-oriented, I do not consider it within the category of the *eela*.

11 The term is not in general use in Whalsay. The *shott* was the stern 'room' on the *sixern*, where the catch was held. Fenton reports that in Fetlar the fishing ground itself was called the *shutten* (1978, p. 587).

12 Elsewhere in Shetland, *meiths*. Old Norse *miða*, to mark a place.

13 I am indebted to Mr Brian Smith, Shetland County Archivist, for bringing this article to my attention.

14 Stewart and Fenton both report, and explain differently, two further terms: *reead* or *raid* (Old Norse *reitr*, Old Scots *reid*), and *saet* or *seat* (Old Norse *saeti*, Norwegian *seta*). For Stewart the first is another navigational device, a single bearing in which two landmarks are aligned; for Fenton (p. 587) it is a fishing area allocated to a crew. Stewart says that the *saet* is a *meyd* referring to a general area of water rather than to a highly specific point. For Fenton it appears to be a generic term for a fishing ground. Stewart can be regarded as the more reliable authority so far as Whalsay is concerned. However, neither of these two additional terms seems to be in current use.

15 If one adds their knowledge of sailing and boatbuilding, acquired and reinforced through their devoted pursuit of competition sailing, they must still approach the summit of Frake's scale of seafaring accomplishment.

16 Summarily, 'We are obliged at all times to locate our bodies in relation to external co-ordinates which are unaffected as we move about, and it is in relation to these co-ordinates that we entertain token-indexical beliefs as to our current location in space, and the locations of other places relative to ourselves' (p. 279).

17 The water off Lunning Head is deep – fifty fathoms or more – and good haddock ground. It is just off the coast of Mainland, as far from Symbister as this crew ever go on the *eela*.

18 *shoormil-brokken droo*: seaweed scattered above the high-water mark; *proil*: booty; *smoared*: smothered. These verses are abstracted from Mr. Peterson's poem, and are published here by kind permission of the author, and of the editor, *The New Shetlander*.

19 According to Jakobsen, *hallow* is an anglicisation of the Norwegian *halge*, 'a bundle of eight sheaves of straw'. *Windlin* is lowland Scottish and may derive, he speculates, from the Old Norse *vindli*, or Norwegian *vondul*, a bundle of straw.

20 The sieve was fashioned by stretching and tacking a wet sheepskin, with the fat removed from it, over a hoop. As it dried it contracted and tightened, and was then perforated.

21 Apparently found in Aith, on Shetland's west coast, as *trumskit* ('sulky, unsociable'), and related by the author to the Faroese *trumsutur* (Melchers, 1983, p. 19).

22 Jakobsen gives the possible derivation of *galbou* as follows: 'The first part of the compound is O.N. gal, n. *bawling*. The second part is uncertain; might be a shortening of O.N. baul, n. *bellowing*.'

23 Melchers reports this in Aith as *raamist* (1983, p. 19). *Chambers' Scots Dialect Dictionary* gives 'Rammish, rammaged' as the very opposite: 'to go about in an

almost frenzied state'; 'to go about under the influence of strong passion' (Warrack, 1911, p. 441).

24   Cf. Jakobsen, 'gan . . . looking vacantly' (p. 210).

25   On 'owning words' see Sansom (1981).

26   The recent volume edited by Ranger and Hobsbawm (1983) is a salient historio-graphical case. Among anthropologists Evans-Pritchard was an early exponent of the argument (1949) and more recently it has been revitalised by Sahlins (1985).

27   A nickname which almost certainly refers to 'doziness'. Cf. Norwegian *dura*, 'to sleep lightly'.

28   Jakobsen notes *toilter* as a nickname for 'a short, thick-set person'.

Chapter 5

Whalsay, and the ways of the world

In the last chapter, we found that Whalsay people use the indigenous/extraneous opposition as a means of evaluating aspects of 'tradition' and of 'modernity'. In the present chapter we shall explore further the use of this opposition to see how it sustains a sense of Whalsay's difference from other communities and wider society. Our earlier argument has been that the community's boundary inheres in that sense of difference, the maintenance of which is therefore crucial to the community's survival.

We shall look across a range of issues, some of which will appear to the outsider as obviously important; others, as relatively trivial, so that their inclusion within the same discussion may seem odd. My defence is that when people's sense of the integrity of their community – of its authentic difference – is at stake, nothing is trivial. Any breach of its integrity may appear to be the thin edge of an insidious wedge. People have to be able to bring the scale and pace of social change under their conceptual control if it is not to induce a condition of collective *anomie* – of normlessness, of utter disorientation – and the exercise of such control requires them to dig deep into their cultural reserves.

The operation of the indigenous/extraneous dichotomy is the master technique. It serves as a kind of template for the evaluation of modernity and change. These are initially seen as alien and, therefore, as negative, even if irresistible. This evaluative division does not only mark Whalsay's external boundary but also intrudes into the community. As a consequence, those members who are seen by others as relatively quick to embrace change are also seen as having thereby become 'less Whalsa'' and more 'like da folk sooth'. It will be evident from the discussion which follows that I am deeply sceptical about such judgements, and I shall argue that the movement which some Whalsay people may *appear* to make towards outside values is largely illusory, for it is motivated by their intention of reinforcing the community boundary and maintaining the cultural difference which it marks. This is not to say that the culture does not change, for of course it changes continuously

The MFV *Antares*, at 187 ft the largest of the new pursers in the Whalsay fleet. [Picture by Robert Johnson]

and substantially. But, to this observer, such change does not entail the loss of distinctive identity and its dissolution into 'sooth' anonymity.

The struggle to accommodate change and to maintain the boundary requires Whalsay people to be constantly vigilant, and to be prepared to fight for the preservation of their community. In this chapter we look at a number of such campaigns, and will find that, although they may appear to be issue-specific, they have to be placed within the broader context of the community's survival. Thus, while the fights may appear to be for improved fish prices or catch quotas, or for harbour works, they are more accurately seen as struggles against attitudes and policies which might deprive the community of its economic viability. Similarly, while people appear to embrace alien modernity in such forms as, for example, changes in women's roles, in a willingness to be policed, and in enthusiasm for a local pub, they are, more profoundly, fighting against the spurious attractions of life elsewhere and are recasting these alien forms into distinctively local terms.

But, sensitive as people are to the continual need for vigilance, they can be discomfited by what they perceive as gratuitous or excessive militancy in the defence of their community. Such over-assertiveness is itself seen as non-Whalsay conduct. This is apparent in their ambivalence towards their most vocal campaigner, who is discussed below. Their reservations about his methods illustrate a key theme of Whalsay attitudes to change and to the aggressive defence of local interests: both are contemplated only when the alternative is perceived as a dire threat to the community's viability.

Finally, we shall touch on one of the most intriguing, if intractable, questions which surface frequently in studies of social change. It relates to differences of attitude within a community towards change. Social scientists have pondered long (and not very fruitfully) over this, and I have no desire to leap into their theoretical morass. I would simply make the point that things are not always what they seem to be: an apparent inclination to change may often conceal a certain conservatism; vice versa, the disparagement of change does not always indicate an unalloyed traditionalism.[1] The expression of such views in a close community has to be understood as more than a conflict of philosophies. It needs also to be seen in the context of segmentary social relations. Moreover the very process of formulating and expressing such attitudes is a device of orientation, for obtaining a hold on events which seem to be continuously subject to flux. It is a means by which the *anomie*, referred to above, is averted.

Fishing, fer bugger-all

'. . . for these communities especially dependent on fishing, a decline in the industry would probably prove disastrous in both social and economic terms'. [Coull, Goodlad and Sheves, 1979, p. 13]

Despite the adventurousness of their investment in the fishery, Whalsay people see themselves as rather conservative. This conservatism is a mixture of caution and of commitment to what are seen as traditional values. Clearly, they have changed considerably. Yet, though change may have resulted in material benefits, it is not welcomed unreservedly. Rather, people see change as having been forced on them by the pressure of circumstances which dictate that the community must change or else face disintegration. They see themselves as having had change thrust at them by a world ignorant of their circumstances, and as having resolved to manage its disruptions with greater care and intelligence than may have been evident elsewhere. They have thus accepted the financial and technological constraints of modernity, but have not embraced it wholeheartedly. Their reservations are apparent in some of the conventions already noted: the antipathy to conspicuous consumption, the retention of 'customary' social and economic forms, and the rejection of unqualified materialism.

This wariness about modernity, together with the historical experience of the depredations of the lairds, have instilled into the fishermen a stronger commitment to conservation than is apparent among their competitors in the North Sea and northern North Atlantic. Their sensitivity to the imperatives of conservation has to be set against the financial pressures on them to maximise the boats' income; the restrictive regulations imposed by government and international bodies, which they see as often more politically motivated than informed by considerations of the eco-system; and the reckless destruction of fish stocks by their foreign competitors on the same fishing grounds. They distrust official evaluations of the state of fish stocks as essentially uninformed, and as revealing the kind of blithe and arrogant ignorance with which they are generally oppressed by the outside world. Their conservationist attitude is an aspect of their relationship with the outside world: it expresses *their* greater knowledge of local conditions, and their view of the wanton exploitativeness displayed by the outsider. Moreover, they correctly regard themselves as more vulnerable to the imposition of these restrictions and as more conscientious and honest in their implementation than their competitors elsewhere in Britain and Europe.[2]

This is not the appropriate place to present a recent history of fishing policy and its effects on Whalsay crews. My concern throughout the research and in this book has not been with the fishery *per se* but with its role in the community: with its embeddedness in and influence on culture and social relations. As suggested earlier, the fishing crew should be regarded as 'the community-at-sea' rather than as a qualitatively distinct and discrete entity. An indication of this embeddedness can be gleaned from the manner in which people's views of the state of the fishery affect, and are affected by, the tenor of community life, rather than relating strictly to the biological circumstances and economic conditions of the fishery. Between 1974 and 1985 I found an almost annual variation in people's estimations of prospects and in the general mood about the fishery. The confident optimism of one year would swing to despairing pessimism the next, and, in the following year, would swing back to a more sanguine view.

This instability of opinion is not obviously related to a corresponding changeability in the abundance of fish or in the state of the market, nor even in the perceived wisdom or otherwise of the latest regulatory policies. The trend in catches of demersal species in Shetland waters throughout the latter 1970s and 1980s has been one of serious decline (see Coull, Goodlad and Sheves, 1979, p. 44). In 1976 a complete ban was imposed on North Sea herring fishing. With one or two notable troughs, the trend of earnings for the same period has been upwards.[3] Moreover, this has been the period of the heaviest investment by Whalsay crews, and of the greatest intervention by regulatory bodies. The decision in 1978 by two crews to invest in one of the new generation of £1¼ million pursers was regretted in 1980 by the mate of one as ill advised (see Cohen, 1982a). Yet by 1984 he had decided it 'was the best thing I've ever done'. Again, the reversion to optimism cannot be accounted for solely by the buoyancy of earnings, nor by the happy failure of predicted bankruptcies to materialise. People do not express confidence about the long-term stability of their earnings; nor about any increasing enlightenment in EEC policy. The cost of gear continues to rise and crews complain that they are having to 'run harder just to keep still'. Every year brings its own crises: disputes with the EEC over subsidies and quotas; arguments with the East European buyers over prices; conflicts of interest with the Scottish Fishermen's Federation and producers' organisations (from which the Shetland men eventually seceded). Therefore it seems clear that we have to look beyond the fishery itself in order to explain people's attitudes to it.

The period since 1972 has seen such fundamental change in the administration of the fishery that fishermen have had to acquire quite new ways of thinking about it. Until that date they could plan their strategies around obvious variables: the state of the fish stock, the weather and the buyers. The white-fish prices at Lerwick were fixed, and the large buyers and exporters manipulated the market to suit themselves. The Shetland processors struggled; the fishermen's incomes, reasonable in gross annual terms, looked rather more moderate when reckoned on an hourly basis. Nevertheless, their bearings were clear, and strategy was relatively straightforward. But this all soon changed. The Lerwick market was 'opened' in October 1972, initially giving fishermen's earnings a boost; but, later, considerably augmenting the buyers' capacity to manage the market. The Common Fisheries Policy was painfully and inconclusively negotiated and renegotiated, prior to its projected introduction in 1982. The transitional arrangements ushered in the era of rapidly changing regulations governing 'TACs' (total allowable catches), quotas, subsidies and prices. By the end of the decade earnings, which had once vaguely conformed to the interplay of supply and contrived demand, now responded more to wholly artificial intervention. Highly restrictive quotas on some species, far from depressing earnings, led to their inflation. The stockpiling of white fish in cold stores removed the obvious association between the size of catches and quayside earnings. The availability of subsidies rather than the state of world demand or of cost–benefit analyses effectively influenced investment decisions about type and size of catching technology. The negotiation of these policies ended the previous simple opposition of fisherman and buyer: it now led to temporary alliances within national groups which rapidly broke down under the pressure of local interests. Thus large producers' organisations came into existence,[4] and then fissured into much smaller regional blocs.

Even within Shetland itself, the growth of specialisation within the industry broke the basic commonality of interest which had previously inhered in the typical adaptation of winter white-fishing and spring–summer herring fishing. The first generation of pursers, built during the late 1960s and early 1970s, were dual-purpose vessels, convertible to white-fish trawlers. When the North Sea herring ban was imposed in 1976 it was only this versatility which kept the boats viable. They turned, first, to industrial fishing for the feeder stocks of sand eel and pout, and later to mackerel. But their adaptability involved a compromise: the hold space necessary for carrying boxed white fish limited the quantity of mackerel they could carry in bulk, forcing them to return frequently to market from the fishing grounds. So they converted into pursers only, and were succeeded by a new generation of boats on which the conventional hold was replaced by refrigerated bulk tanks. These much larger boats fished farther afield, spending months at a time at 'da Channel', off the Cornwall coast. When fishing in the north their skippers could pick the optimum market, having the storage and fuel capacity to sail for Danish, Dutch or Norwegian ports if the prices there were above those in Scotland. For example, the Whalsay boat *Research* began in 1984 to land catches regularly in Denmark, earning £170 per tonne for herring, as opposed to the £110–£130 available from the East European 'klondykers' in Lerwick.

This period witnessed a clear stratification of income levels within the fishery. The world demand for herring, and the covertibility of bulk pelagic catches into fishmeal, meant that the pursers were constantly working to a relatively buoyant market. Although the fish may have become comparatively scarce, prices remained very high. Indeed, the prices available for herring during the period of the North Sea ban – itself regarded in Shetland as ill informed in several respects – had the perverse effect of depleting other stocks as well. In 1978 a rule was introduced which permitted crews fishing for mackerel to sell a 5% 'by-catch' of herring, with the supposed justification that it was technically unavoidable to take some herring in the purse-net, even though the target was a shoal of mackerel. But this was seen locally as inducing crews to catch more mackerel than they would be able to sell, since fifty units of herring, allowable as a by-catch, would fetch as much at market as a thousand units of mackerel. Not surprisingly, the mackerel were overfished and the market was soon glutted.

In 1980, when the second generation of steel-hulled pursers had begun fishing, the fishery was regarded locally with the greatest pessimism. Like the mate referred to earlier, some of the crews had grave doubts about the wisdom of their decision to order the new boats. Everywhere on the island there was talk of the gross earnings which would be required by crews just to 'break even'. People worried that 'this time, they've gone too far . . .' and 'dey've surely overstepped da mark.' But within five years they had confounded the sceptics and exorcised their own doubts, to the extent of again committing huge sums of money to having their boats lengthened, first to 140 ft, later to over 180 ft, using the increased storage to stay longer at sea and to sell farther afield. In 1984 the 'half-catch' earnings of one crew, reckoned locally to be a reasonable average of all the purser crews, was in the region of £18,000 per man. This excludes the additional income notionally accruing to them, as owners, from the 'boat share'. It is this scale of earning, and the taxation it attracts, which makes the logic of reinvestment so compellingly rational in financial terms. Yet at the same time people recognise that financial logic and the long-term interests of the fishery may be incongruent. One purser fisherman–owner commented in 1977, 'Well, boys, we've murdered da herring. We'll mebbe go an' wipe oot da mackerel noo!'

However, this growth in the incomes of the purser men did not extend to those of the white-fish crews. Indeed, the attractions of the herring and mackerel fishery led to a depletion of the white-fishing fleet in Whalsay, which is now rather overshadowed by Burra fishermen, who, during the last five years, have replaced their old fleet.[5] A young man, on a purser, with five years' experience, is now likely to earn rather more than his fisherman–owner father on an 80ft white-fish boat. The landing prices for white fish are subject to considerable fluctuation. They may sink so low as to make the catch quite uneconomic; indeed, there have been several periods during recent years when boats have been unable to sell their catch at all. The alternative strategy of switching to 'industrial fishing' for the fishmeal factories is also limited now by market conditions and quotas.[6] The very nature of the work differs. Purse-seining obviates the tedious chores of gutting, salting, boxing and storing fish, and frequently avoids the scramble for market. It keeps men away from Whalsay for extended periods at sea but also gives them more frequent, and longer, breaks at home.

Although the bifurcation of interest is not expressed in obvious animosity, there is evidence of a growing sense of difference and of some resentment. Some purser skippers may be referred to witheringly as 'tycoons'. Of some, it was said in 1985, 'Da bigger da boat, da bigger da heid!' And the resentment is not reserved to the men: 'Deir wives are jus' da same. Da folk are nae like Whalsa' folk nae mair. Dey gets less 'n less like Whalsa' folk.' The perceived change is more obvious to the sensibilities of Whalsay people themselves than to the anthropologist. They do not identify explicit indications of change; they just have 'a feeling' about it. I have to reserve judgement, for, to my eye, the friendships, solidarities and disputes seem to have remained much the same. However, even if the justification for the assertion of change is insubstantial, the fact that it is genuinely sensed has to be taken seriously.

It would be simplistic to assume that, in the past, fishermen who prosecuted different types of fishery shared material interests sufficient to outweigh those which divided them (see Cohen, 1978a, pp. 460–1). Yet, prior to the definitive separation of pursers and trawler-seiners, the common term 'fisherman' did embrace the specialisms of herring, white fish, industrial fishing and the shell fisheries sufficiently well to make 'da fishing' an essential referent of collective identity in Whalsay and, therefore, a prominent 'landmark' on its boundary. They could utter, and identify with, statements distinguishing them in common from people elsewhere. In 1974, following the miners' strike: 'Da folk 'at talks aboot mining as da maist dangerous wark in Britain . . . dey've never wrocht ipo' da deck o' a fifty-foot boat dat's heavin' aboot da Nort Sea i' da winter.'[7] In 1976, following a ruling by the Inland Revenue that money accruing to the 'boat's share' and held on deposit should be taxed as investment income: 'You're oot there, miles frae shore on an aakward day, workin' da pout, an' you wonder what fae? Fer every one hunderd poond du taks aboard, you can only keep twenty-two.' In 1975, with prices in a trough, and government regulations favouring the importation of Norwegian frozen fish: 'What are we killin' wirsel's fae? We're oot yonder, in da gales an' snaa' an' aa' dat shite, an' dere's naebody worryin' aboot us. We're fishin' fer bugger-all.'

I doubt whether any Whalsay fisherman would regard themselves as adequately compensated financially. As suggested earlier, their earnings have to be seen in the context of what is frequently a ninety-hour week. They take enormous personal financial risks in their investment and, by the very nature of their occupation, face continual physical danger. The work can be tedious, the living conditions at sea physically and mentally trying. It is an arduous life, exacerbated by the complications of international politics, Shetland's peripherality, and the petty but inevitable frictions which occur even within the local fleet. Thus, however affluent the purser men may appear by comparison with other working-class occupations, and whatever the present financial disparities between them and the white-fish men, they too could reasonably claim, and indeed *do* claim, to be 'fishing for bugger-all'. Whether demersal fishermen would regard this comment as applying similarly to their purser kinsmen and neighbours is a moot point. But I would suggest that to so regard oneself is part of the occupational ethic. Moreover, it is a reflex of the community boundary and of the state of relations between Whalsay and elsewhere.

So, too, is the mood which prevails at any moment about the state of the fishery. In 1979 and 1980 this mood was one of deep despair. In 1984 and 1985, crises notwithstanding, it was confident. What had changed? By various means the new boats had survived and prospered. But that itself begs the question. I would suggest a twofold answer. First, Whalsay people had learned to take crisis in their collective stride. As indicated in an earlier chapter, the ramifications of loan networks, and of sentiment, within the community are such that the failure of any one boat would be felt across the entire community. There is a general concern about every crew, though this is obviously intensified in the case of one's own associates. In the late 1970s, with huge sums of money being committed and personal assets being mort-gaged to new projects, people had an almost overpowering sense of vulnera-bility to forces beyond their control. It was a reassertion of the deeply ingrained consciousness of their powerlessness with respect to the outside world which we noted earlier, Whalsay fishermen know that they are more than a match for their competitors so far as the skills of fishing and seamanship are concerned. But the struggle seemed to be less with the sea and the fish, and more with powerful international vested interests, faceless bureaucrats and 'Eurocrats' and remote politicians. They had a long-nou-rished aversion to political militancy, little taste for or experience of collabo-rative lobbying, and a lack of conviction in their ability to affect the decisions of those who exercised authority over them. Every new policy proposal emanating from Whitehall, Brussels or the other European capitals was thus seen as a total crisis. However, together with councillors and officials of the Shetland Islands Council, and with their own Shetland Fishermen's Associa-tion, they weathered these crises, acquired a reputation for professional and political expertise, and gradually regained the self-confidence which comes with the survival of successive crises. They thus learned to defuse crisis by treating it as routine.

The issues over which they have fought have been many and various: the implementation of a regional policy, under which a Shetland authority would regulate fishing within its own fifty-mile limit; conservation measures which would regulate net-mesh sizes, catch quotas and licences in accordance with local expertise rather than with arbitrary and ill informed rules imposed by the government; the recognition of traditional fishing rights, and the effective policing of the more rapacious fleets, such as the Danes and Icelanders; a system of grant and loan for new vessels to encourage young men into the industry; the reconfiguration of the 'pout box', an area within which industrial fishing would be limited in order to protect edible species; and so forth. However, their arguments are misunderstood if regarded as oriented simply to the protection of the industry or of its specialised aspects. Rather, the fight is for *the community*, for, as Goodlad *et al.* correctly observe (above), Whalsay fishermen make a complete identification between the fishery's health and the community's survival. Their attitudes to aspects of fishery policy can be seen as grounded in their sensitivity to the vulnerability of the community.

Giving evidence in 1977 in Whalsay to members of the Trade and Industry Sub-committee of the House of Commons Expenditure Committee, Skipper Josie Simpson introduced his remarks by saying, '. . . this island has nothing but fish. We rely 100 per cent on fishing.'[8] This statement does not suggest that the entire work force is engaged in the fishery, but that without the fishery the community would not be viable. It is obviously correct. It is from this perspective that any impairment of the fishery's prospects looks like an assault on the community itself. Josie Simpson went on to express in revealing terms his indignation at the North Sea herring ban. 'I have been forced away from home; I have been forced to the Minches . . . I have been forced out of Shetland . . . I have been forced out of Shetland and made to go elsewhere to make a living. . . . I have been forced away from home' (*ibid.*, p. 1118), a telling and lucid expression of the sentiment that the fishery is not seen simply as an economic adaptation, but as the very quintessence of local identity. Its regulations were seen as an intrusion into the heart of local affairs, a breach of the boundary, an affront to local integrity.

Josie Simpson's sensitivity was general throughout the community and was based on the well-grounded fear that any harm to the local fishery could trigger a process of out-migration, especially among the young, which would be difficult to stem. We have encountered this topic already, but it is worth reiterating the contemporary circumstances which justified his anxiety. The demand for sea-skilled and other labour at Sullom Voe, and the possibility of commuting to work there afforded by the ferry service, was already making itself felt in Whalsay. Secondly, the inadequacy of harbour facilities at Symbister might have persuaded crews to base their boats in Lerwick – and they, too, would have followed. Some of their members might then have abandoned the fishing to work ashore. Third the age structure of the active working population suggested the imminent scarcity of berths on fishing boats for school-leavers. These, together with the government's policy of restricting the future growth of the fleet by withdrawing grant-and-loan facilities might have forced the young men into leaving the island to find work.

The spectre which loomed continually over these issues, as also over the dreadful possibility of bankruptcies, of the destruction of fish stocks, or the inability to compete with other fleets, was that of depopulation and the demise of the community which would inevitably ensue. The threat was made all the more convincing by a feeling that the government, in so far as it thought about Shetland at all other than as an oil base, saw its future as

having been secured by oil, and regarded its traditional industries as anachronistic irrelevances. There has never been a British government which has
taken the owner–operator fishery seriously, and Shetlanders are all too
painfully aware of their electoral impotence. While the government was
misconstruing the requirements of Shetland, the media and a steady stream of
peripatetic academics and consultants were misrepresenting the impact and
benefits of the oil industry in Shetland. It all combined to engender a feeling of
some hopelessness among Whalsay people.

The fishermen just managed to hang on. Some crews had an easier time
than others, largely through the success with which they timed their investment to minimise their indebtedness. Others lurched from crisis to crisis,
helped out by the Shetland Islands Council and by *ad hoc* arrangements with
the Norwegian financial authorities. Eventually they were able to turn their
survival from a day-to-day struggle into a positive resource. They found new
grounds on which to fish, markets they had not hitherto exploited, high prices
to compensate for low catches; and, most important of all, the experience of
coping with crisis. They could take heart also from the comparative failure of
mainland Britain. As unemployment soared in the south, it grew at a very
much slower rate in Shetland, and effectively removed any incentive to the
young to leave the islands. The demand for labour ceased at Sullom Voe as the
construction phase ended and permanent jobs were filled. The Shetland fish
processors, Whalsay's among them, provided new cold stores and expanded
their plants. Indeed, the expansion of Whalsay's factory was partly financed
by the sale of equal shares to some forty Whalsay fishermen. Somehow the
locality seemed to have been reminded of the futility of expecting help from
elsewhere, and to have renewed its conviction in its capacity to survive.

Whether this prompted, or resulted from, an upturn in the fortunes of the
fishery has to remain a matter of speculation. My inclination is to the former:
a community reaches a depth of uncertainty and crisis at which it somehow
recognises that it has either to assert itself in vigorous positive action or to 'go
under'. One might expect such a descent to result in desperation; but it seems
rather to induce a sense of confidence (see Cohen, 1985a, pp. 104 ff.; Paine,
1982, p. 90), a sense of the need to 'keep going'. In his evidence to the
parliamentary inquiry already cited, the late Geordie Hunter, the first
General Manager of the Shetland Fishermen's Association, told the committee, 'We are not asking for a lot. We are asking for enough to keep the local
industry alive' (Expenditure Committee, 1978, p. 1135). The measure of
what is enough to 'keep going' may or may not be intelligible to accountants.
But it is readily understandable to islanders: they may be 'fishing fer bugger-
all', but so long as fishing remains a more attractive prospect than anything
else the community is relatively safe.

Henry, and the eternal campaign

Attention has been drawn throughout this book to the traits of reserve and political quiescence characteristic of Whalsay people. However, one person is a prominent exception to the general rule. Regarded for many years within Whalsay itself as idiosyncratic in the strength and conviction with which he propounded his views, he has also now loomed large for some years on the wider Shetland stage as Whalsay's vociferous county councillor, uncompromising in his espousal of local causes and in the somewhat eccentric manner with which he pursues them.

Henry Stewart has to be described as 'larger than life'. Everyone on Whalsay has a fund of 'Hendry' stories, but these apocrypha do not adequately suggest the immensity of the living legend. They relate his single-minded prosecution over thirty years of a campaign for a new harbour in the North Voe; his brief but vigorous and innovative career as a fisherman; his late, but devout, conversion to sailing; his absent-mindedness; his antipathy to religious dogmatism and to school teachers; his sudden enthusiasms, and his barely concealed disappointment when they are not shared by others; his penchant for exaggeration; the impression he contrives of being overwhelmed by his family of six daughters; his increasing cantankerousness; his resolute refusal to be cowed by the conventions, alliances and elitism of the council. These stories combine the predominant, if contradictory, sentiments which Henry seems to evoke in his fellow islanders: exasperation and affection. The first is a bewilderment at his readiness to be so assertive, and the deeply ingrained fear that no good can come of such openness; the second is a recognition of the sincerity of his convictions, of his lack of personal ambition, and of his unreserved commitment to the community's welfare. Throughout his life Henry has seen this as inseparable from the prosperity of the fishery. This view has made him one of the best informed and most far-sighted advocates for the Shetland fishery during the last thirty-five years. Indeed, his prescience about likely developments has been uncanny. But the sheer unlikelihood of some of his predictions – eventually to be fully vindicated – made it difficult for people to take him entirely seriously at the time. He foresaw the advent of 100 ft and larger boats in Whalsay (the largest now is 187 ft) at a time when few could envisage anything larger than 55 ft as economically viable. He was an early and unrelenting opponent of British entry to the EEC, and accurately foresaw its implications for remote and vulnerable communities such as Whalsay. He has been continually alert to the deficiencies of official policies concerned with the regulation of the fishery. Now in his late sixties, and having triumphantly survived serious illness, the fervour of Henry's campaigning has not diminished. Two of his present (1986) causes are the construction of a new school and the creation, in the old school premises, of a regional fisheries training centre.

Henry A. Stewart, Islands councillor for Whalsay and the Out Skerries.   [Picture by Gordon Craig]

Henry was born in 1919, the youngest of the nine children of Magnus Stewart and Janet Anderson of Brough. As a boy he won a place at the Anderson Institute in Lerwick. Some people identify the origins of his unconventionality in his education way from the island. Moreover, his early postschool years also kept him away from home. He worked as an engineer for the Post Office, stationed for some time in Orkney; and he served throughout the war as a signals engineer in Africa. He spent one further period out of the community as a clerk of works on the construction of the reservoir and mains water system in Unst, a job he had undertaken in Whalsay. All his siblings were known as distinctive characters.[9] His brother John settled in Aberdeen as a teacher, but returned home frequently to conduct archaeological, historical and linguistic research. Another brother, Tommy, noted for his humour and for his physical endurance, went to sea (as had his brothers Magnie, a merchant navy officer killed in the war, and Peter) and, on coming ashore, worked first as a fisherman and later for the council. He too is the subject of many affectionate stories. His sister, Margaret, was a much loved teacher, first in Brough and, following the amalgamation of the island's two schools, at Symbister.

While he was still a full-time fisherman Henry took on a variety of parttime posts: as agent of the Symbister Estate and of the old Zetland County

Council; as clerk to the district council, and representative to Whalsay and Skerries of the Ministries of Labour and Pensions. When his employment on the water schemes came to an end he took a job, with which he was permanently disenchanted, as manager of the Co-op stores at the Hillhead, a business which he eventually purchased. He was also a crofter and, for years, continued to fish Whalsay Sound from his *fowereen*, during which time he set 'turbot' lines single-handed. He became Whalsay's representative on the Shetland Islands Council in 1978, and was the first locally resident Whalsay person (other than the laird) to serve as councillor.

Running through all these activities has been his overriding concern and passion for the fishery. This interest is one aspect of his fascination with the community. He is steeped in its lore and language, has been an avid prac- titioner of its skills – as sailor, boatbuilder, sail-maker – and is always engaged by some topic in its history, whether a nineteenth-century disaster at sea, the details of an early herring drifter or of some long forgotten land transaction. It is clear that fishing and the sea caught his imagination early in life. Albums which survive from his boyhood are full of his lightning sketches of the Lowestoft drifters as they sailed through the Sound, and of drawings of boats under sail. Indeed, he recalls having twice 'been aff' on sail boats, the *Research* and the *Valkyrie*, as a boy.

During the several years he spent as a fisherman after the war Henry did not have a permanent berth, but worked in several boats as 'spare man'. Stories abound from this stage of his career of incidents which, in the public domain, have been made to express his eccentricity, regardless of the actual circum- stances of their origin. These humorous anecdotes aside, his fishing career was marked also by his substantial contribution to the development of seine-netting grounds. He mapped much suitable 'hard bottom', working out *meyds* then unfamiliar to many local skippers. His experience of the fishing left him with a profound admiration and respect for the tenacity and commit- ment which marks the successful crew. In answer to my question about what makes a good skipper, he doubted whether seamanship and 'fishiness' alone were very significant. But 'Drive – that's it! Drive! Keeping at it. Working a boat hard. *Keeping going*. A fisherman, if he's going to do any good, 'is always got to be looking for an excuse to go off.'

His concern for the fishery has not made him an apologist for the fisher- men. He was vitriolic about the destructive implications of the industrial fishery, arguing, first, that the catching of the feeder stocks must diminish the edible white-fish species and, second, that it was impossible to fish pout 'cleanly' – that is, without taking vast numbers of immature white fish as well. In his public pronouncements on the matter his ostensible targets were the Danish, Faroese and French fleets. But his remarks were clearly intended also as a warning to local fishermen.[10] He had no patience with the protestations of purser fishermen that, fishing offshore, they were only taking 'clean pout'.

'Dere's no clean pout! You're only getting unmixed pout offshore because the white fish out there have been fished out!'

He was impatient with the fishermen's stubborn antipathy to co-operation; doubtful about the financial wisdom of some of the new pursers; scathing about the general decline of interest in the sea and fishing among the contemporary generation of fishermen.[11] He was scornful of the pretensions of some skippers who, he said, saw themselves as 'little tycoons'. There was a lot of vanity about. 'Mind, dere's aye been some o' dat here. Oh yes! Dere surely has. Dey see themselves as above aa' da rest o' wis.' But this criticism has all the more bite precisely because of his commitment to the fishermen: he wants them to do so well, and therefore resents what he sees as their lapses.

Ironically, the cruellest blow of his career was suffered at the hands of the local fishermen. In 1975 he sought election to a full-time post as the first General Manager and Secretary of the Shetland Fishermen's Association. He did not expect to secure the post, but wanted it badly. When the votes were counted, he came second to the late Geordie Hunter. Local speculation about the outcome was rife. Among the reasons offered for his defeat were that, unlike Hunter, he was not a Freemason, and Freemasonry was powerful among the Shetland skippers; also unlike Hunter, he was not a fisherman; the largest electorate was in Whalsay, and it was suggested that Whalsaymen would rather vote for an outsider. With regard to this latter point, it was also widely supposed that a majority of the Burra men would have followed a similar inclination, voting for Henry rather than for Hunter, a Burra man. But among the Whalsay fishermen there was also a certain fear of what they saw as Henry's dogmatism and wilfulness. 'Dis is da ting wi' Hendry. He gets fixed on something, an' he'll go efter it fer years an' years until he's got it. He'll never let it go.' 'If Hendry gets an' idea in his heid, we'll – da fishermen 'll – not be able to do a ting aboot it.'

Whatever the reason was for his defeat, it was a bitter disappointment. Not only had he been a tireless spokesman for the fishermen, he had also helped them privately in innumerable ways: drafting letters, briefing them for meetings, helping them to complete applications for financial assistance, smoothing their claims for unemployment benefit, and so forth. Many non-fishermen in Whalsay were critical of the fishermen's decision. Henry himself tried to remain philosophical. 'It disnae' mak' nae difference ta me. I'm not oot o' a job. I'll jus' go on fiddlin' aboot wi' groceries fer da rest o' me time.' A sympathetic friend remarked, 'I 'spect if du'd been dün on da water front at Lerwick, Hendry, wi' your left trooser leg rolled up, it micht hae been different.' 'Yeah, mebbe. An' I expect if I'd been some stupid idiot gaain' aroon' wi' a collar an' tie, dey'd aa' hae voted fer me.' Within a few years there were indications that many local men regretted their opposition to Henry's candidacy. One esteemed senior skipper admitted, 'I think we maybe made a mistake and voted the wrong man in.'

Since becoming the island's councillor Henry has pursued the cause of the fishery from his official base, serving on the council's Fishery Group and on the Lerwick Harbour Trust, becoming actively involved in negotiations with government Ministers and officials and with the EEC. He has participated in official delegations to places far and near, from the Faroes to the Aleutian islands. He remains apparently inexhaustible in his advocacy of local interests, and is ever more outspoken in the council chamber.

When Whalsay people smile over some story of Henry's contrariness there is more than amusement in their reaction. Contrary he is, indeed: 'If een o' da Sandwick men said to Hendry, "You need no' bother settin' tatties yonder," for da weeds or somethin', you can be sure that Hendry would jus' go an' set dem right dere,' – and not only in his crofting. Many of his sailing exploits are recalled for his insistence on doing things differently, whether it was the design of a course for racing, the best way to measure boats for handicapping, or some innovation in sailing technique. (For example, when the conventional method proved unsuccessful he once sailed a Shetland Model stern-first!) Henry won his share of trophies; but he also possibly had more than his share of capsizes: 'We were carryin' too much sail. Well, na, it wis nae ower muckle sail. It wis da boom. We were jus' experimenting!'

But they also recall the social consequences which can result when a campaign is waged unremittingly in so small and isolated a community. The one great divisive issue in Whalsay since the last war has been the battle over the location of the harbour. The new Symbister harbour was officially opened by the Queen in 1961, but the years before its construction were marked by a bitter and pervasive struggle between the protagonists of two adjacent locations, the North and South Voes. (See Fig. 13.) Henry was, and remains, the principal protagonist of the North Voe. The South Voe faction was led by the

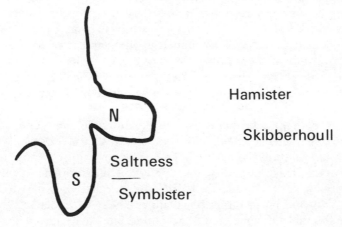

Fig. 13 The North and South Voes

late J. W. Johnson, a Skerries man who bought the Symbister shop, located at the head of the South Voe, from Hay's in 1951. The argument split the community and is said even to have divided families. By the mid-1970s the community was said by some to have 'just about recovered'. Although the harbour was eventually sited in the South Voe, Henry has never ceased to argue the greater merits of the North Voe, and has still not abandoned hope of its eventual development. As we shall see later in this chapter, it has remained a live issue.

I have never really understood why the argument aroused such passion. With hindsight it seems clear that the North Voe presented technically the better site: it is much deeper at the shore, and would have provided more adequate berthing for today's deep-draught vessels. But it is also obvious that when the harbour was planned no one other than Henry seriously envisaged the advent of such vessels in Whalsay; nor could they have reasonably been expected to do so. The North Voe also offers greater protection from the north-easterly gale which the fishermen now see as a real threat to their boats. But, again, the value of the fleet when the debate was at its height would not have animated the imagination of the planners. There is some innuendo in people's present speculations about the intensity of the conflict: that each side had some vested interest in its own cause. But this is not convincing, and does not bear serious examination.

One can imagine that the argument had a certain snowball effect: once launched, it mobilised segmentary alliances to the degree that it became a matter of social hubris rather than of technical and geographical merit. This does not account for the claim that the dispute split families, except in the case of those families which had ties of blood and marriage to the opposed camps. (Indeed, the two camps are themselves now closely linked affinally.)

The rather unsatisfactory explanation I would offer is that, because the dispute, and Henry's relentless pursuit of his proposal, were both so unprecedented, people simply did not know how to cope. The very unfamiliarity of the situation may have undermined their customary reserve and control, and blown the lid off long suppressed tensions. The strife which ensued left people apprehensive about any further such argument and, perhaps, wary of the intense singlemindedness with which Henry espouses his causes.

There is, perhaps, a further reason for the mutual incomprehension which sometimes characterises Henry's relations with Whalsay people. While they have learned painfully to cope with, and even to routinise, change and crises as they occur, Henry has always anticipated them. His insistence on the folly of the decision not to develop the North Voe revealed a depth of understanding all too obviously lacking among planners: he saw instinctively that a new harbour should be designed not to accommodate the needs prevailing *at the time* but to cater for *future* development in the fleet which the new facility would itself stimulate. This failure of foresight among planners accounts for the almost immediate inadequacy of new facilities on their completion. The novel demand which they make possible rapidly outstrips the supply they make available. Henry's prescience in this matter, as in his prediction of the scale of fishing operations, was founded on his characteristic inclination to take the long-term view of the community's needs. It may be for this reason that his diagnosis of problems, and suggestions for their remedy, have seemed far-fetched to Whalsay people.

But, while he may embarrass his fellow islanders by his militancy, Henry galvanises and personifies for them their collective confrontation with the outside world as no one else has ever done. Caricatured almost weekly in the *Shetland Times*, he makes no concessions to style. The battered suitcase and jacket, and his commitment to 'garnsey' rather than collar and tie, which physically mark his attendance at council meetings and official functions are complemented by his uncompromising (and doubtlessly exaggerated) Whalsa' speech and manner. When he goes to Brussels wearing his carpet slippers or his sea boots he is uniquely and idiosyncratically 'Hendry'. 'Na, dere's nae other body like Hendry. Dere never was, an' I doot dere never will be anidder een!' As the political, if voluble, personification of the boundary which separates Whalsay from the rest of the world he is definitely 'wir Hendry', taking on the world while using some of its unfamiliar ways to fight for Whalsay.

Fishing, militancy and local identity

There can be little doubt that one of the factors accounting for Whalsay's social coherence is the readiness of its members to observe its conventions of restraint. There is much about each other which they refrain from discussing among themselves. Outsiders may assume that neighbours know each other's business – but this is not strictly true. Everyone's knowledge is limited by what is released to the 'public treasury' (see chapters two and three). But people do not pry. The ethnographer (whose research is necessarily based on his irritating and often distasteful compulsion to pry) is frequently surprised to discover things which people do not know about each other. A further dimension of this silent restraint is a reluctance to make explicit commonly held assumptions, or assumptions which are believed to be held in common. The public expression of private certainties always carries the risk of weakening them and, thereby, of shaking the secure foundations on which people base their lives. This is a restraint which Henry must often seem to them to reject, and which therefore causes discomfiture and sometimes disharmony. The customary reticence of Whalsay people is not a product of complacency but, rather, of their apprehension. Making things explicit exposes them to the possibly malign effects of scrutiny and critical appraisal.

There is also a sense that to be too vocal about grievances and demands may tempt fate (or the government) to even more injurious action. Whalsay people neither wish nor expect to be noticed: they feel, justifiably, that life progresses in a smoother manner when they are left to get on with it free from external interference. They require a good deal of persuasion about the desirability of bringing themselves to the attention of 'the authorities'. In this respect the customarily high profile of Henry's campaigning is at odds with them. Hence, when they *are* provoked to assertive statements and actions by some change in the administration of the fishery, it may well be imagined that they must feel extremely strongly about it. They tend to see it as not merely inept or unfair but as an attack on their integrity and an assault on their very way of life. That sense is clearly conveyed by the vehemence of Josie Simpson's remarks.

In order to achieve an appreciation of this depth of sentiment, it has first to be understood that Whalsay people do not see fishing as simply an occupation. Fishing is everything, not only in economic terms but in the sense that it is inextricable from the very notion of 'being Whalsa''. To 'be Whalsa'' is to fish, or to have fished, or to be among folk who fish, and to have fishing as a constant element in one's world view. To fight for the fishery is thus to fight for the very viability of the community, rather than for any narrow occupational interest. It is possible to correlate with the occasions of fishermen's militancy circumstances beyond the fishery itself which are seen as affecting the community in some essential respect.

Alone among our informants Henry knew that in 1892 the Whalsay fishermen had struck against the Lerwick merchants Hay & Co. An inspection of the contemporary newspapers[12] revealed the circumstances to be that nineteen skippers signed a resolution affirming that they would not launch their boats until Hay's guaranteed minimum prices of 6s per basket of ling, 5s for cod, 4s for tusk and 2s for saithe. They were also to maintain the previous year's price for turbot and, in addition, to pay a bounty of 4s for every ton of whole fish which was landed. Not surprisingly, perhaps, this event is glossed over with some blandness in Hay & Co.'s house history (Nicolson, 1982, p. 124), but was clearly dramatic at the time. The strike lasted a month, and provoked the government into the ludicrous over-reaction of despatching the gunboat *Watchful* to Symbister. Henry was fairly certain that three policemen were drafted in. He further recalled that Farmer Hamilton, who rented farms from the Symbister estate, recruited blackleg crews from Unst to man his two boats, but they refused to cross the Whalsay men's picket line, and returned home. The *Shetland Times* of 7th May 1892 reported an amicable settlement of the dispute in the men's favour.[13]

It is appropriate to wonder why, after enduring so many years of virtual enserfdom to the fishing lairds, the fishermen should have proved so resistant

Henry mobilises the troops: some Whalsay fishermen, gathered at Symbister Harbour.   [Picture by Dennis Coutts]

on that occasion. The answer, I would suggest, transcends the fishery itself and marks a new sense in Whalsay people's perception of the relationship between themselves and the world at large. Twenty years before the strike the Truck Commissioners had published the results of their inquiry, after which there followed successive Acts of Parliament outlawing the system of truck and presaging the gradual demise (slower in Shetland than elsewhere) of fixed-price agreements (Truck Commissioners, 1872). Hay's had taken over the Whalsay 'fishings' (originally leasing them) from the Symbister estate in 1864. When the commissioners took their evidence eight years later they reported that, while they had not received any complaints from Whalsay people, the fishermen were 'bound to deliver their fish' to Hay's, and described them as having been only recently 'emancipated from a very primitive kind of tenure' (*ibid.*, p. 7). In 1883 the Napier Commission began the work that was to lead to the legislative reform of crofting, beginning with the Act of 1886, and the establishment of the Crofters' Commission, giving crofters increased security of tenure and considerably diminishing the power of the landlords. Thus on the two economic fronts of most relevance to Whalsay, fishing and the land, a long overdue and revolutionary change was taking place: the utter powerlessness to which the people had been accustomed for centuries was beginning to be ameliorated.

Having seen the Symbister estate collapse into virtual bankruptcy as a consequence of profligacy, Whalsay people had to endure mercantile exploitation by Hay & Co. which was no more benevolent than that of the fishing tenures under the lairds for being more efficient. The company was sensitive to shifts in market demand for fish and kelp, often leaving Whalsay fishermen and curers without the outlet which must previously have seemed assured. They would therefore be left without any means of support, apart from further indebtedness to the company. To be thus yoked into another captive relationship so soon after having escaped from the first must have been intolerable, especially when Parliament had at last begun to recognise their plight. Moreover, a reminder, if they needed one, of the risks they ran in order to keep their masters profitable came with the disaster of 9th December 1887, when seven Whalsay lives were lost at sea in a massive blizzard. This local tragedy followed close upon the heels of a devastating storm in 1881 when more than sixty Shetland fishermen were lost (*Peace's Almanac*, 1905, p. 40). Moreover, an apparently successful strike by herring fishermen against the Lerwick curers in July 1891 may have served as an instructive precedent (see Ratter, 1983).

These historical circumstances may not have been sufficient in themselves to propel the Whalsaymen into their 1892 strike. It is likely, however, that they gave added bite to the alternatives which confronted Whalsay: to prosecute the fishery successfully, or to follow the rest of Shetland and export vast numbers of its younger population. Between the mid-nineteenth and mid-twentieth centuries the population of Shetland halved. As noted in chapter one, Whalsay was untypical in not suffering depopulation. But one may well imagine that if the fishery had appeared to the men to offer little but renewed servitude the story might have been very different. The 1892 strike coincided with the kind of stark choice we noted earlier as a condition of collective militancy (Paine's 'to be – or not to be?'): stand your ground or sink forever.

A similarly bleak choice may have been perceived when Whalsay fishermen next took comparably militant action, although, on this later occasion, they acted in concert with inshore fishermen throughout Scotland. Nevertheless, there are good grounds for supposing that the issues which animated the national protest were interpreted in a peculiarly local fashion by the Whalsaymen. From 31st March until 4th April 1975 Whalsay fishermen joined in the blockade of Lerwick harbour, an action repeated in all the Scottish fishing ports.[14] The Scottish fishermen had decided on the action in their frustration with their inability to make any progress in their attempts to influence government policy on a number of issues. They wanted an end to the importation of cheap Norwegian frozen fish; they opposed one of the provisions of the proposed Dock Labour Scheme, which would have given to shore porters monopoly rights in all ports to unload boats for market.[15] They sought the renegotiation of the Common Fisheries Policy, the imposition of an exclusive British fifty-mile limit, and a redistribution of government subsidies to inshore vessels. Although the Whalsay fishermen felt strongly about these issues, their indignation is not an adequate explanation of their decision to participate. None of the many fishermen with whom I discussed the matter at the time believed that the protest would secure its objectives. Nor, at that time, did they express much solidarity with fishermen elsewhere in Scotland. Moreover, there are several factors which make their participation something of a puzzle. First, as we have seen, Whalsay people are not inclined to militancy: they do not believe that any good can come of it. Nor do they believe in collaboration, and certainly not in the kind of collaboration which would require them to subordinate control of their own boats to an overall command. The topography of Lerwick harbour is such that, unlike the Scottish ports, which could be closed by simply roping the vessels together across the harbour entrance, the Shetland boats had to lie at anchor in open water. With the severe weather and strong tidal conditions which prevail at that time of year, such an exercise called for considerable seamanship. It risked damage to the boats and danger to their crews, the very kinds of risk which Whalsay fishermen would not normally contemplate. Moreover the protest challenged another fundamental tenet of Whalsay ideology: it wasted time which might have been used productively.

For the Whalsaymen, therefore, their participation in the blockade required them to contravene their own customary values in an action whose

Part of the blockade of Lerwick Harbour, 1975

efficacy they doubted. In an earlier discussion of the event I have described in detail the manner in which they seem to have recast such unfamiliar behaviour into familiar idiomatic terms. But this 'Whalsification' explains more than the process of the event itself: it also suggests a peculiarly local dimension to their decision to participate. It is reasonable to assume that they filtered local sentiment and interests through the highly generalised statement of the Scottish fishermen's aspirations; and, again, that this local refraction of a national campaign was tantamount to stating the conditions for the *community's* survival, rather than for the industry's health and success. Moreover the directness of their action, unmediated by councillor or Member of Parliament, made it an authentically grass-roots statement, the community speaking for itself.

Customary Whalsa' intruded itself on to the proceedings in a number of ways. In radio communication among the crews early in the blockade the usual segmentary associations were obvious. Later, when the weather worsened and boats dragged their anchors, becoming entangled with each other, Whalsay crews invariably blamed the misfortunes on the inadequate seamanship of crews from elsewhere in Shetland, exonerating their Whalsay colleagues. Much of the shipboard conversation was concerned with exclusively local matters, in particular with a wedding due to be held at the end of the week. Most significantly, Josie Simpson, the Whalsay skipper who had been elected by Shetland skippers to command the Lerwick blockade, used characteristically *local* idioms of seamanship and command to manage the transformation of the atomised fleet into a locally anomalous phenomenon of a unitary and solidary entity dependent upon his authority. (See Cohen, 1982b, pp. 306 ff.)

A graphic analogy of the transformation of national issues into local sentiments in the blockade may be to see the community boundary as a prism fracturing the five national demands on one side into a myriad parochial issues on the other. When the blockade was held, there were in the Whalsay fleet ten boats less than seven years old; six of them were less than four years old. These boats represented the first major wave of reinvestment in the fishery, and the risks they entailed were still unfathomed. Members of the community took great pride in, and showed much goodwill towards, the adventurousness of their crews, many of them young men still only in their twenties. People knew that it was a critical time. If the adventure failed, Whalsay would have to reconcile itself to becoming a backwater of modern fishing, an eventuality which could mean the community's rapid demise. The issues behind the blockade were seen less as maximising the opportunities of the new fleet than as attempting to minimise the disadvantages imposed upon it by the government.

Moreover, most of the new boats were at that time tripping to the mainland markets at Peterhead, Fraserburgh and Aberdeen to take advantage of the superior prices available there. This strategy involved getting the catch to the day's early market, which itself meant being in the optimum position to unload quickly, and then to make a swift departure in order to minimise lost fishing time. All this was felt to require the goodwill of the mainland skippers and their crews. If they were to feel let down by the Whalsay men's refusal to participate in their blockade they could make life unpleasant. On both these grounds there was feeling that in order to protect the interests of the crews, and therefore of the community itself, the remainder of the fleet had no alternative but to comply with the Scottish call for a nation-wide blockade.

As in 1892, the spectre of depopulation loomed over the community. The construction phase in the development of the oil-related facilities was at its height, with jobs available in construction itself, on the oil-rig service bases, and in the service industries. Permanent jobs for sea-skilled men were promised on the Sullom Voe tugs and oil-rig support vessels. The oil industry was still a novel phenomenon in Shetland, so that its negative aspects – loss of independence and tedium foremost among them – had not yet been widely perceived. Employment elsewhere in Shetland – indeed, elsewhere in Scotland – thus appeared to be a viable alternative to a failed fishery, albeit one which would almost certainly entail significant departures from the community. There was explicit concern that the young people must be retained against the superficial attractions of the town and other amenities which had followed in the wake of oil. (See Cohen, 1978b.) Outsiders may perceive the industrial transformation of a community in physical, economic and infrastructural terms. But for the members of the community the changes have another, more pressing aspect, one which is all the more fearful since it can only be the subject of speculation. It is the possibility presented by development of irrevocable change to an established mode of life, to secure values, to all those certainties which make an arduous life on the periphery tolerable. The anticipation of oil, with all the exaggerated forecasts of increases in Shetland's population, the transformation of its landscape, the atrophy of its apparently soon to be redundant traditional industries, sparked off an intense cultural stocktaking, an introspective examination of local life and of commitment to the locality. This process was not confined to those areas of Shetland which were immediately proximate to the oil developments, but was general throughout the county, and was certainly evident in Whalsay. It culminated in a renewed commitment to the community: in the massive reinvestment in the fishing fleet; in the construction of a new fish-processing factory; in the creation of other local businesses; in the substantial improvement of recreational facilities, and so forth.

The blockade was a crucial element of the cultural audit conducted in Whalsay, and signified people's recognition of it as a watershed: much as they were irritated and bored by the blockade itself, and even though they recognised it as a token act, it was one to which they had to assent. Whatever their misgivings, every Whalsay crew participated.

When the blockade was lifted, the government had not changed its policy on any of the charter issues. It had merely indicated willingness to meet the fishermen for talks. Among the Whalsaymen there was a feeling of relief that it was over, a conviction that they had done as much as they could, and a discernible embarrassment at their self-subjection to Josie's command. But the action had longer-term effects. Although men expressed the hope that 'that's the last bloody blockade I'm ever on', they had broken their fear of militancy, and were to become far more actively involved in fishery politics than they had ever been previously. Almost immediately after the blockade Josie became chairman of the Shetland Fishermen's Association; he and two other Whalsay skippers became directors of the Scottish Fishermen's Federation. The Shetland body became active as an effective lobbying, marketing and research organisation. Although there has been no subsequent action of a similar scale and duration, the fleet did strike briefly in 1981, and in the winter of 1985–86 the Shetland pursers, led by Whalsay crews, broke ranks with their Scottish colleagues to fight for improved prices from the East European buyers.

Such action is not just an expression of occupational self-confidence among successful fishermen. It is also an indication of a new sense of assurance within a community which has faced and weathered crises whose outcome might have been disastrous. It is in precisely these respects that the fishery and Whalsay are identified with each other in people's minds. The sheer unlikelihood of so remote a community having such economic success and revealing such enterprise is itself an instance of the way in which local consciousness turns the world symbolically on its head: Whalsay becomes Centre; everywhere across its boundary is Periphery. This reversal is accomplished with an ironic finesse: *in extremis* people use what they see and despise as the ways of the outside world – such as militant action – to reaffirm their commitment to the anomalous community.

A *public meeting*

Militant action of the kind described in this chapter is only very rarely taken by Whalsay people. It betokens a general perception of dire crisis and is contemplated only as a last resort. Whalsay people do not feel comfortable with militancy, and recall it with some embarrassment. For most of the time they accept the necessity of living with the frustrated knowledge that the needs of the community as seen through their own eyes, and through those of outsiders – and especially of officials who are outsiders – differ. The difference does not lie so much in a divergence of priorities as in their respective recognition of what renders the community vulnerable, of the importance attached to local expertise and values and how these should be weighed against bureaucratic contingencies. Whalsay people and outsiders end up by talking straight past each other.

In spring 1975 the county councillor for Whalsay, a retired English colonel who had lived and crofted in Whalsay for three years, convened a public meeting which he had persuaded the council's General Manager and its Director of Construction to attend. The principal business of the meeting was to discuss harbour improvements. The councillor, well intentioned but often impatient with local sensibilities, was clearly disconcerted to find that Whalsay people were reluctant to say in public, and in front of outsiders, what they frequently told him in private. He had persuaded the officials to attend in order to impress on them the fierce insistence of the Whalsay fishermen that the development of a new harbour in the North Voe must begin without delay, and that they would not brook failure to heed their determination. He had rehearsed a senior fisherman in statements he should make at the meeting. He resembled a conductor who believes the orchestra will interpret the score exactly as he does. But in the event the performance proceeded in a very different manner. The players were reluctant to acknowledge his cues. When they did, they offered an interpretation quite unlike his own.

He had the greatest difficulty in persuading anyone to speak first. This is not surprising, for not only does a public statement entail social risk but to offer oneself with alacrity as the *first* to speak flouts egalitarian convention. Moreover, he seemed unaware of the sensitivity with which Whalsay people viewed the fraught issue of the harbour. He had relied heavily on Henry for local information – indeed, had told me a year earlier, having just been 'dragooned' on to the council, that Henry really ought to be doing the job. Thus, because Henry told him that it was necessary to develop the North Voe, and may have given the impression that this view was held throughout the island, he accepted it and appeared to remain ignorant of the long and controversial history of the proposal. Having convened the public meeting to 'clear the air' about the North Voe plans, as he put it in his introductory remarks, his own baton cue gave people present the opportunity to talk instead about improvements to the *existing* harbour in the South Voe. As we shall see, the men's hesitation about raising again the question of the North Voe was veiled at the meeting and was apparently lost on the colonel. He was further discomfited by the General Manager's revelation that the Shetland Fishermen's Association had not listed any work in Whalsay among its priorities for fishery pier projects in Shetland. Even after the meeting he still failed to understand what had transpired, how the subject of discussion had shifted, and why. Mystified, he saw it all as proof of the fishermen's political ineptness.

The colonel had revived the issue of the North Voe with the county council at the urging of Whalsay's district council. The clerk of the district council was Henry. At the colonel's behest he drafted a paper claiming to show the inadequacy of the existing harbour, and the colonel submitted it to the county council. Its Construction Department was instructed to carry out basic investigative and design work so that an approach for funds might be made to the government. The Director of Construction, a Shetlander who would certainly have known something of the historical conflict surrounding the harbour, reported on the progress of his investigation, but also slipped in to his opening statement the news, significant for a later stage in the proceedings, that the council had contracted with a dredging company to carry out some work on the existing harbour. Rather optimistically, perhaps, the councillor concluded, 'From that, you will have gathered that they [i.e. the council] have accepted that the harbour isn't large enough . . . and that they have begun the basic groundwork for the construction of a breakwater in the North Voe.' He asked for questions or comments.

Silence.

'Well, there *must* be *some*body?'

Silence.

'Look, when I talk to the fishermen privately they have a lot of questions! Why aren't they talking now?'

Silence. Eventually a young man who was closely associated with the South Voe camp (a man who, like Henry, had lived and been educated away from the community, and is less constrained by its conventions), asked, 'How about alternatives? You don't seem to be considering any alternatives!'

Colonel. 'Oh. Well, what they do have to do is to take all the possible alternatives. Now there has been a suggestion . . . for an extension of the present harbour running out to sea, with an arm coming across and taking in a great deal more water. That has to be investigated: a survey has to be made of the [sea] bed there to see if that is feasible – not in fact, I hope, to prove that it *is* feasible, but to prove that it's *not* feasible. This is to prevent the government officials coming back and saying, "Well, now, you're attempting to build a new harbour when you've got an existing harbour, and we feel you're throwing your money away. . . ." We're trying to look at the alternatives in advance. Anybody want to shoot on that one?'

Silence.

Colonel. 'Where's Henry?'

Silence.

Colonel. 'Anybody?'

No one (other than Henry, who had chosen to absent himself) could have intervened at this stage, when the alternatives of North and South Voes had been so baldly introduced. Fortuitously the colonel, probably unwittingly, then neutralised the issue, with the consequence that attention was to shift wholly to the question of improvements which might be made immediately to the existing harbour. He raised in detail the question of the congestion of the existing harbour and concluded, 'Now, how about you fishing people telling us where we're going wrong, and what you want doing?'

Silence. Then his 'rehearsee', a fisherman associated with the North Voe faction, said, somewhat hesitantly, 'We want a breakwater a' Nort Voe as quickly as possible. It's as simple as that.'

Colonel. 'You think . . . that the present harbour in its congested state is in fact extremely dangerous, with the amount of shipping we've got in here?'

Fisherman. 'Most certainly, yes.'

Colonel. 'And the value of the boats here is eight or nine million pounds [turning to the General Manager]? So we're not asking for something for no reason. We've got eight or nine million of private money invested in boats here. Now, has anyone else something they'd like to say?'

Silence. Eventually a senior skipper rose, a man closely related by marriage to the old South Voe faction.

'Well, speaking for my own part, I've nothing against the breakwater in the North Voe. . . . But surely you've seen the state of the harbour right now? We could be in the middle of another winter and nothing will have happened about this. . . . Surely [the county council] can do something in the meantime to help us over another winter, to ease the berthing space before this breakwater is finished in the North Voe? Certainly go ahead with your breakwater in the North Voe. But we must have something in the immediate future to ease our berthing space.'

The colonel now embarked on a disquisition which killed further discussion of the North Voe development stone dead. He explained that the process of obtaining government approval and funds for a new harbour would be lengthy: he doubted whether it could be brought to fruition in anything less than three years. 'So what you are asking for is some form of alteration in the harbour to assist over that period? How much space has got to be found in the harbour to make it safe? I'm asking this because if we try to establish any point for further development in the South Voe harbour you'll have the greatest difficulty in justifying the extension into the North Voe. So let's keep our requirements down to a minimum. Now, what would be the minimum amount of extra berthing that's got to be created in the South Voe?'

Now the players seized the initiative, while still denying their partiality – 'Let me mak' it clear, I'm not gaain' ta stand up here an' go after stoppin' da breakwater a' Nort Voe, don't get me wrang!' – and the colonel found himself listening to what was probably a rather different tune to the one in his score. Fishermen insisted that the risk to their boats in the habour from a north-easterly gale was such that some *immediate* action had to be taken. Three proposals emerged: that the 'wave screens' and shingle baskets on the outside of the pier should be restored, to permit berthing on the end of its inner side; that a temporary jetty should be erected in the inner harbour to accommodate the shellfish boats, and that additional dredging should be carried out.

The colonel, to his apparent surprise, now found himself a little at odds with the officials, since the first of these proposals was supposed already to be in hand, and the Construction Director began to sound an excessively cautious note about the costs of the latter two. He also started to weave a labyrinthine web around the complexities of council procedures, and to be pedantically defensive about the past actions of the council. It was at this point that outsiders and Whalsaymen conclusively lost track of each other. For the officials the problem was how to squeeze an extra few thousand pounds out of the budget whilst not complicating the accounts. For the Whalsay fishermen it was how to physically protect the investment on which the future of the community rested. They could not take seriously the bureaucratic preoccupations of the officials as against the enormity of their own adventure. One sensed that the officials simply could not fathom the depth of feeling among the fishermen, and had to regard them merely as contestants in the kind of political game they witnessed daily in council committees. They warned that improvements of the kind being demanded would decrease the 'impact' on the government of their proposal for a new harbour in the North Voe. The colonel, showing some impatience with the officials, confessed himself 'lost for words'.

A succession of suggestions followed from the floor about the location of the temporary jetty, given more point by one questioner who successfully elicited from the colonel the admission that completion of a North Voe harbour would probably be considerably more than three years distant.

The General Manager then intervened, in a manner which revealed that he

too was misreading the fishermen's intentions. Telling them how impolitic it
would be to press for improvements in the South Voe, he clearly failed to
recognise that they would greatly have preferred rapid improvement of the
existing harbour to the vague prospect of a new one at some indefinite time in
the future. Nor would they have been heartened by his implication that they
were, or should have been, motivated by considerations so trivial as calculations of political advantage. He sounded the wrong note by introducing his
remarks with a defence of the crucial role he had played in negotiations with
the oil companies for financial compensation, maintaining that his aspiration
was to secure a financial base for the protection of the traditional industries,
including fishing. But practitioners in these industries throughout Shetland –
among them the Whalsay fishermen – felt the greatest resentment that it was
oil, and not the inherent value of their own industries, which had brought
Shetland to public attention. To defend oil because it might ease the plight of
the fishery was to miss the point: the fishery and its pre-eminent communities
deserved support because of their intrinsic merits. The General Manager,
who had achieved national fame as the David who supposedly slew the
Goliath of the oil companies (and who went on to become chief executive of
the British National Oil Corporation), never appeared publicly to appreciate
the degree to which people felt thus slighted and neglected.

He followed this unpromising opening by figuratively dangling before the
audience the letter, received the previous day, from the Shetland Fishermen's
Association, stating the Association's priorities for fishery pier development,
'and making no mention whatsoever of any work here in Whalsay'. The tone
of his remarks suggested that the Whalsaymen were therefore being less than
candid in protesting the urgency of their needs. 'I fail to see where a better
body [than the Association] can be found for telling us what the real priorities
are,' a remark which once again betrays the gulf of misunderstanding. At the
time the Association was still regarded by the Whalsaymen as marginal,
dominated as it was by Mainland and Burra fishermen. To suppose that
Whalsay people might recruit outsiders to articulate their community's needs
ignored the principles of self-sufficiency, independence and distinctiveness
which stood (and stand) at the very heart of the Whalsay self-image and
ethos. It revealed the outsider's view of Whalsay as 'just another community'.
To its members Whalsay was obviously more than that: it was, as it remains,
the centre of their world. The episode is a precise illustration of a failure by
those on the outside to perceive a social boundary in any other than structural
terms and, therefore, to see its symbolic implications.

The General Manager's homily was greeted with a frigid silence, broken by
the colonel, who brought the meeting to a close without making any further
reference to the North Voe, merely summarising the improvements proposed
for the existing harbour.

The North Voe never has been developed. The extension to the South Voe harbour, which the colonel hoped would not be feasible, was built soon afterwards. The pressure on berthing space was thereby eased – but the men began to acquire much larger boats, so that space was soon at a premium again and the inadequate depth of water remains a problem. So too is the harbour's vulnerability to a north-easterly gale. The proposal at present before the council is for the construction of a new breakwater from the opposite shore of the South Voe, which would give the necessary weather protection, and for further dredging. The battle continues within Shetland for priority work on fishing harbours.[16] For Whalsay people the struggle to inform the assumptions of bureaucrats and politicians is a permanent imperative and one which they do not expect ever to accomplish. The unwillingness of outsiders to be thus enlightened is itself proof of the boundary's reality.

Much as they may have wanted and needed radical improvements in the harbour facilities, the greater imperative of maintaining local harmony required them to resist the colonel's invitation to be vehement and assertive in public. Had they accepted his invitation, the old arguments and hostilities might well have flared anew, and it is plain from the proceedings of the meeting that the old loyalties had not disappeared.

The fishermen accept the inadequacy of the harbour as a cost of their continued residence in Whalsay. I think they also suppose that this acceptance is an indication of their distinctiveness: that people elsewhere would be less prepared to make the compromises entailed by the enlightened discipline of community. It is one further respect in which they dissociate themselves philosophically from the way of the world.

'Da folk we ken't is aa' gan frae wis'

Fishing militancy reveals Whalsay's people's preparedness to use the world's devices, albeit with reluctance, when there seems to be no acceptable alternative. But the world then misinterprets Whalsay actions by treating them as if they were reducible, after all, to its own schemes of meaning. They are not; Whalsay people may resort to the world's forms, but they still infuse them with their own meanings.

The disparity of form and content creates discordant interpretations within Whalsay itself, between generations and among segments. As we have seen already, some people are inclined to regard their juniors as having deserted the Whalsa' ethos by their loss of traditional skill and language, their apparent materialism, and generally by a perceived change in their mode of life. Yet the people who are thus denigrated, while accepting that they may have changed, (indeed, in some cases seeing themselves as the forces of change) do not thereby see themselves as having become any less 'Whalsa'', or as having lost their essential distinctiveness. To take on some of the world's ways is not to diminish or compromise their own authentic 'Whalsayness'.

The tension between the 'supposedly old' and the 'apparently new' pervades much of Whalsay life. We have already noted its impingement on fishing, and on the customary work and skills of the island. But it is not limited to such functional behaviour. Rather, it is seen as essentially a matter of attitude.

Discussing the spree, we heard earlier an elderly woman comment on the difference between the spreeers of her own generation and those of today. 'Da folk we ken't is aa' gan' frae wis.' Here she laments the passing not only of friends and family but also of familiar and cherished values. The denigration of her successors which this kind of remark innocently implies is resented by them: it is hurtful. Nevertheless, it is a philosophy which abounds. It attaches to all aspects of community life, but it can be illustrated briefly with respect to three topics, all of which have been frequent subjects of comment since this study began in 1973: changes in gender roles, and the advent first of a local policeman, then of a local pub. With each we shall see that an *apparent* move in terms of *structure* away from the 'customary' pole towards what is perceived as the alien pole does not decrease the distance between the two in terms of *meaning*; on the contrary, it keeps Whalsay clearly and firmly distinct.

1. Aspects of gender. Whalsay gender roles, both in the domestic and in the economic spheres, are not easily comparable with those elsewhere. While generalisation is rash, it is reasonable to say that there are few gender-specific aspects of household management. Women bear the major responsibility for the care of infants, but men become closely involved in the care of older children. Cooking is not exclusive to either sex. Boys usually begin their fishing career as cook, one of the most arduous jobs on a fishing boat. On Whalsay boats, as elsewhere, a skilled cook is a prized man. Moreover, men frequently cook at home as well. Many who work ashore are active knitters, using machines to make the plain elements of garments on to which women will graft Fair Isle patterns (see chapter three).

This sharing of tasks is a residue of an earlier mode of economic life which persisted until after the last war. As we have noted, women laboured alongside men on the croft and the peat bank, and prepared the lines for fishing. They also provided much of the labour in the herring stations. Fishing itself is the only economic activity in which they have never engaged – indeed, their presence on a fishing boat was one of many celebrated taboos.[17] They were also supposed to avoid stepping across a fishing line. During the last few years the idea of women going to the fishing has become broachable – the work having become increasingly mechanised – though its realisation is unlikely in the near future. (See Aberdein, 1986.)

The 'traditional' domestic economy thus involved women's participation in the production of subsistence: they worked within the same economic spheres as men but, with the exception of crofting, performed specialised tasks within them. Present-day accounts of the archetypal traditional household deny the women time for purely domestic chores. The earth floors might have been swept once weekly. Laundry, too, would have been done no more often than once a week and required the assistance of men to carry the washing to and from the loch. While women knitted undergarments and guernseys, men made and mended footwear, and, skilled with a needle from years of repairing nets, would repair the heavy outer clothes and oilskins. In this genre of recollection the present domestic fastidiousness over the cleanliness of houses and of children's clothes is regarded as 'modern' and as symptomatic of the lack of 'real work' required to be done by women.

There are four benchmarks offered locally for this domestic transformation: the disappearance of *kye* from the croft; the installation of mains water in 1954 and of mains electricity ten years later; and the growth in fishermen's incomes during the late 1960s and early 1970s. The demise of the kye obviated the daily chores of milking, mucking out and preparing dairy produce. It also decreased considerably the amount of intensive cultivation necessary on the croft. The provision of mains services enabled the use of labour- and time-saving machinery at home. Both, incidentally, contributed to the privatisation of the household. They made unnecessary the frequent visits to the well for water and to the shop where generator batteries were recharged and paraffin was purchased. These chores had provided occasions for social contact and might also have been shared among neighbours. Throughout the 1970s the island's housing stock was almost completely renewed. Old houses were rebuilt and extensively remodelled, and many new homes were built, a process which further stimulated the supposedly recent 'house-pride'.[18] During this period women continued to knit, usually on a 'contracted out' piece-work basis. But by the mid-1970s their earnings had become marginal in the direct production of income. Three or four women were employed in the island's knitwear factory; about twenty unmarried girls worked as packers in the fish factory; three older women were employed at the school as cooks; another half-dozen or so worked as shop assistants. The only other women in full-time employment were schoolteachers and the postmistress. Girls tended to marry within two or three years of leaving school, and gave up their paid employment.

Women became increasingly involved in voluntary associations. A daily play group was established, in which mothers assisted on a rota basis; the local Scottish Rural Women's Institute flourished; committees proliferated to raise funds for the extension of the public hall, and for the construction of a licensed club; evening classes in joinery, country dancing and traditional fiddling were heavily patronised by women, and several became stalwarts of the Shetland Country and Western Club. Older people seemed to regard all this as a kind of freedom from responsibility, and to disparage it. However, it was hardly a meaningful 'freedom', for, apart from seasonal labour with peat and hay, it reflected the diminution of the woman's role in the household economy to that of unpaid housekeeper and carer, a narrowing of role emphasised by the longer periods fishermen were spending at sea. There was a dire shortage of paid employment for women. Even the seasonal labour at the herring stations had long since disappeared.

The expansion of processing at the fish factory and the creation there of casual work transformed the situation. Some forty new jobs have been created during the last ten years, of which all but three are filled by women.[19] The addition of part-time and casual jobs for married women enables them to stay at home during school holidays or when their husbands take their breaks from the fishery, and to modulate their hours of work to domestic commitments. For the part-time workers the cash contribution to the household budget may be relatively slight: but, as noted earlier, employment provides the opportunity for non-domestic economic and social activity which had been lacking. Moreover, its financial significance is significantly enhanced during those periods when men are ashore while their boats are being refitted or repaired, when the weather is too severe to permit fishing, or when the fish are scarce.

The development of the specialised full-time fishery has clearly resulted in a more obvious discrimination between men's and women's roles than at any time since the demise of the fishing tenures in the mid-nineteenth century. Apart from the changed nature of marital relationships, it has meant that for much of the time the island is denuded of more than half its men of working age, and is only fully reconstituted at Christmas and New Year and during the summer Regatta break. When the purser fleet is fishing in the Minch or the Channel its crews may return home only every third or fouth weekend.

There is an intriguing irony here. This transformation is seen by some older Whalsay people as marking the community's increasing slippage towards the world's ways. Yet the maintenance of the community when substantial numbers of its men are physically absent in, and have increasing contact with, that very world suggests the existence of an even stronger sense of commitment to Whalsay, and of difference from the world, than might otherwise have arisen. The Whalsay crews are said to keep to each other's company when they are away, and not to mix extensively with non-Shetlanders in the 'unken' ports. There is a daily flow of news between the boats and the island, so that intentional effort enables the ties of family, friendship and community to bridge physical distance and to sustain a sense of cultural distinctiveness.

2. *The policeman.* Another respect in which the world was regarded as having intruded its undesirable ways was in the increased consumption of

alcohol at weekends. The problem was not one of drinking *per se* but of late-night driving by youngsters thought to be under the influence of alcohol. A further aspect was the attraction of the island as unpoliced territory to young Mainland drivers and motor cyclists. During the mid-1970s the problem was elevated into something of a crisis. With the fishery expanding and profitable, young men could afford to buy cars within a year or two of beginning their working careers. Under-age driving was common, and there was some abuse of a Ministry of Transport concession which permitted unqualified motorists holding only a provisional licence to drive unattended on the island. There was a steady incidence of Saturday night accidents in most of which vehicles were injured far more seriously than their occupants. But there was a genuine fear of what might occur if the problem remained unchecked. People confessed to being 'terrified of what we might find one Sunday morning'.

In 1974, therefore, some of the islanders began a campaign to have a policeman stationed permanently in Whalsay. The issue was perceived as falling within the process of social change, since, with the exception of a very few known individuals, drinking behaviour had normally been highly disciplined. Drink was never carried on fishing boats (a voluntary and unusual embargo which remains the general rule) and fishermen tended not to drink during the working week. The big sprees and settling days were accepted as occasions for some over-indulgence by certain individuals but, these special occasions aside, drunkenness was, if not wholly unusual, certainly not a problem. The sudden appearance of undisciplined drinking among the young folk was therefore regarded as a product of Whalsay's changing relationship with the world at large rather than of entropic forces.

But the idea of having a policeman in the community aroused serious misgivings. There had not been a resident law officer since the demise, with landlordism, of the notorious *rancelman*, the bailiff charged with maintaining the laird's peace and rule, often with little regard for justice or delicacy (e.g. Smith, 1979, p. 16). The very idea offended people's sense of the integrity of their community as a disciplined society in which the importance of self-restraint and reasonable behaviour was generally recognised and in which people strove to maintain harmonious social relations. To submit voluntarily to being policed was tantamount to abdicating responsibility for such self-regulation. Against this was the argument that it was precisely because of the overriding concern with social harmony and egalitarianism that an outsider had to be recruited to impose an impartial authority: too many feathers might be ruffled, or relationships strained, by an attempt to do it locally. Finally, some people were apprehensive that a policeman would have little option but to apply laws which were regularly flouted and on whose considered neglect rested the viability of life and work in the remote community. For example, tractors would have to be taxed, and proper sets of tractor tyres purchased and maintained to serve the different conditions of road and *hill* – requirements which would instantly render the already irrational economics of crofting a complete nonsense.

In April 1975 a petition was circulated calling on the district council to request the provision by the Northern Constabulary of a policeman for the island. The prime movers were thought to have been the Church of Scotland minister, then resident in Whalsay, and the then headmaster, who was also the church's session clerk. It attracted sixty-two signatures, and the council duly sent it forward. The police decided, however, that their occasional presence, especially on Saturday nights, would suffice. When they eventually made their first sortie, on 4th July that year, their every movement round the island was tracked and reported by telephone. Defective, untaxed and uninsured vehicles were hastily concealed, as were any other materials which might have attracted attention, only to re-emerge as soon as the police were reported safely embarked again on the ferry. The roads, which at the time of the year should have been busy with tractors hauling the peat home from the hill, were deserted. There was a brisk trade in new and reconditioned tyres. People were scathing about the petitioners. 'Dey're waantin' a psychiatrist, not a policeman!' 'Dey don't see that it's a privilege to live without a policeman.' 'You canna live life on an island without breaking some laws.'

The visit had its humorous moments. One local driver who was waved down by the police thought that he was simply being acknowledged in the manner in which drivers on the island always signal to each other as they pass. So he waved back and drove happily on. One of the island's most celebrated women was reported to have finished her Saturday night spree by flagging down the police Land Rover and demanding a lift home. Taken aback, they replied that they could not: they did not even know who she was. 'Well, I'm da midder o' da wife you're bidin' wi' – so tak' me hame!' And, seeing no reasonable alternative, they did.

There was considerable satisfaction that several of the signatories were among those 'booked' for offences relating to the condition of their vehicle. But there was also genuine anger about the inconvenience which had been caused. In particular, Magnie had been charged with having defective tractor tyres, although he deliberately used ones with a worn tread when cutting grass, believing that they caused less damage to the ground. Moreover, old 'Robbie Linty', whose income, such as it was, was augmented by a few taxi runs each week, was forbidden to drive again. It was said that people had been looking for an opportunity to 'put him aff' the road.

The occasional police visits petered out fairly quickly, and the matter was dropped until some three years later, when, in 1978, it was again raised after a number of unpleasant incidents caused by youngsters from outside. The concern persisted the following year after a number of young children only narrowly avoided being hit by reckless young drivers from Mainland. In 1979 there had also developed among the youth an infatuation with air rifles. People were worried that a serious accident could not be long delayed. Thirty married couples, many of them with young children, including the doctor and his wife, signed a letter renewing the request for a constable to be permanently stationed in Whalsay. This time the request bore fruit, and by 1980 a policeman and his family had taken up residence in a Symbister council house.

People now looked anxiously for the consequences, but there hardly seemed to be any. The policeman was said to be popular among his neighbours but, apart from being personable and helpful, this seemed to be principally because he appeared reluctant to exercise his authority. The shooting continued as before, and after some early caution the drunken driving also seemed unabated. One man who had 'dumpéd his car' in anticipation of the policeman taking up his post regretted having been so hasty. The officer had a passion for fishing and for Pentecostalism, and policed only when strictly necessary. Not surprisingly, his seniors saw the lack of charges as evidence that permanent policing in Whalsay was extravagant, and after a while he was withdrawn to Mainland, where the force was badly stretched during the period of oil-related construction. There has been an incumbent since, but the case for permanent policing is still unproved and controversial.

People remain ambivalent about the desirability of having a police presence. That the matter should even be seriously considered is seen by some as evidence of the deterioration in Whalsay life to the standards of wider British society: people, it is said, behave with less consideration than they should, and their seniors are regarded as reluctant to exercise proper authority over them. It is a deterioration which, they feel, would make 'da aald folk blide ta be gaan fae wis'. Yet, even by comparison with other areas of Shetland, Whalsay is peculiarly law-abiding. Theft and fights are very rare; violence is virtually unknown. No one can recall a criminal charge being brought against an indigenous Whalsay person. Even in their drinking behaviour a comparison with almost any other district of Scotland would reveal Whalsay as being abstemious. In an interview for the local school magazine Henry observed that modern youth behaved more considerately towards their elders than had his own contemporaries. He recalled the sport of baiting elderly people, which 'led to serious disorders and was a dangerous pastime', and confessed his incomprehension at the improvement in the behaviour of the young in this respect, 'as there seems to be a much greater tendency among mothers, especially, to stick by their children whether they are right or wrong. In olden days, the child was never right.' (*Mareel*, p. 19.)

Anthropologists and others concerned with social identity have long recognised that the perception of identity is relational: the sense of self is founded, at least in part, on a sense of the other. There is an historical dimension to this as well, because, of course, temporal concepts are also relational. People's sense of the present and of themselves in the present is founded, at least in part, on the way in which it is contrasted to their sense of the past. In Whalsay it would seem that the past has to be conceptualised as *qualitatively*, as well as *temporally*, different, simply in order that people may orient themselves to the present. I do not propose this as a universal condition of social identity, but it would not be altogether surprising if the recent history of intensive social change in Whalsay had heightened people's consciousness of and sensitivity to change. It culminates in a discriminatory model which identifies the negatively valued aspects of life as 'modern' and as extraneous in origin (the way of the world); the positively valued aspects of life as 'traditional' and indigenous ('Whalsa''), and thereby complements the view of social and technological change established in the previous chapter. The cognitive model juxtaposes Whalsay and the world, with their respective associations of past and present. Aspects of customary social life are then weighed in this balance. Depending on their general view of modernity, people habitually observe a bias in the scales towards one side or the other.

My own observation, as evident in this discussion, inclines me to a rather different view. It distrusts 'past' and 'present' as categories, since they are so contingent, and sees the scale continually heavier on the Whalsay side – not because the extraneous is rejected but because it is assimilated, transformed and recast in a distinctively Whalsa' mode. Just when it looks as if the community has succumbed to the ways of the world it reformulates them and then triumphantly displays them in distinctive garb. Whalsay folk can thus claim that however they may have changed to *apparently* resemble those elsewhere, gender roles in Whalsay *are* distinctive. By the same token the community may have moved from its former proud self-regulation to subject itself to policing; but people see policing in Whalsay as quite distinctively Whalsa'.

3. The club. As a final illustration of this argument I turn briefly to 'Da Club', a recent accession to Whalsay life but one which has quickly become important as a focus of social activity. Ever since we first stayed in Whalsay, people have raised with us the question of the desirability or otherwise of having a pub on the island. There had never been licensed premises in Whalsay, and it seemed to us in 1974 that the weight of opinion would be opposed to one. A range of arguments were advanced against the idea. It would encourage drinking, especially among the youth. It would strain relationships, since the maintenance of order would require the exercise of authority. It would transfer sociability from the domestic hearth to the public bar. The second of these generally led people to conclude that only an outsider could run a pub, since he or she would be free of local ties and would not be trammelled by the protocols of egalitarianism. But the very idea of the pub was seen as controversial, as likely to generate argument, and was not seriously pursued.

The Whalsay Boating Club existed primarily to organise the annual regatta and the 'points' races held weekly through the summer, and to manage the Whalsay teams participation in Shetland's Inter-club Regatta. During the local regatta the crews were provisioned in a former fishing boat, used as a kind of messroom. They could go aboard between races for a cup of tea or a dram, and their meals were served aboard. As the number of crews proliferated, this facility became too small, and the club bought a section hut from the county council which was erected on the pier. In 1979 the idea emerged of erecting a permanent building which might be used throughout the year as licensed premises. Hence 'Da Club' was born. The idea was criticised, just as that of a pub had been. Moreover, its critics doubted whether it could be financially viable. It was seen as evidence of Whalsay trying to imitate Lerwick, but 'Lerwick is just entirely different as a way of life' and 'If you want a pub, why not go and live in a town?' 'It'll be da ruin o' da young eens.' 'Dey say dey wants somewhere ta tak' deir friends when dey come ta Whalsa'. Isn't it ridiculous! Instead o' sittin' in here an' haa'in' a tin o' beer, like wis, dey want ta be able ta say, "Let's go down ta da club and hae' a pint"!'

However, a club had one distinct advantage over a pub. It would be a collective enterprise and, while it might call for the exercise of authority, it would not be the authority of an individual but that of the collectivity essentially regulating itself. Moreover, no individual would profit from the susceptibilities of others. During the following three years money was raised by various means, and the club was eventually opened in its harbour premises, immediately opposite the ferry pier, in 1983. Contrary to some fears, it has not become unduly associated with the youth of the community. The management committee has sought to involve all adult ages on the island by putting on special 'nights' for different groups. The responsibility for serving members (and, by implication, of refusing to serve some when appropriate) is shared among a number of people so that the problem of authority is effectively surmounted. The club is also used occasionally as a venue for concerts and for other social functions, thereby easing the pressure on the public hall.

The early sceptics doubtless remain unconvinced, the critics unappeased. The club has become established as an integral element in the fabric of social life. Its accession obviously constitutes a change in the community, but whether it really subverts Whalsay's distinctiveness is entirely a matter of opinion. True, it is divisive in that a substantial number of islanders are not members, and have never patronised its facilities. But, by the same token, there have long been places and activities on the island that some people have steadfastly avoided. Further, it is not exclusive, since all adult islanders are eligible for membership. My own judgement is that it does not represent an insidious slide into a para-urban and non-domestic sociability. Rather, it provides an additional milieu for sociability and so contributes to the life-giving business of community. The nature and personnel of its management make it a recognisably Whalsa' milieu. Moreover, it may have removed one further incentive for people to move off the island for their recreation and, thereby, to become increasingly town-oriented. If this is correct, then, like the modernisation of the fishery and the provision of other recreational facilities, it is, as noted earlier, a further defence of the boundary.

The topics raised in this chapter have been various and dissimilar. They range from the economically crucial to the politically fraught; from the extraordinary and aberrant events of militancy to the mundane and relatively trivial issues of leisure. But all these have in common their popular perception as signs of fundamental change in the nature of Whalsay life and culture which derive from increasing contact with the world at large and, therefore, from the blurring of the community's boundary. The argument has been that, while all these phenomena do indeed signal important changes in the community, they do *not* suggest any diminution in Whalsay people's perception of its distinctiveness. Rather, they see in the changes a means of reasserting Whalsay's viability, and use their idiosyncratic adaptations of the new forms to express that distinctiveness. When they fear that it is being threatened from without (as by the possibly deleterious effects of new fishing regulations), or from within (as by Henry's unconventional and discomfiting campaigns), they resist stoutly. They thus nurture a view of their own eccentric modernity. They do not see themselves as having turned their back on the ways of the world. Rather, they use the world's ways to bolster their own fastness and to keep the world firmly at bay.

Notes

1   This observation is hardly novel for social anthropologists. However, it often seems to fall outside the neat theoretical contrivances of other disciplines concerned with 'development'.

2   A recent example is provided by the anger among local fishermen following the arrest in Shetland of a Danish skipper who was found to have been using small-mesh nets. These nets catch immature fish and jeopardise the regeneration of the stock. The Danes and Icelanders had long been vilified for their use of such destructive methods. Following the financially difficult years during the closure of the North Sea to herring fishing, their renewed destructive assault was a particularly bitter and resented blow. See *Shetland Fishing News*, 5th March 1986. The threat posed to the local fishery by the politically powerful British distant-water fleet, following the exclusion of the latter from Icelandic waters, was recognised (somewhat half-heartedly) in a study of the British fishery by the House of Commons Expenditure Committee (Expenditure Committee, V, 1978, p. 46).

3   The following figures for the Shetland fishery illustrate this trend dramatically in respect of white fish:

Year	Tonnes ('000)	Value (£ million)
1982	15·14	5·06
1983	15·30	6·60
1984	13·00	6·13
1985	13·00	8·00

These figures show a decline in catch of 16% but an increase in value of 58%. During the same period the pelagic catch increased in weight by 76% with the re-opening of the North Sea to herring fishing. Its value increased by 88%. The total catch for all species fell by 14% but rose in value by 49%, from £10·82 million in 1982 to £16·10 million in 1985. I am indebted for these data to Mr J. H. Goodlad, Secretary and General Manager of the Shetland Fishermen's Association.

4   The producers organisations were created to administer the EEC market support system. This sets 'intervention prices', a device which compensates fishermen when quayside prices fall below a stipulated minimum. They later became more actively concerned in fisheries management and marketing (see Goodlad, 1983).

5   Their recent reinvestment in the fishery seems to refute Byron's suggestion (1986) that the opening up of geographical and kinship boundaries in the Burra community of Hamnavoe dissipated the 'culture' of fishing and led to the decline of the Burra fishery.

6   The sand-eel catch by Shetland boats declined from 52,640 tonnes (worth £1·57 million in 1982 to 17,300 tonnes (worth £0·5 million) in 1985. (J. H. Goodlad, personal communication.)

7   For graphic descriptions of such conditions, which threaten the most modern of boats, the reader is recommended to read, *inter alia*, Byron (1986), Thompson *et al*. (1983) and Warner (1984).

8   Minutes of Evidence, Thursday, 1st December 1977, *The Fishing Industry*, p. 1112, Expenditure Committee (Trade and Industry Sub-committee), hereafter Exp. Comm., 1978.

9   One of his brothers, Davy, is reputed to have expostulated at the conclusion of a characteristic family political argument, 'Ye've aa' had an education, mebbe, but ye've nane o' ye ony midder's wit!'

10   See, e.g., his letter to the *Shetland Times*, 28th March 1975.

11   In 1978, when fish were very scarce, Henry commented that if there were any fish 'It'll be da aald men dat comes among dem. Dose men ken every scratch o' da paper,' i.e. the marks on the echo-sounder.

12   Made by Dr Bronwen Cohen, to whom I am indebted for the information which follows.

13   Although a present-day writer maintains that the strike disintegrated for want of local solidarity (Ratter, 1983).

14   The Whalsay men's participation in the blockade is described in detail in Cohen (1982b). The national protest is surveyed in Cargill (1976).

15   The 'lumpers' or shore porters had such rights at Aberdeen, a major reason why Whalsay boats tried to avoid the Aberdeen market. Allegations abounded about the lumpers' abuse of the fishermen's dependence on them. In particular they were accused of extortion and favouritism.

16   See, e.g., the report commissioned by the council from Dr C. A. Goodlad, submitted in June 1984. In his recommendations for harbour improvements Goodlad gives first priority to Whalsay.

17   The anthropological literature is replete with instances of societies in which women are regarded as a source of danger, or as unpropitious in some way. The

Shetland fishing case is slightly puzzling, however, since women were so closely involved in other economic activities which, while not so dangerous, were nonetheless subject to the vicissitudes of the elements. Moreover, women did bait and prepare the lines to be used at sea, and boats are referred to in Whalsay, as elsewhere, in the feminine gender, although they tend not to be given women's names. It is possible that the taboo developed less from superstition *per se* than from the compulsion to maintain the distinct nature of categories. The boat at sea was a male domain: the category would be confused by the presence of women. For perhaps the same reason clergymen also were taboo. As Jorion (1982) has argued, the gender associations of the priestly role may appear to be ambiguous in a fishing society.

18 Quite how recent this domesticity really was is a moot point. MacDiarmid (1939), writing before the war, comments on the 'comfort' of Whalsay cottages despite their unprepossessing external appearances.

19 I am most grateful to Whalsay Fish Processors Ltd for the following figures:

	1970		1980		1985	
	Men	*Women*	*Men*	*Women*	*Men*	*Women*
Full-time/supervisory	22	20	24	37	25	48
Part-time/casual	2	10	2	16	2	19
Total	24	30	26	53	27	67
	54		79		94	

Chapter 6

Final glimpses . . .

This book opened with a naive view of Whalsay. As it has progressed, successive layers of naivete have been stripped away to reveal ever greater complexity. The complexity is in the mind of the indigenous beholder, by whom its communication to the outsider must be almost impossible. Our personal experience suggests that when, as individuals, we are invited to respond to the enquiry 'What kind of person are you?' we have the greatest difficulty in readily formulating an intelligible and concise response. What can we reply? Each of us, from his or her own perspective, is just too complicated. So we frequently feel ill served by other people's descriptions of ourselves, offended by the requirement to condense our own complexity into the discipline of an application form or a curriculum vitae, frustrated by the dissonance between our own and others' views of our selves. A similar difficulty confronts the anthropologist and the people upon whom he or she has intruded. If it produces nothing else, the experience of fieldwork should always impress on the anthropologist, and has certainly left the present practitioner in no doubt, how very little he knows. Indeed, the greater his familiarity with the people he studies, the more complex do they appear and the more obvious to himself is his ignorance about them.

From such positions of enlightened ignorance anthropologists have for years delivered themselves of dogmatic descriptions of, and portentous theories about, the societies they have studied. It is an odd discipline which can claim to do for entire communities what, as individuals, we can hardly manage to do for ourselves, and all on the basis of such relatively brief acquaintanceship. I do not dare to hope that I have managed to convey in this book the complexity of social life in Whalsay; however, I hope that by this late stage, the reader will have gathered that it is neither so familiar nor so easily understood as may have appeared from the first selection of portraits in chapter two. The strategy of the book has been to 'situate' the material of these sketches by progressively revealing more and more of the social and cultural context, and thereby attempting to replicate the anthropological learning process. By giving substance in this way to the Whalsay people I have described I hoped to suggest the problematic nature of their lives, and to dispel any assumption that these problems respond simply to the application of some deterministic cultural logic, such as those which anthropologists have naively (perhaps, even, ethnocentrically) attributed to other societies.

There is no *dénouement* to the strategy. I conclude the descriptive section of the book by taking up some of its dominant themes in a final selection of brief sketches. I will not attach further commentary to them. If the strategy has been successful, such an amplification would be redundant and the reader will not need any further guidance to make an interpretation. If it has failed, more words at this stage will not redeem it.

'I'm jus' a simple fellow'

Social life in Whalsay is very exposed. There is little cover, nowhere to hide. People are in full public view for most of the time. Mistakes are difficult to conceal, and privacy is at a premium. On this spotlit stage people have to battle with their self-doubts and life's uncertainties, as well as with the more rarified issues of community. Evaluations of their behaviour both by others and by themselves almost always have a comparative dimension, explicit or implicit, and thus emphasise the overarching nature of shared public knowledge. People seem to measure their individuality against the community rather than against other individuals, as they struggle to locate themselves in the Whalsay ethos.

In 1974, at twenty-seven years of age, A. was among the youngest Whalsay skippers. Indeed, when he and his crew bought their first boat five years previously, he was the island's youngest skipper. They made a great success of their venture, and were eventually persuaded by their agents to order a purpose-built vessel, one of the first of a new generation of 70+ ft white-fish boats. In spite of his success, A. seemed uncertain of his own abilities as a skipper. Quietly spoken, he exudes goodwill and is reluctant to assert himself unless absolutely necessary: 'I'm not a very authoritative kind of fellow.' He compares himself continually to one of his elder brothers, also a skipper, whom he regards as his mentor. He sees his brother as more accomplished and more determined: 'I'll never come up to him.'

His self-effacement has been a feature of his career. As we have had occasion to note before, a persona, once established, becomes almost impossible to change in Whalsay, for it is publicly owned. A. is just old enough to have served the years of his fishing apprenticeship on the earlier generation of boats, before the dramatic improvement in the fortunes of the fishery. Like most men, he began his career at sea as cook: '. . . da worst job i' da boat. It's bad enyoch cookin' fer a bunch o' men. But when da boat is rollin' aa' ower

da place, an' you're haa'in' ta dodge oot an' spew, man, it's hellish.' To add to
this discomfort, the cook at the drift-net fishing also had the job of coiling the
bush rope, cramped into the fo'c'sle for hours on end. A. spent six months on
an Aberdeen seiner, and then several years of 'filling in' on a variety of local
boats, accumulating experience of different techniques and different
skippers.

He was then approached by some friends, all contemporaries at school,
who suggested that they should form a crew and that he should be skipper. 'I
dinna ken why – it seems funny. I s'pose dey tocht I wis cut oot fer it.' Once
persuaded, he had to attend navigation classes and to obtain his skipper's
'ticket'. But the early years of success, of plentiful catches, high prices and low
expenses were a poor preparation for later hazards. After fishing for five years
with their second-hand boat, and ending one season 'top of the fleet', they
ordered a new boat at a time when prices were high. 'We just couldn't go
wrong.' When the boat was finally delivered in 1974 it cost rather more than
the estimate, and landing prices had tumbled. Added to this, the boat had
early teething troubles which cost them much lost fishing time. To meet the
running costs, interest payments, and so forth, they had to gross a weekly
average of nearly £3,000.

During the first year of the boat's operation A. was shocked by the
immensity of the difficulties, and depressed by their apparent intractability:
'If we could get jus' one good trip soon, I wouldnae' feel so bad. Jus' one good
trip. . . .' Although it was a collective endeavour, and he always went to great
lengths to consult his crew about strategy, A. seemed to feel that he should
take the full responsibility for his colleagues' misfortune. Their plight
weighed heavily on him. The constant requirement to decide where to fish, at
a time when fish seemed to be scarce everywhere, imposed a morale-sapping
strain.

'You can never get awa' frae it. When you're ashore at da *helli* [weekend],
you're aye wond'rin' whaar da hell ta geng a' Monday. . . . When times is bad,
it's difficult to keep it up. I tell da boys, "When we can't afford ta bide ashore,
an' it disnae' really pay ta geng ta sea, aa' we can do is keep fishin!" ' But they
had their moments: 'Oh, when du sees a foo' bag come aboard – ah! dere's
naathin' ta beat da fishin'. I feel great then.'

The pressure experienced by a skipper in A.'s position must be considerably exacerbated by the knowledge that the eyes of the community are on him.
To some onlookers his occasional spree may suggest that he is not treating the
problem with sufficient seriousness; others will it regard as evidence that he is
cracking under the strain, and taking to the bottle! Whatever the circumstances, some people will find no excuse for the crew's misfortune. Such
criticism would only ever be made in private conversation, but is none the less
irksome. Further, the skipper is conscious that it is not only his crew's
livelihood which is at stake, for all its members will have had to raise some

financial support among family and friends.

Under such circumstances a skipper can drive himself relentlessly. A. recalls standing for a continuous stretch of thirty-six hours at the wheel as he steamed from place to place, desperately trying to make up enough boxes for 'a trip'. When, eventually, they were on the way back to Whalsay and the crew persuaded him to go below to rest he was quite unable to sleep. Though he prided himself on his fitness, A., in his late twenties, like most of the young skippers, looked rather older than his age.

He and his crew continued their struggle successfully, frequently changing their strategy to maximise the moment's opportunities. They spent one season pair-trawling with their 'sister' boat. Some years later they collaborated with A.'s brother's purser crew in the herring fishery. They then decided to merge with this latter crew, and to invest in one of the new pursers, a decision which was eventually to be fully vindicated. As a consequence of the merger, A. ceased to be a skipper, without regret – 'I never much likéd dat wheelhouse waark, onywye' – and looked forward to losing weight under his brother's regime.

A.'s self-depreciation went beyond his skipperhood. I once found him chuckling in incredulity over how badly he had managed to clip one of his ewes. He said he had had great difficulty in catching it in the first place: he did not know how to *caa'* sheep properly, and had chased it, 'fer it fell doon jus' exhausted!' He is a man entirely without pretension. Explaining why he had never voted in an election, he said, 'Well, it seems stupid to me. I'm jus' a simple fellow. How süd I ken better as dey do what's best fer da country?' a sentiment which, like his general demeanour, speaks less of 'simplicity' than of modesty, a quality by which he intuitively measures other people. He recalled meeting, and being deeply impressed by, a Scottish Nationalist Member of Parliament with whom he had immediately felt an affinity which he could not imagine for other politicians.

'I could talk to him! He could understand what I was saying. He's a crofter, an' I'm a crofter – an' a crofter's jus' like a fisherman, onywye – an' we talked aboot sheep. I canna' imagine talking to Grimond [then MP for Orkney and Shetland] aboot sheep! He wouldnae' ken wha' I wis on aboot. An' he wouldnae' care, either. But Hamish, well, you could jus' talk to him, he wis on da sam' level. He even looks like a fisherman, sort o' squat-faced.'

A.'s moderation, as well, possibly, as his experience of struggle, makes him impatient with people who take themselves too seriously, or who seem to want more than their fair share. He is a successful and knowledgeable competition sailor, but does not pursue the sport with the single-mindedness displayed by some other Whalsay men. In 1978, when he was collaborating in the mackerel fishery, he commented that the earnings made by some of the boats fishing off the Cornwall coast were ridiculous. 'Aabody's got ta mak' a living – but £70,000 a week! Who needs dat? It's jus' no right!'

His self-effacement, perhaps combined with his sense of Whalsay's peripherality, is sometimes manifest in a certain lack of self-confidence, notwithstanding his athletic prowess, intellectual ability and experience as a skipper. Once in 1976, having sold his catch at the Aberdeen market, he was walking up to Union Street in the city centre, but the crowds on the pavements caused him to lose his nerve and he turned back to his boat. And when, in 1975, he had to take the boat to Denmark for repairs, he told me the trip there would take two days and added, only half-jokingly, 'if we *ever* get there!'

So his claim to be unfit to vote is entirely in character. 'Yeah, well, dat's da wye I look at yon, I'm jus' too simple ta mak' a decision aboot foo ta govern da country!' a humility which might discomfit those of us who are too seldom assailed by such self-doubts, and which must be severely tested by the relentless gaze of the community. One night, when there was 'a braa ebb', A. had touched bottom bringing his boat past the treacherous Berga Skerry at the entrance to Symister harbour. The boat following him ran aground on the skerry. A. had not warned her helmsman by radio that he had himself hit the bottom 'because I felt so silly. I would hae likéd to run five miles awa'!'

A football match

Whalsay are to play Unst away in the semi-finals of the Parish Cup. The party leaves Symbister on Saturday afternoon aboard the fishing boat *Fortuna*. The team is accompanied by twenty people who are close relatives of the players, officials of the club, or just interested spectators. Among the men, conversation on the outward voyage is mostly concerned with fishing. The talk is of high costs and low prices, of the need to economise. The skipper contacts two local boats, still trying to make up their week's trip, and the news of their progress swiftly circulates among the company. Inevitably the older men reminisce about the fishing of the past, and especially about the drift-netting. They all agree it was 'da best fishing': demanding of seamanship, entirely lacking the boredom of long trawls, giving plenty of time ashore, and physically active. 'Aye, ye had nae belly left at da end o' da summer.' 'Man, in dose days, we wis aa' fit. I mind eence me an' Davy haalin' a huge catch 'at we landed jus' a back o' dinner time. Den we tore up ta Unst ta play fitba', an' den back ta Lerrick an' went ta sea da sam' noit.'

The party lands at Belmont, and is taken by bus to the pitch at Burrafirth. The passengers look avidly at the passing countryside, trying to identify landmarks and speculating who might occupy the crofts we pass. When we arrive, there is some critical comment about the absence of changing facilities 'fer da boys', 'no like wir groond', though the indignation is possibly tempered by enjoyment of the opportunity to make such unfavourable comparisons.

Most of the team are closely related to each other by kinship or marriage, and a number are crew mates. At its core are four brothers, two of their first cousins, and two close affines. (See Fig. 14.) During the match the spectators make encouraging noises, although with three exceptions (two officials, and the mother of one of the players) they are undemonstrative. They comment quietly to each other, but there is no criticism of the Whalsay players. Much is made of 'how well they do' considering that they spend all week cramped into fishing boats, without the opportunity to practise or to exercise. One of the club officials, noted (and satirised) for his eagerness to make himself prominent at public gatherings, strides officiously and noisily along the touchline, bellowing at players and referee, and worrying loudly about half-time refreshments and a meal afterwards for the players. His Whalsay companions seem to shrink away from him in embarrassment.

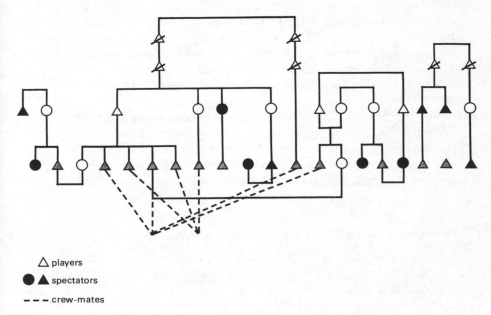

△ players

● ▲ spectators

– – – crew-mates

Fig. 14   Whalsay team and spectators in Unst

The Whalsay team play below their best form. Bungled chances, miskicks and obvious sluggishness elicit only sighs of 'aye, aye' from the supporters. Some mutter wistfully that the players do not seem to be as big or as strong as those of former years. However, they eventually win 3–2 in extra time, to general satisfaction, and bottles of whisky immediately appear as the entire party makes its way back to the coach to drive to the Baltasound Hotel for refreshment. The earlier sombreness has entirely dissipated: players enjoy the congratulations of their supporters, and laugh over their own mistakes. The talk is of a spree, rather than of fishing, and they pleasurably anticipate the allotted hour in the pub.

On arrival this conviviality is abruptly punctured by the noisy official who tries to divide players and officials from the rest of the party, insisting that he has made eating arrangements only for the former. This causes acute discomfort among the entire group. There is a feeling that it would be quite unacceptable to make such a discrimination, but how can the situation be remedied? Who could take the initiative, and how could they do so without showing up their officious and insensitive colleague? After some indecision and uncertainty the landlord comes to the rescue. Of course all can be accommodated, if they would not mind waiting a little? Everyone puts £1 into a kitty, to pay for the extra food and drink. The earlier jovial mood is restored, albeit with some figurative head-shaking over their deliquent compatriot.

The bus journey back to the *Fortuna* is spent in ribald high spirits, with the Whalsay party accompanied by some Unst men. The boat leaves Belmont pier with the skipper clanging the bridge bell, and much good-natured banter shouted between hosts and guests. Most of the company promptly disappear below to the cabin for the serious business. By the time we reach Symbister, only a handful are sober.

News of the team's victory elicits only mild expressions of approval. Some interest is shown in the performance of the younger and more inexperienced members of the team; but the established players are not singled out for discussion. It may be that the football team is seen as being too heavily oriented to a single segment to be regarded as representative of Whalsay as a whole.

Dere's never been a fiddle sooned in dis hoose fer fifty years

'The tune with no name', transcribed from the playing of Alan Tulloch by Vimalan Jesudason

The fiddle is Shetland's musical instrument. The bagpipes have strong Gaelic associations; the accordion is Scottish. While Shetlanders enjoy Scottish piping and country music, it is over fiddle playing that they wax really lyrical. Scottish musicians are inclined to talk of a 'Shetland style'. But fiddlers in Shetland reject this monolithic concept, and emphasise the differences among themselves. Those from other parts of Shetland may speak of a 'Whalsa' style', but Whalsay fiddlers eschew any such notion and remember the noted fiddlers of the past as distinctively individualistic. However, they do distance themselves from the style established in Lerwick by the celebrated Tom Anderson, as rather formal and overly strict in tempo. All the experienced Whalsay fiddlers are self-taught. During the last three or four years several women have attended an evening class in Shetland fiddle-playing conducted by a teacher from Yell.

The most accomplished fiddler in Whalsay is Alan Tulloch of Brough, now in his fifties, who has played since his early teens. As a young man he gained a considerable reputation throughout Shetland, but he gradually curtailed his public appearances, eventually even giving up his place in the island's band, which played at all the local weddings and dances.

He began to play again in 1984, using fiddles made on the island by Jimmy Arthur. Jimmy is not a fiddler, but he is a craftsman with wood. Some years earlier he had acquired an old set of home-made chisels, and promptly set to work making some Shetland spinning wheels, following the traditional design. As word of his new interest spread around Whalsay, he was soon inundated with wheels in need of restoration and repair, excavated from attics and sheds where they had long lain neglected.

Unable any longer to do heavy joinery, he gradually conceived the desire to make some fiddles, never having previously done so. The challenge was formidable, for not only had he to master the technical complexities of the violin's construction but, first, had to fashion the necessary tools. He made two fiddles in quick succession, slightly varying their design in order to experiment with tone and volume. He later modified them, but not before Alan Tulloch had played, and been delighted by, them. They were to reawaken his dormant interest in playing and, eventually, Jimmy made for him a Norwegian-style Hardanger eight-stringed fiddle, intricately carved and meticulously decorated. Between them Jimmy and Alan have saved the Whalsay fiddle tradition from virtual extinction under the onslaught of the 'country and western' craze. As with wheels, so with fiddles: Jimmy's front room soon became a hospital for the island's derelict violins.

Alan insists that there was never any orthodoxy in Whalsay fiddling. He regards the late Andrew Polson of Marrister as the most accomplished local fiddler he has heard, but says he had an imitable style of bowing, quite different from that of anyone else.[1] 'Aald Glybie' is recalled as having an extensive repertoire and a vigorous style. The old Isbister men even held the

James Arthur of Sodom, fiddle maker.   [Picture by Gordon Craig]

Alan Tulloch, fiddler extraordinary.   [Picture by Gordon Craig]

fiddle differently, balancing it at the breast rather than under the chin or, like some country fiddlers elsewhere, in the crook of the arm. 'Robbie Linty' was said to play softly, and to *sneush* – to breathe heavily through his nose – while he played. As one man observed, 'Da wye Robbie played, da more he likéd it, da looder he sneushed,' until the fiddle was barely audible. Others had characteristic ways of stamping a rhythm or of varying tone or key. Knowledge of Shetland tunes, *springs*, is becoming scarce. One elderly lady, 'Betty o'Houll', is known as one of the island's experts, and can 'la-la' and name innumerable examples. Robbie Linty claimed to know of a hundred authentic Shetland reels, but there are not many, and they are not widely known. Alan is sometimes accompanied on the guitar by John 'o'Burns' (Hutchinson) who is rapidly acquiring a reputation throughout Shetland as a fine musician, and whose father, 'Gibbie O'Creeds', is himself an accomplished and highly-regarded fiddler.

Over the years Alan has accumulated countless tunes but, unable to read or write music, he has to learn them all by ear and memorise them. Once 'da mood is ipo' him' and his fingers are moving easily he becomes unstoppable, the music flowing ceaselessly – reels, laments, waltzes, polkas. If he comes to a temporary halt, he can always be nudged. 'Can du mind "Da Caald Nights o' Winter"?[2] Can du mind him?' 'Oh, aye, dat een. I dinna ken if I can mind dat . . .' and away he goes. Among the assembled company, feet tap, bodies sway, heads rock involuntarily to the compulsive rhythms.

Sometimes he will interject impressions of other fiddlers well known to his audience, the mimicry containing a gentle satire similar to that in Whalsay yarns. The more that people praise his playing, the more he will praise the fiddle, and sometimes presents himself almost as a mere accessory to the instrument. 'Jimmy, dü's surely mak'd a fine fiddle.' 'Well, it soonds aa' right when *dü* plays ipo' him.' 'Na, na. Dis een plays itsel" – and, indeed, he sometimes appears amazed at what he has just played: 'Well, well. I never minded dat I ken't dat!'

The authentic folk tradition in Whalsay is still close enough to evoke strong sentiments. For the younger generation of Shetlanders, folk music has recently become a matter of revival and performance, as elsewhere in Britain. But older Whalsay people might still recall the fiddle being played in their own homes during sprees, and will know from hearsay, if not from personal recollection, of its centrality to the wedding celebration (e.g. Flett, 1971). When Alan plays to them, they are therefore not just listening to a virtuoso performance but to a reminder of their own past, a past which Alan, fiddler, and Jimmy, fiddle maker, have helped to keep alive. Just how easily it can be lost was summed up in a remark Jimmy made one summer night in 1985. Alan had played for some hours in our cottage, the very house where Jimmy was born. When, finally, he finished, Jimmy commented, 'I believe dere's never been a fiddle sooned in dis hoose fae fifty years!'

'I laach'd fer da waater cam' ta me ee'n'

Much of the joking in Whalsay conversation and stories would be quite unintelligible to the outsider; at least, what causes hilarity among Whalsay folk could be only mildly amusing to outsiders. The reason is that it tends to rest on exclusively local referents, usually on the publicly allocated personae of Whalsay people. It may be used as a means of reinforcing the conventions of egalitarianism, by puncturing pomposity or the assertion of self; or it may simply celebrate a person's known and publicly acknowledged traits – for example, absent-mindedness, or a tendency to dwell on particular aspects of the past. Such humour simultaneously marks *community* and social boundary, for its very humorousness is itself evidence of the degree to which knowledge is shared *and* is exclusive to Whalsay people. It is also a matter of internal social relations: the gentle satire of intra-segment humour may be considerably sharpened when the subject belongs to another segment.

This kind of deflating comment was described by an elderly Lerwick woman, who had been closely associated with Whalsay throughout her life, as 'pokey humour'. Three men are discussing the news that X. has bought an old cottage. His brother is putting in the plumbing for him. 'What? Dat man shouldnae' be alloo'd near tools!' 'Jus' a quarry pick, dat's aa'.' 'Na, gie him a quarry pick an', man, he'll dig hisself in!' A man known for his occasional and voluble self-importance had just bought one of the little islets in the Sound. An affine is greeted with the comment, 'So, ——, dü's gotten a laird i' da family noo.' 'Aye, aye, wir X. is Laird o' da —— Isle!' Nominating the same man for a committee post, his proposer slyly remarked, 'At least we can aye hear him!' During the 1960s a crew had to modify their boat in order to bring it down to the size of vessel which their skipper was qualified to command. Part of the alteration involved the installation in the hold of a suspended wooden floor. Soon after, a local woman was broadcasting the news that her son had obtained his full Master's ticket and, she bragged, 'He can tak' oot ony boat i' da world – even da *Queen Mary*.' A fisherman made the deflating observation, 'It'll tak a braa piece o' wood ta get da *Queen Mary* doon ta size.'

By contrast, joking among close associates is affectionate, and emphasises shared opinion and mutual belonging. 'Does dü mind dat Saturday night, back o' las' Easter? We wis aa' in, an' den W. comes alang wi' his bottle. You mind dat? He comes in an' says, "Boys, I'm aafu' drunk." He'd been t' a weddin' a Lerrick. He gies wis a dram, an' den he says, "Boys, I doot I'd better wen heim." I says to him, "Man, dü're no' able." "Yes, yes, I'll be aᴀ' roit." But he collapsed afore he reached da grind. So den wir P. said he'd tak' W. heim. Does dü mind dat? An' when he cam' back . . .' (the company, recalling the incident, are already giggling and anticipating the climax) '. . . he says, "Boys, W. is surely braaly drunk." "What wye, P.?" "Well, man, he keepéd tellin' me dat da road ta his hoose wis dis side o' C.'s." "Well," I says, "it is, P." ' All except the narrator are now rocking with laughter. ' "Is it? Boys, I tocht it wis da idder side!" He'd mad' W. try ta wen doon da idder side o' C.'s hoose, an' dey'd baith o' dem fallen ower da fence into da bog. Mind dü dat, G.? Dü said, "P.! I doot dü're jus' as foo' up as W." '

'Dat's roit, oh man, oh man, dat wis funny. Wir P., when he's had a bit o' a dram in, he jus' disnae' seem ta ken whaar he is or what's gaain' on.'

'Aye, aye. He looked dat *stumsit* [bewildered], I jus' laach'd fer da waater cam' ta me ee'n!'

I hesitate to tread the ambitious paths of earlier anthropologists and psychologists in theorising about the functions of joking in, respectively, the regulation of social relations and the management of personal stress. I draw attention here only to the symptomatic nature of Whalsay humour in its social and cultural contexts. There is a further typical mode of joking which relates to the commonality rather than to its component social relations, and which exploits people's enjoyment of their verbal creativity. We have already noted the improvisatory nature of much Whalsay dialect, and the latitude allowed to people for verbal idiosyncrasy. Indeed, their inventions sometimes become important ingredients of their public identity. This delight in language and linguistic dexterity extends throughout Shetland, reflecting the oral nature of the islands' tradition. The kinds of saying which are repeatedly retailed in Whalsay are not inherently funny, yet they are clearly the source of much pleasure. One can only conclude that their humour resides in their very familiarity and that of the characters with whom they are associated; and that, like the topics discussed in chapter four, they are mnemonics of the collectivity.

One example we have already encountered was in the iconoclastic dismissal of orthodoxy in peat-cutting: the comment that, however well or ill cut the peats may be, 'dey'll aa' dry, an dey'll aa' burn'. Another is the often rehearsed verbal cunning of a young boy to his grandfather, with whom he had been fishing from the banks. By the irresistible force of his (untranslatable) humour, he obliges the old man to carry home the load: 'Age must hae' honour; an' Da [Grandad], tak' heim da büddie!'[3] —— the *büddie* being a basket used for carrying fish.

A final example is of the kind of saying which obviously celebrates local characters. In 'daa ald days', when they were 'caa'in' da sheep', the women would run after their dogs, shouting and flapping their skirts to urge them on. There is a story that 'an aald wife' at Challister got carried away by enthusiasm and threw a peat at Willie Leask's dog, felling it and knocking it unconscious. As they came up to the prostrate animal, Willie said to it, 'Dat's da tanks dü gets fer da day dat dü's had!' It may well be that this is *all* that is now remembered of Willie Leask, although it has secured him lasting fame. But it is less significant as a personal memorial than as an implicit statement about the community as a whole, in this case suggesting its shared, quirky wistfulness and eccentricity.

Much of this kind of humour seems to point to the suspension of cultural normality and, in particular, to the temporary failure of the customary disciplines of personal control and self-sufficiency. When it is directed across segmentary boundaries it is, as we have seen, barbed, and ridicules the delinquent. But when it concerns close associates or the collectivity, it gently suggests the aberrant nature of the behaviour it narrates and, thereby, implicitly reaffirms 'normal' values.[4] This may be why it seems so often to concern incidents of drunkenness. These are presented as inherently funny but, also, as 'out of character' and, therefore, as excusable. (By contrast, inter-segmental stories about drunkenness are unambiguously critical, and would depict the subject as uncontrolled, silly or spendthrift. In these stories the aberrant nature of the incident stands out in relief against the frequent references to the everyday world of familiar landscape and people, mundane incidents and, in the coda, a reflection on the aberration. These stories could sustain a variety of interpretations. However, it seems clear that without the contrast between normality and abnormality they would have no motivation:

Ertie's night out[5]

Ertie is a taciturn old man, a bachelor, with no living relatives in Whalsay. Almost skeletally thin and bent, with gaunt features, he lives alone in a dense cloud of pipe smoke, and in the same 'garnsey 'n' breeks' that he has worn for as long as anyone can remember. The incident recalled in the story had occurred some fifteen years earlier, when he would have been in his early sixties.

'Dis night, it wis "second night" [the spree] of X.'s wedding. Some o' da boys said I wis ta come ta second night. I says, "All right," an' we went doon ta da hoose. Noo, I don' believe Ertie'd ta'en a drink fer years – 'less a glass o' beer, mebbe. Onywye, we had some beer, an' den da whisky started gaain' roon'. Well, dese boys mad' oot ta Ertie dat dey were drinkin' da foo' glass, no' jus' sippin' it. So Ertie, he says, "If dose boys can drink a glass, so can I!" An' he drinks it. An' den he drinks anidder, an' so on. He's sittin' in dere, in his aald army greatcoat dat he had frae da war when he wis in da Heim Guard. An' he's sittin' in here, in dis coat an' cap, an' knockin' back dis whisky.

'An' den some een says, "Well, boys, what aboot some dancin'?" Dere were nae' music, o' course, jus' some een singin'. So dey gets dis Shetlan' reel, dis eightsome, gaain', an' Ertie's in dere, in his greatcoat an' cap an' rubber boots, dancin' awa' . . .

'After dat, some een suggested we wen' oot, so Ertie says, "Okay." Noo, I dinna ken was it da caald air dat hit him or what, but he seemed ta be gettin' a bit giggly-wye. But he wis aye knockin' back aa' dis whisky. . . .

'We tocht we'd gae doon ta da Haa'. Somebody waanted ta caa' in at X.'s folk a da Crudens fer a bottle, so we went by dere an' it started ta rain. Well, Ertie be noo wis jus' foo' up. I s'pose it wis mebbe da caald air got ta him again, but he was haa'in trouble waalkin' noo. I says to Charlie, "I tink we'd better get Ertie heim." "Yeah, dü's roit. We better will," he says. He wis fairly drunk hisself, but he cam' alang. So he took Ertie a' een side, an' I took him on da idder. I tocht, it wis dat dark an' wet, we'd better go roon' by da Crudens an' doon ta da Sneugins road dat wye. . . .

'Well, dere wis dis rain, an' Ertie, he wis gettin' heavier an' heavier wi' dis greatcoat gett'n' soakéd an' jus' haad'n da waater. Den his cap would keep comin' aff . . . an' I'd go back fer it in dis rain an' look fer it and den jam it doon on his heid. I dinna ken was it da wye he wis waalkin': his legs were seemin'ly gaain' up i' da air, an' heid up 'n' doon, but dis hat keepéd camin' aff. His legs were pumpin' awa', but he wis na gaain' far'ard avaa'. I says, "Dü're no' maakin' muckle heidway, Ertie." An' he wis jus' gett'n' heavier an' heavier. Den, aa' o' a sudden, he sort o' bent roit i' da middle, roit i' da middle! Dü kens, jus' like a muckle angle iron – an', well, dü kens what a *wenglit* [ungainly] body he is – an' we couldn't get him straightened up. He wis noo an aafu' weight ta haa'd, an' he'd started laachin', so he wis jus' shaakin'. . . .

'Den we gets ta da *grind* [the gate] an' aa' o' a sudden, Charlie – an' he wis jus' as drunk as Ertie – he gets his foot in a hollow, an' he goes ower into da *gutter* [mess] an' he pulls aald Ertie doon wi' him. An' dey're baith o' dem lyin' dere, roarin' wi' laachter. Dey were absolutely helpless wi' laachin', an' dey giggled an' *spreckled* [legs kicking the air, as when a dog's belly is tickled]. . . .

'So, onywye, we gets trow da grind an' up ta da hoose, an' Ertie' 'n' Charlie by dis time dey're jus' a horrible mess o' gutter – aa' black an' wet. An' da door was keyed. Well, Ertie wis propped up sort o' diagonally wi' his heid leaning o' da door, an' seemingly if he had his foreheid agin' da door he could keep up. Charlie wis at his side jus' roarin' awa'. Well, I starts ta go trow da *pooches* [pockets] o' dis greatcoat fer da key. Dere'd be a muckle key. Na, dat didn't fit. A bit o' black twist. Some sweeties, a bit o' paper, a *niall* [a cork to plug the drainhole in the keel of a boat]; twartree used matches. Anidder key, no good. Ertie's pipe, an' so on. Aa' dis time da rain's camin' doon an' Ertie's roarin' awa'. Well, at las' I foon' da key an' got da door open – an' hadn't realised dat Ertie had been propped agin da door – an' as I got it open he jus' went in, whoosh, heid first, an' lay dere on his face. Man, I tocht he wis died.

'But den he starts ta snore an' ta laach, baith at da sam' time. Boys, sic' an on-carry, he cackled jus' like yon' aald turkey o' Robbie's. An' he's roit oot, completely unconscious. We never ken't what to do avaa'. Onywye, we jus' dragged him across da floor ta da bed. We got dis greatcoat pulled aff, an' it jus' weighed a ton. Den his boots – dey were rubber eens, but not dose long eens, jus' sort o' laced up ta da *coot* [ankle]. Den he had on two lots o' long johns, so we got dem aff too. An' he had on his aald waistcoat, done up roit ta da *oxters* [armpits]. We jus' dumpéd him on da bed – he wis awa' snorin', jus' completely unawaar o' it aa'. Oh, aye, an' we got him a bowl ta spew in, an' we left.

'Well, next day was Sunday, an' I saw nae sign o' life avaa'. Den Monday, I still saw naathin', no smoke camin' oot o' his *lum* [chimney]. So I tocht I'd better wen doon. So I went doon an' dere wis Ertie at da grind. I says, "Mornin'." He says, "Mornin'." I says, "Foo're dü feelin' today?" "Oh," he says, "I'm caamin' tae mesel' noo. *Dastreen* [yesterday] I could dae naatin' avaa', 'cept crawl ipo' me haan's 'n' knees tae a bottle o' aspirin. But today I'm caamin back tae mesel'." He couldn't mind comin' by da road 'stead o' across da *park* [field]. 'Cos he'd skinned his knees, an' he said ta me dat "I never ken't dere were muckle stanes yondru da size ta dae yon'." '

Two styles of command

1. It is 4.30 a.m. The crew appear silently out of the blackness and step aboard the boat without a word to each other. They immediately go about their tasks. The skipper was one of the first to arrive and cleared some rubbish from the galley before going up to the cramped wheelhouse. This is one of Whalsay's older boats, built soon after the last war, and is now used almost exclusively for seine-netting. At the centre of the crew are four owners, men in their fifties. The skipper is anticipating his retirement, and dreading the possibility of a long trip away to the Bergen Bank if he cannot find fish closer to shore. 'I'm gett'n ta like me heim comforts. I don' believe in killin' mesel' nae mair. Why süd I? Da bairns is aa' growed up. Noo it's deir turn ta waark deirsel's silly, like we did when we were young. I'm seen me oot yonder on a bitch o' a day, haalin' lines fer me haan's were bleedin', an' da skin freezin' ta da lines, jus' ta try an' beat da nex' boat. Noo it's aa' by, I don' hae ta dae dat.' But he feels great pressure to maintain the boat's performance, 'ta keep up wi' da young eens', for otherwise he could lose the good young half-catch men among his crew. 'Da proper wye'd be fer aa' da older eens ta fish tagedder, an' aa' da younger eens ta fish tagedder.'

We steam for two hours. The crew went below as soon as we left the pier, and none has come into the wheelhouse to talk to the skipper. 'Dis is an aald boat. Aa' da equipment in here is aald. Like yon echo-soonder: we süd hae bocht a new een. But if we bocht een noo it'll be oot o' date nex' year.' During this long 'steam' he has been talking at intervals to another local skipper on the ship-to-ship radio. They complain to each other about the Scottish trawlers we have just passed. He calls them 'Sunday fishers': they fish the area over the weekend, when the Shetland boats are lying up, so that on Monday there are no fish around. Before the advent of the Decca navigator 'outsiders' could not exploit the traditional inshore grounds, simply because they did not know where they were. He reserves his strongest criticism for a skipper from the north of Shetland who now commands an Aberdeen trawler. He came from a crofting family, and gained all his experience with Whalsay skippers. Now he uses it against them. 'He'd nae ha' done dat if he cam' frae a fishin' family. He's a bloody sinner. If he'd been brocht up tae da fishin', he wouldnae 've done dat. Leastways, not if he wis a Whalsayman.'

Finally the moment comes to shoot the net. Without any command being given, the crew come up from below, having been alerted only by the slowing of the engine. The mate, 'John', goes forward to throw over the warps. First he throws over the flag buoy which has attached to it a radar reflector. The rope follows, gradually uncoiling as the boat steams ahead slowly in a huge circle. The net is paid out and the second rope goes over; eventually we come alongside the buoy again. John now throws over a grappling iron to catch the first rope so that it can be hauled aboard to be secured to the forward winch. His first attempt fails. The skipper mutters, 'Oh, John!' The manoeuvre has been delicate, for we are in thick fog. At each stage the skipper has been taking the navigator readings so that, allowing for tidal drift and so forth, he can be sure of locating the flag buoy again. John succeeds at his second attempt.

They make six shots during the day, each lasting about ninety minutes, but catch very little. The mood at the mess table is sombre. When, briefly, the skipper is relieved at the wheel in order to snatch some breakfast and dinner he is scathing about the Scottish trawlers. Perhaps for the ears of the younger deck hands, engrossed in their comics, he emphasises that we are doing no worse than any other of the local boats today.

As we steam for home, the skipper joins the crew gutting the last shot, and dispels the gloom with a joke about the aphrodisiac qualities of the skate we have just taken aboard. 'Wha's gaain' t'eat yon? My Christ, after da day we've had, any body wha eats yon'll kill hisself!'

Throughout the entire day, there has been no strategy discussion between skipper and crew, and not a single instruction given. The entire operation is a perfected routine. The crew disperse as quietly as they gathered, after a perfunctory statement from the skipper. 'Be here at six [o'clock] da morn's morning, boys. G'night noo, boys.'

2. The boat, one of Whalsay's newest, is ready to leave Lerwick, where its young crew have been loading fuel, ice and water.[6] All the crew are present, apart from the mate, who is at home in Whalsay, and are drinking tea at the mess table. They expect to be spending the night at home, then taking the boat to Scalloway, on Shetland's west coast, to be slipped for a minor repair,

before setting off for the week's fishing. But the skipper has just reported their agent's opinion that, having taken on their fuel and so forth, they will be too heavy for the Scalloway slip.

'What're we gaain' ta dae, den?'

Skipper. 'Well, I s'pose we *could* unload.' He hesitates, waiting for a reaction? There is a jabber of contradictory opinions. 'What aboot if we do wir *trip* [i.e. week's fishing] an' sell at Buckie, an' den get slippéd dere? It's jus' a suggestion, like. I'm no mindin'. What does dü tink, boys?'

Voices murmur, 'Dat soonds aa' roit,' and 'Yeah, we could do dat,' even 'It's aa' roit wi' me. I'm no carin' een wye or da idder.' Then someone asks, 'What about —— [the mate]?'

Skipper. 'I'll wen an' see if I can speak wi' him on da 'phone.' He returns after twenty minutes: 'I spak' wi' ——, an' *he* tinks we *süd* geng aff. I tink he's roit. We canna get slippéd a' Scallowa', so we moit as well get wir trip an' geng ta Buckie.'

Everyone agrees. Now they are approaching Symbister's congested harbour. When all the boats are ashore, as now, they have to tie up three or four abeam. Where should they berth? Three men besides the skipper are in the modern wheelhouse, and all volunteer opinions. The skipper remains silent and impassive throughout the debate.

B. says, '[Skipper], I tink we süd geng ootside o' da *Azalea*; den we can steam oot da noit ahint da *Athena*.'

J. 'Yeah, yeah. But if she disnae' geng fer seven, we'll hae an aafu' job ta get wirsel's clear. Let's geng alangside o' da *Korona* on da inner pier. I heard Peter sayin' dey wis gaain' oot a' six, sam' time as wis.'

A. 'We canna geng ootside da *Korona*, fer da *Unity* 'll tie up ootside o' da *Serene* on da breakwater, an' den dere'll be nae channel trow.'

J. 'Aye, man, dat's roit enyoch. Well, I dinna ken, den. Mebbe we could go in aboon da *Azalea*, fer da *Adonis* is nae' yonder.'

A. 'Na, na. Da *Adonis* is gaain' ta tie up yondru ta tak' in her trawl.'

The skipper does not contribute to these exchanges. He simply enters harbour and, executing a difficult manoeuvre, berths the boat in a position which is obviously better than any of those which have been mentioned. He makes no comment on his decision, and neither do any of the crew, until they have tied up. Then J. says, 'Well done, [Skipper].'

As they prepare to disperse there is much joking and banter among all the men. The skipper is solicitous, and wants to be sure that they are all content. Although he is the same age as his crew, he nevertheless appears to be considerably their senior, and adopts an almost paternal attitude to one or two of them. After satisfying himself that all is well, he sends them away with 'Cheerio, then, me boys. We'll see dee later.' 'A' six, [Skipper]?' 'Aye, man, we'll try ta geng oot at six.'

Whalsay triumphant

I hope the ethnography in this book has vindicated my early remark that generalisation about social behaviour in Whalsay would be foolhardy, since its apparent orthodoxy is only superficial. It is a gloss by means of which Whalsay people mark their community's boundary and represent themselves to the outside world; but it only thinly conceals the diversities in social behaviour and attitudes within the community. The lines of this internal variation have been drawn here at the segmentary boundaries of the kinship–neighbourhood–crew nexus, but that is itself a device of simplification. These segments do not leaven the difference among their constituent members but, rather, aggregate them. No doubt, as in any family or small group, their own differences from each other are of crucial importance to their individual members. Anthropology tends not to dwell on such a fine level of individuation, for to do so could lead logically to the extreme conclusion of defining society and culture out of existence.[7] In the specific case of Whalsay, moreover, I have argued that the public acknowledgement of individuality is confined to, and expressed in terms of, segmentary boundaries. The 'community' as a *conscience collective* thus manages a tricky balancing act: of collectivity and individuality, of similarity and difference, of the simple mask adorning the complex face. I have represented the dichotomy in analytical terms as one between form and meaning in symbol and structure. I think that Whalsay people themselves would see the distinction as between 'public' and 'private'. Part of their triumph is to reconcile the two. As distinct dimensions of thought and behaviour they are complementary, rather than opposed, to each other. The ethos of 'being Whalsa" on which the simplified collective identity is based provides the frame of reference within which people strive to make the much more complex internal definitions; and, in turn, the manner in which they formulate these internal evaluations, and the consequences of such judgements, inform the perception and expression of the community's self-image. Of course this dynamic interplay is not conducted in isolation, for there is an abiding consciousness of the world beyond Whalsay: of how, people suppose, it sees Whalsay, and of how they see themselves in relation to it. The triangular interrelation – between community 'as a whole', its parts, and the world beyond – builds dynamism into the island's social life.

This dynamic generates a further test for the community, the successful negotiation of which constitutes another element of its triumph. It compels Whalsay people to think about how they must change the ways in which they live and work in order to keep their community viable. But they have also seen that such viability depends on accomplishing something much more difficult than the adoption of the world's cultural and material forms. Rather, it rests on a consciousness of cultural selfhood, of vitality and distinctiveness, in order that they can *trans*form the world as they bring it across the community's boundary: to make it respond to *indigenous* values and concepts. Whether or not the Whalsay models they use in this exercise are 'really traditional' is a question for historians and folklorists to ponder. From my point of view the question is interesting but unimportant. What matters is that people regard them as traditional or customary, *they make them so* and, in so constructing them, they make them do the work of tradition: to engender a sense of continuity and, thereby, to perpetuate the cultural identity. This essential security provides a stable base from which people can make the further adaptations they judge to be necessary, again without courting anomic disorientation and endangering their sense of cultural self. The measure of this accomplishment was stated in the opening chapter: that Whalsay has undergone massive change, yet retained its distinctiveness and an authentic consciousness of its difference. It has accommodated the world's demands without compromising itself into anyonymity or effective dissolution. The manner of its accomplishment has been our subject. If Whalsay's achievement has been conveyed with any success, it will have impressed the reader, as it has this observer, as being a veritable triumph.

Notes

1 Andrew Polson may be heard on a recording made by Peter Cooke, *Scottish Tradition, 4. Shetland Fiddle Music*, School of Scottish Studies, University of Edinburgh (Tangent Records, TNGM 117). In his notes to the record Cooke says that it is Andrew Polson's technique of the 'rhythmic "driven-up bow" that makes the performance so resonant and rich in harmony. Also interesting are the slight hesitations and syncopations found usually only in the first "turning" of each tune. This is said to be typical of older styles in Whalsay – the dancers matching their reeling steps to these rhythms as they make the figure-of-eight pattern.'
2 See Moar (1947), pp. 36, 40.
3 This is found, with variations, throughout Shetland and probably beyond. Its historical origins and distribution are irrelevant; what *is* significant is the claim to its possession which is made by Whalsay people.
4 The efficacy of symbolic 'inversions' and ritual 'reversals' as means of discriminating between normality and pathology in social behaviour, and in reasserting the former, has been widely noted by social anthropologists. It would perhaps be over-stretching the point to place Whalsay joking in this category of phenomena.
5 A slightly abbreviated and less vernacular version of this story appeared previously in Cohen (1986). In that earlier publication I tried to follow a suggestion made by J. W. Fernandez (*personal communication*) and speculated briefly on the possible symbolic significance of the items of clothing referred to in Ertie's saga. On this occasion I refrain from any further analytical intervention: readers are invited to make their own sense of the story and, if they care to do so, to send me their results.
6 Parts of this sketch appeared previously in Cohen (1977).
7 Although for intriguing attempts see Rapport (1986, 1987).

. . . and last thoughts: making sense of Whalsay

Fieldwork and the exhausted self

The term 'field work' implies observation of people and things *around* the investigator. What is observed, and how, depend upon the location and inclination of the investigator in the field. Indeed, the self of the investigator is inseparable from the subject of the investigation. Readers may find in this statement an echo of the 'post-modern'[1] sentiment that ethnography must now be written in a manner which clearly reveals the integral role of the ethnographer in constituting the culture which it purports to describe: that is, it must be explicit about the relationship between observer and observed, for this relationship creates the field of study. (See Dwyer, 1982, p. 272.) But in this final chapter I shall follow a slightly different argument, one which is personal rather than prescriptive. I will suggest some parallels between the processes of sense-making and interpretation in Whalsay and in contemporary anthropology, and will conclude by speculating on how they might assist our understanding of quite different milieux.

Most anthropologists would agree that their experience of fieldwork has taught them much about themselves, quite apart from what they may have learned about the societies they have studied. One finds limitations and capabilities within oneself which had not previously been revealed or acknowledged. But the self intrudes in a more significant way than through this personal discovery. It is the storehouse of experience which is used to apply a sense to what one sees and hears, to render it intelligible, to shape it. In the process of 'observation' the ethnographer processes data so that, rather than simply watching what other people do, one watches oneself watching them, just as all bounded entities – cultures, ethnic groups, and so forth – watch each other through the lenses of their own conceptual systems (cf. Boon, 1982; Geertz, 1984; Cohen, 1985a). So far as fieldwork is concerned, there is no alternative to this mediation if we accept that our task lies in *interpretation* rather than in a vacuous recording of actions.[2] (See MacIntyre, 1962.)

Anthropological data have no meaningful existence and truth independently of the anthropologist. Whilst I hope that I have presented the reader with substantial illustration, even 'evidence', in this book, it must not be regarded as self-less data. It is, rather, such stuff as *I* have been able to gather and to render intelligible to my*self*. As noted in the opening chapter, it is version, *my* version. I do not see how anything more reliable might have been offered.

But it may not be very reliable at all. Another common experience of anthropological fieldwork (as opposed to, say, journalism), especially if it has been conducted over many years, is the conviction that the more one knows a society the more one is aware of how little one knows. With increasing familiarity, the society appears to be ever more complex; the temptation to qualify statements about it grows increasingly insistent, until one is reluctant to say anything at all. The decision has then to be confronted either to keep silence, at least so far as publication is concerned, or to air one's version, however partial or selective it may be judged. This is not to say that I believe there is a strong likelihood that the judgements I have advanced here may be demonstrably false. Quite the contrary; I am convinced of their validity. My conviction remains intact as I write this chapter in August 1986, having just returned from a further visit to Whalsay during which I received comments from a number of local people on the preceding chapters.

However, it does suggest that an element so far missing from my version is any explicit acknowledgement of my self (in so far as it has constituted the data of this study). If my self is inseparable from the field, it behoves me to say something about how I believe it appears in Whalsay, and how this may have affected my 'fieldwork'. This is not a 'reflection' in the masterly manner of Paul Rabinow (1977),[3] nor a rehearsal of the dialogue between anthropologist and 'informants' of the kind commended by anthropologists such as Tedlock (1983), Dwyer (1982) and Crapanzano (e.g. 1980, 1985). It is a cursory history of social relationships which may assist the reader in evaluating my version of sense-making and segmentation in Whalsay.

Considerable emphasis has been given in this book to the importance of segmentary groups in Whalsay. Although lacking kin in the community, I strongly suspect that we (my wife and myself) would be seen as principally associated with the Whalsay neighbourhood in which we live; in particular, with various of its households. The members of these households are our closest friends; but we have close friendships beyond them and beyond the neighbourhood. When we lived in Whalsay in 1974–75 the range of such relationships covered most of the island. My wife's friendships were more extensive than mine. It may be that our scope for making close friendships was less restricted than if we had been tied by blood or marriage in to local segments. However, we were conscious that our principal commitment should be to our own neighbours, would be seen in those terms, and has grown in that way over the years. Whilst my observations of, and information

about, Whalsay were not restricted to our neighbourhood, I would not claim
to give a 'representative' view of the community. As was made clear in
chapter one, I doubt whether such a perspective could have any substance. At
the beginning of the research I had thought it might be possible to work with a
cross-section of fishing crews. However, it became apparent than even this
aspiration was unrealistic, might be harmful, precisely because of the
segmentary character of the community. The two boats on which I spent most
time had owners among my neighbours. After the first such excursion I would
occasionally be asked for news of the boat in question: in the public mind I
seemed to have become associated with it, however marginally. To seek an
association with other boats might well have been regarded as fickle, as
would the deliberate neglect of the other segmentary boundaries of kinship
and neighbourhood. It might have created mistrust, since I could be regarded
as a source of information about other boats which was not generally
available. There was rather more stability then in the composition of crews
than there is now.

During 1974–75 we knew most people on the island, and were certainly
known by them. These relationships ranged from mere acquaintanceship to
very close friendship. As time has passed, our close friendships have
deepened; the range of our acquaintances has decreased. It has been impossible to sustain such extensive relationships during the five or six weeks we
spend in Whalsay each year. Our close friends, with whom we maintain
contact throughout the year, treat our return flatteringly as a home-coming;
for other people, it is just a brief visit. Many people we knew well ten or
twelve years ago have since died. Many whom we knew as children playing
around our neighbourhood are now married and bringing up their own
families. Our age peers have grown into middle age as we ourselves have,
and as their own relationships have altered so, accordingly, have ours
with them.

A further source of change in my relationship to Whalsay should be
mentioned. When we first went to live on the island I made it plain that I was
there to do research and that I hoped eventually to write about the community. Our own orientation to Whalsay changed quickly: we ceased to
think about it primarily as a place to study; it became 'home'. Our attachment
to its members became personal and emotional rather than academic. Our
hosts appeared to forget our transience, and to accept us as permanent
settlers. Personal knowledge of us displaced our identity as slightly eccentric
intruders. Eventually, however, we had to return south, although for the next
four years we managed to spend two or three months each year in Whalsay. In
1977 I began to publish papers in academic journals based on the Whalsay
study. A steady stream of articles followed which were seen by a few local
people but were not widely known. However, in 1982 a volume of essays was
published under my editorship in which I included two chapters on Whalsay.

These were read by many people on the island. Although little was said to me direct, I sensed somewhat mixed feelings. Our own friends seemed quite untroubled by anything I had written; other people professed themselves 'amused' or 'interested'. There were rumours of some muted concern among one group and from one or two other people whom I knew hardly at all. One night in 1984 a young man to whom I had previously rarely spoken and who was not connected with anyone about whom I had written, questioned me pointedly (most un-Whalsa'-like behaviour) in the club about my own kinship and ethnic origins.

By that time I had already come to have misgivings about some of the material I had published. I had decided early on against any attempt to disguise the community, since its identity, like that of its individual members, would be obvious to Shetlanders. But I felt that I had identified some people when it may not have been necessary to do so; and, though I had tried to avoid making any obviously offensive remarks, I had perhaps not thought sufficiently hard about what might cause offence. I hope this failing at least is remedied in the present book. On reflection I decided that what, if anything, was really offensive, was not the *content* of any statement I had made so much as the fact that I had said anything at all. When the business of so tightly bounded a community as Whalsay is broadcast to the outside world, people may feel that they have somehow lost control over it. The purveying of such information might therefore be seen as, at best, intrusive and, at worst, a betrayal of trust, particularly if people have forgotten with the passage of time that one had always intended to write about them.

All ethnographers have to come to terms with this quandary. Those of us who write about the people who are also our readership have to face it as one of the conditions of our work. We will all square our consciences in our own ways (see, e.g., Messenger, 1983). For my part, I understand the sensibilities of my detractors in Whalsay but feel that I am justified in writing about the community. As I hope has been shown here, it is an exceptional society, exemplary in its sense of identity, its values, skills, self-discipline. It has survived and prospered, economically and culturally, where so many comparable communities have died or deteriorated into fraility and dependence. The world ought to know about Whalsay. My chief reservation is whether I have managed to do justice to its remarkable qualities.

I suspect that most Whalsay people would sympathise with my defence. They are aware of their special character and have more than an inkling of the extent of their extraordinary achievement. Most of its members would endorse my suggestion that they have much to teach the rest of us.

I suppose that the publication of this book will again alter the attitude of some Whalsay people to this interloper. It breaches their boundary (though, I hope, does not weaken it); and that, of course, is the eternal problem of anthropological fieldwork. The ethnographer moves between different worlds (cf. Geertz, 1975; Strathern, 1986a, pp. 16–17). The self perceived by those about whom he writes is necessarily partial. Such partiality should not be regarded as deceit.

One respect in which the self of the fieldworker differs from its other manifestations is in the 'self'-consciousness which it perpetually exercises. One may not continue to be consumed by the near-paralysing self-consciousness which characterises the early days of one's field research, but it does not disappear. Indeed, it is a necessary condition of fieldwork: one continues to use one's self to make sense of the society and to verify one's interpretations. Did I behave correctly or otherwise? Did I understand? Did I anticipate accurately? Did I make myself understood? The self is *the* essential element of anthropological fieldwork. In a sense, it is by observing his own self performing (as the 'post-modernists' would have it, 'in discourse') that the fieldworker 'discovers' the culture he studies. 'Facts', 'data', 'documentation', all are constituted by the ethnographer's self (cf. Geertz, 1975). That may be unsatisfactory scientifically; but it is the limitation, and the strength, of anthropology.

A brief summary of the progress of this monologue to date may be helpful. This ethnography is ethnographer-centred. It is therefore mediated by the ethnographer's native culture, his interpretive abilities, his social relationships in the 'field', other people's perceptions of him, their reactions to his public judgements about them, and their apprehensions concerning what he might say about them in the future. Further, in the *writing* of the ethnography the ethnographer's self acknowledges a quite different imperative: to present his judgements about one group of people in a manner which will be persuasive to another – that is, to create a 'persuasive fiction' (Strathern, 1986a). Here the anthropologist is like an alchemist, even though too often in the present case he turns gold into lead rather than vice versa. These two orientations of the ethnographer's self are resolved by his interpolation into the conceptual mediation of 'an anthropological framework', a peculiar mode of thought which, he supposes, differs from lay analysis. Moreover the anthropologist claims that this conceptual matrix is actually founded on, or has at least been fundamentally influenced by, his need to make sense of a particular society – Whalsay – to which, therefore, it must bear some kind of congruence. The self thinks in a manner which it believes to have been generated by its experience of those about whom it thinks.

Others may judge this to be a self-induced confidence trick. I do not. I see the crucial discourse in the anthropological enterprise taking place not between the ethnographer and the informant but between the selves of the ethnographer: one of which interacts and, hopefully, communes with those among whom he lives; the other of which struggles to make, and to communicate, an intellectual sense of them which is qualitatively different from (neither inferior, nor superior to) the kind of sense appropriate to his interaction with them. The first is a communion; the second, a detachment. The second feeds greedily on the first. When the hunger is assuaged one ceases to think about them *qua* anthropologist and relaxes instead in communion. The act of translation, whether between cultures, conceptual schemes or minds, is the essence of anthropology.

So far as Whalsay is concerned, this fieldworker is sated: the motivation to maintain an anlytical detachment has long since foundered in the stronger currents of friendship and personal sentiment. The post-modernists in anthropology have properly called into question the authorial nature of the ethnographic text and the manner in which it privileges and lend *author*ity to the perspective of the ethnographer as opposed to those of his informants (see Marcus and Cushman, 1982; Clifford, 1986; Strathern, 1986b). In the light of this critique it seems obvious that the anthropologist's view is not superior; it is different. They go on to argue that in order to expose the way in which this different perspective affects the formulation of an ethnographic text the ethnographer should reveal the course of his or her interaction with 'informants' through which the culture is elicited. The demand is for a record of the observation/interaction, rather than for the analytical, *post hoc*, conclusions (in Tedlock's terms, following Bakhtin, for the 'dialogic' rather than the 'analogic'). The critique then deteriorates into typical academic internecine squabbling over 'how' and 'how far' such a demand may be realisable. My sympathy stops at the critique. The demand to 'see' the ethnographer in the field can be reformulated as curiosity about what interpretations, other than those offered, may be possible or plausible. But that can be a gratuitous exercise. If we accept ethnography as a personal statement, a product of the self, it is obvious that different ethnographers are likely to produce different statements. Of course, this begs the question of how we should discriminate among them. If all we can produce is *version*, is any one version as good as any other? The question does not bear serious examination. We test versions for their plausibility: it is the method of everyday life, the means by which, as Geertz (1975) says, we distinguish the wink from the twitch. Of course, that in turn begs the question, and the answer remains the same: plausibility responds to our interpretive predispositions, whether as members of kinship–neighbourhood segments in Whalsay, or of theoretical, methodological and 'paradigm' segments in academic anthropology.

I referred earlier to the doubts which are induced by deepening familiarity with the society, a familiarity which reveals such a plethora of plausible accounts. Many circulate within the community, quite apart from those which outside observers may proffer. Somehow, though, one has to plot a discriminating course among them. The exhaustion of my Whalsay-analytic self amounts to the confession that the rest of me has decided to be content with my version and to be satisfied that it is plausible.

Symbol, segment, boundary

There are certainly as many plausible accounts as there are segments within
Whalsay, and no doubt far more still. Every group has its conceptual tag on
people and events mediating its members' observations and interpretations.
They are rehearsed within a group, but are only whispered or rumoured
beyond it. Competing versions are somehow known about, suspected or
imputed but are rarely made explicit, for fear of undermining the superficial
consensus of the community. The terms of inter-segment communal
discourse must be such as to permit all parties to assent to them whilst still
allowing them to attribute their own segment–specific meanings to them.
This kind of symbolic manipulation is replicated both at more and less
inclusive ends of the segmentary series, *within* Whalsay groups and *beyond*
the community itself.

The claim of any one group to speak for the community as a whole, or in
some way to pre-empt other views, is ill regarded. Despite its forcefulness and
effectiveness, Skipper Josie Simpson's complaint to the parliamentarians,
reported in chapter five, is said to have provoked some critical muttering. His
detractors apparently did not object to the substance of his advocacy, but to
its terms: in particular, to his repeated use of the first person singular.

The acceptable vocabulary of community life – its symbolism – clearly
imposes a considerable discipline upon members. It constrains them in
thinking about them*selves*, as well as in thinking about others. Their formulation of 'I' is tempered by the continuous and insistent preeminence of 'we':
kin, neighbours, crew, ultimately Whalsay itself. Individuality blends and
blurs in the public mind into segment, which, in its turn, merges into the yet
more amorphous generality of the community. But this sense of belonging to
a larger communal whole, through the more intimate mediation of family and
friends (see Cohen, 1982a), is the dominant characteristic of Whalsay and the
strongest marker of its difference from other communities in Shetland and
beyond.

The three organising themes in this book, symbol, segment and boundary,
all have well established but separate pedigrees in anthropology. But as they
are used here, in a clumsy attempt to replicate a version of Whalsay life, they
are not separate but, rather, crucially interdependent. For Whalsay people the
symbolism (or whatever other word readers might prefer to apply to 'the
ideas behind the words') of Whalsay culture takes its vitality, its very
meaningfulness, from their perpetual experience as members of segmentary
groups *within* the bounded community of Whalsay. The boundary marks
them off as different from people elsewhere; the symbolism formulates and
celebrates the terms of their difference; and it is through the segmentation
that each individual participates in these differentiating items – values, skills,
proclivities – and experiences them. Of course, the individual is more than a

member of a group, just as the groups and the community as a whole are each more than the sum of their various parts. But, by and large, it is by reference to their 'groupness' (their public identity) that other people make sense of their behaviour. The indigenous theory of segmentation is a primary sense-making device, a 'folk model' (see Holy and Stuchlick, 1981), for Whalsay people.

This is all rather pedestrian. I raise it again here briefly because it is relevant to a persistent tension in Whalsay life. It runs throughout the ethnography of this book, but is the basic problem for sociological analysis. The empirical issue is how individuals resolve the contending claims of individuality and communality. The theoretical problem is the relationship of the individual to society. For forty years or more following Malinowski's Trobriand field-work, British social anthropology was beset by fiercely competing approaches to this problem as it related to the subject's then central objective, the explanation of social organisation. This objective was gradually displaced by increasing concern with the symbolisation of culture and with its associated cognitive and expressive processes. One element of the anthropo-logical post-modernism, referred to in the previous section, has been the definitive turning aside from such a large and abstract issue as how society is structured, to concentrate instead on exploring people's *experience* of social interaction. The intractable methodological difficulty which this presents is as old as the *verstehende* sociological tradition: how to elicit and understand another mind's experience without constituting it by one's own, without fictionalising it in one's own image. It is a perennial concern of anthropology. Elsewhere it is presented as a problem of 'intersubjectivity'. After I had publicly agonised over a similar difficulty with respect to the interpretation of symbolism (see Cohen, 1986), a most distinguished and senior anthropolo-gist generously consoled me with characteristically wise advice. Many of the fundamental problems in our discipline are insoluble, he said. We must be mindful of the difficulties and just do what we can as well as we can.

Philosophical virtuosos might find such advice a little prosaic. On reflec-tion, I found it increasingly appealing. Moreover the aspiration to accomplish more than this now appears to me wildly ambitious. We face the same kind of interpretive obstacle as lay members of society in our ordinary, non-academic social pursuits. We may strive to know the minds of a few other people who are especially important to us, people such as family and friends, and we invariably lament our inability to do so. We wring our hands and confess our perplexity. With most people we do not even bother to make the effort, but are content to flout our own anthropological canons. 'If I were you . . .' we say, frequently to be met by the justifiably aggrieved response 'But you 're *not* me!' Why should we delude ourselves into thinking that the task might be more achievable when the minds in question bear other cultures, belong to other societies?

Moreover the people we study face the same difficulty, though they may be wise enough not to conceptualise it in our terms. All of us use our own experience as our principal interpretive device. Some people claim particular sensitivity, meaning that they are better able than others to penetrate other people's consciousnesses. Perhaps they are; or perhaps they have a greater conviction about their self-less interpretive skills than the rest of us are entitled to have. The point is, though, that the societies we purport to describe are composed of people who constitute the world – including their peers – through their own experience. When that experience fails to fit, they admit their inability to understand. The anthropologist, ignorant of the culture he has just encountered, confronts this inability continuously. Gradually, as one learns to behave in the culture, the feeling of incomprehension diminishes. Later, we discover, it was replaced by *mis*understanding. Eventually we satisfy ourselves that we *have* understood, or at least that we now have the appropriate means of understanding at our disposal: in effect, that we have acquired an interpretive competence similar to that of the people we are observing – and, in addition, we have the anthropological armoury to help us.

A similar competence? But their competence is the application by the self of its experience to *other* people's behaviour. But *that* is what 'intersubjectivists', emic-ists and other post-moderns wish to surpass. The anthropological battery? Techniques of sense-making which rest, in part, on the application of one kind of cultural experience to others – a procedure surely comparable to the lay imposition of the self on to the consciousness of another. The process through which we achieve an understanding resembles that used by the people we struggle to understand. It differs in some respects, one of which I reserve for discussion in the next section. Some of its other differentiating features are that our experience of other cultures may be broader; our awareness of the problems of interpretation sharper; and we may be more concerned to compensate for them. But we should use our experience of these difficulties to understand sense-making *generally*. It is in this respect, rather than in its structural implications, that Whalsay segmentation is significant. It is the context of people's experience of sense-making: the source of the interpretive devices they apply to the cultural symbols around them, and of their capacity to use these symbols to make meaning. In Whalsay, then, symbolism and segmentation are inextricable.

But, further, both are predicated on the senses of wider communality, and of Whalsay's difference from communities elsewhere that have been suggested here in the term 'boundary'. Logically, the very concept of 'segment' implies a whole. For reasons which run right through this version of Whalsay life, the communal 'whole' of Whalsay is continuously reiterated through a symbolic rhetoric which appears to maintain stability in an era of intensive change; to mitigate the inclination of its members to out-migration; to formulate the disciplines of island life; and, generally, to leaven the effects of acculturation. To use a linguistic analogy, people speak the language of Whalsay but comprehend it, and reconstitute it, through the subtly distinctive ways in which it is used by their particular segmentary associations. It is a communality whose claims to orthodoxy are belied in *intra*-community discourse, but are oriented to the community's boundary. A recent study accounts for the 'shared' commitment of Swedish congregants to their church, 'Immanuelskyrkan', by pointing to the church's provision of a *common* framework for the individualistic sentiments of its members' Pietism – a communality which is apparently based on an explicit rejection of orthodoxy (Stromberg, 1986). In Whalsay, far from being rejected, orthodoxy is claimed for most facets of social life. But it is the *existence* (symbol, form) of such orthodoxies which is asserted, not their *content* (meaning). The members of each segment may therefore construct the orthodoxy in the image of its own characteristic practice.[4]

There is an obvious homology between the accounts offered in this chapter of fieldwork and of sense-making. Critics may object that anthropological fieldwork *must* be qualitatively different from lay interpretive processes, and I agree: it differs in the respects, among others, which I have indicated above. But we should also recognise that the further we distance our reasoning and methodological procedures from those of the people we claim to understand, the more we risk mystifying and misrepresenting them, or becoming obsessed by introverted analytical concerns which are quite irrelevant beyond the narrow confines of the seminar room.

Segmentation in modern societies

I return briefly to one further characteristic of the anthropological process: we attempt deliberately, and with intellectual rigour, to illuminate the features of one society with insights gained from the study of others. In common with most anthropologists, the present author sees his research serving different but related objectives: to offer an understanding of a specific society; and hence to contribute towards the stock of experience from which we understand other, quite different, circumstances.

My experience in anthropological research began with fieldwork in a Newfoundland village in 1968. At that time anthropological studies of Western societies were still rather rare. The celebrated tradition of community studies which flourished during the 1950s and early 1960s had come to an end under the impact of misguided criticism and even of some ideological prejudice. We need not dwell on the details here. Some of the criticism was tinged by a curiously ethnocentric bias in its demand that research in Western societies ought to be restricted to locations which were somehow central strategically, or which, in terms of one social theory or another, might be regarded as especially problematic, societies such as those whose industrial bases were becoming obsolete, or which were absorbing large immigrant populations. With one or two notable exceptions (e.g. Worsley, 1966; Nader, 1972), the critics did not make similar demands for political relevance of scholars working in anthropologists' customary stamping grounds. By the early 1970s Newfoundland, although remote from the urban industrial centres of north America, had one of the most intensively studied populations on the continent. Similarly, when the present research in Whalsay began in 1972–73 nearly all the recent and current anthropological research on Britain was located in the remoter regions of the British Isles. It was hardly surprising that such locations should have attracted scholars. They were ideal vantage points from which to observe processes of social change and acculturation. Their distance from the political and economic 'centres' was clearly a matter of culture rather than merely of geography, a distance which both contributed to and was exacerbated by ignorance or misunderstanding about them by those in the 'centre'. But one was castigated for seeking to replicate the anthropological 'bush' in an industrialised economy, for confusing cultural boundaries (bourgeois mystification) with those of class; for bucolic romanticism; for downright irrelevance.

It was not very edifying criticism. Whatever its merits may have been, it revealed a misunderstanding about the nature of anthropological research. Geertz dismisses similarly misinformed criticism thus: 'The locus of study is not the subject of study. Anthropologists don't study villages; they study *in* villages' (1975, p. 22). This is part of the reason why, as noted earlier, they must be Janus-faced. During the last ten years, studies of rural areas in industrialised societies have generated ideas which are transforming our more general understanding of social process. To take one of the classic anthropological topics as an example, kinship has been revealed to us as a cognitive model encapsulating such disparate social ideas as those of class and community, as well as those of familihood (Strathern, 1981); a model which can be sensitively modulated to accommodate economic imperatives and to optimise scarce resources (e.g. Fox, 1978; Segalen, 1985), and to maintain the sense of continuity needed to stabilise a culture in an historical context of pervasive social and economic change (Dore, 1978).

Whether the present study will spark off in readers any similarly general ideas is a matter for hope rather than for prediction. However, it has led the author to speculate. Anthropologists' concern with segmentation grew out of classic studies of tribal organisation in East, West and North Africa. Their authors were concerned with 'segmentary lineage systems' as elements of social structure. They were seen as founded upon material interests, and as manifest in the geographical and/or political relations among tribesmen. Principles of allegiance and antagonism were regarded as reflexes of such relationships. Little, if any, attention was paid to *cultural* disjunctions among segments. (See Galaty, 1981.) One finds similar ideas informing structural–functional sociology in its analyses of the complex organisations of Western industrial societies. Such institutions were regarded as divided among sectors whose competing interests derived from their distinctive functions. The 'administration' was thus distinguished from 'the experts' or practitioners; the resource-acquirers from the resource-expenders. However, in the grand tradition of bureaucracy analysis, these differences of outlook were seen by the analysts as restricted to the performance of specific organisational functions, rather than as being related to, or extended to, more general differences of world view. The members of these different institutional sectors were said to see the institution differently because they occupied different functional niches within it.

An emphasis on culture might well identify other sources for these sectoral differences of view. For example, their members may see the institution differently because they see the world differently; their views of the world beyond the organisation may be affected by their experience *of* the organisation; their articulation of organisational interests may have less to do with their ostensible organisational functions than with the political necessity to formulate a distinctive position; and so on. The possibilities are endless, for this kind of perspective derives from empirical observation rather than from the invention and imposition of abstract analytical devices.

Although structural–functionalism has long since expired, organisational analysis does not seem to have taken any great theoretical leap forward in the direction of culture. There are increasingly sophisticated models of communication flow; of line management; of vertical, horizontal, perhaps even diagonal integration; of corporate structure and identity. But there still seems to be little attention paid to the cultural context of organisational life, in which the corporate message (like the community's collective self-image) is at best a symbolic medium for the expression and interpretation of the disparate (and, often, dissonant) meanings which are generated in the various nooks and crannies of the corporate whole. Rather, culture is still seen as an impersonal and disembodied determinant of the behaviour of all the members of a group who, by virtue of their *structural* incorporation, are assumed to share it and, therefore, to think alike. Few anthropologists would now be able to read the following without wincing:

> The basic idea of culture, including corporate culture, is that it consists of shared meanings and common understanding, and that this culture is variable from company to company [Lee and Lawrence, 1985, p. 104]

It would be tedious to identify the fallacies in so dated and Tylorian a view. But if it represents the conventional wisdom of the corporate world, this naive belief that members of 'a company' share 'meanings' and 'understanding', and are thereby differentiated from the members of other companies, goes some way towards explaining the less than brilliant recent history of British institutions. It is an anodyne and innocent view of the complexities of organisation: 'Just step up the dose of company culture, chaps, and we'll all be united in purpose, and we'll trounce the opposition!' Indeed, the authors cited above approvingly quote another writer who commends just such a remedy: culture, he says, consists of those assumptions which 'have worked well enough to be considered valid and, therefore, *to be taught to new members as the correct way* to perceive think and feel . . .' (*ibid.*, p. 105; my emphases).

By contrast let us take a scenario which appropriates to a problem familiar throughout the country. The National Health Service struggles to operate with scarce resources. To the lay observer its method appears to be to pass the ensuing problems down the line. Thus the Department of Health and Social Security stipulates budgetary limits to its Regional Boards, which in turn pass them on to their own Area Health Authorities. These then allocate budgets to the various institutions for which they are responsible. Eventually the administrator of a general hospital is informed that the hospital has to save £200,000 during the forthcoming financial year. He formulates various proposals: certain wards should close, depriving one or more specialities of their facilities and combining them in a more general unit; consultants should discharge in-patients more quickly following surgery; replacements for staff in certain specialities should not be appointed. These proposals are communicated to the medical staff, who either reject them for further consideration or, too weary for opposition, just try to cope with the increasing work loads and diminishing facilities.

Readers who have experience of institutional life will be able to fill in the gaps in this narrative with ease. Medical staff and administrators will curse each other. Doctors, nurses, technicians and ancillary workers will all examine the implications which the proposals have for themselves; likewise, each of the various medical specialities will consider its own interests, as also will all the practitioners within each speciality. Is it reasonable to suppose that such a fraught situation could possibly be resolved by pumping a little more culture into the committee room? Is it likely that an appeal to the wider interests of the institution ('shared meanings' in the 'company') might be successful? Which institution? The NHS? The Area Authority? The hospital? Pitted against any of these are ideologies which command commitment: to patient care; to the doctor's discretion over appropriate treatment; to 'the manager's right to manage' (a favourite Thatcherite slogan); to the patient's right to decide his or her own preferences; to the Cardio-thoracic Department (as opposed to other specialities); to cardiac transplants (as opposed to other, cheaper forms of heart surgery); to surgery as opposed to conservative treatments – and so on. It is precisely such complexity which is the reality of culture, and it is through such cultural blinkers, Mannheimian ideologies, that the various interests – segments – perceive and interpret the problem as a whole.

Here we have the classic segmentary series. The totality of the health service *vis-à-vis* competing claimants on the national Treasury; competition among regions, their constituent areas, and *their* constituent institutions, for scarce resources. Finally, at the level of the specific institution, there is a collective identity relative to *other* institutions; but one which, far from being commonly understood or shared by its own members, is fractured into variations and incompatibilities by their dissonant interests and personalities. The scenario is not peculiar to the embattled health service. Arguably, it is applicable to a wide spectrum of organisations which are composites of different kinds of expertise and interest, from the multinational corporation to the symphony orchestra.

I am not suggesting that all these are mirror images of each other; such a generalisation would be absurd. However, it seems obvious that we could learn much about organisational behaviour, and about the embeddedness of organisations, if we approached them from a perspective of segmented *cultures* (as opposed to structures) such as the one which has been applied here to the interpretation of Whalsay.[5] Nor should I be read as saying that Whalsay resembles the incoherent organisations discussed above. To the contrary: the point is that Whalsay is an exemplary case of a complex and differentiated society whose members have been astonishingly successful in reconciling individualistic, segmentary and communal interests through their subtle use of community symbols, their conscientious defence of the communal boundary and their sensitivity to any internal excesses by which it might be harmed. Its example should enhance our understanding of the very different world of complex organisations which dominate the public life of urban industrial societies.

Notes

1   I follow Ardener in his application of this term to social anthropology (1985, pp. 50, 54, 62). It refers to the demise of the powerful tradition in social anthropology in which ethnographic interpretations were made as a reflex of theoretical systems, a tradition which embraced systems as various as functionalism, structural–functionalism, Marxism and structuralism.

2   A vacuity demonstrated, for example, in the ethnomethodologists' genre of 'conversation analysis'.

3   A premature reflection appeared in Cohen (1978c).

4   Similarly, the events of community life are susceptible to widely varying interpretations which spring from the different vantage points of local groups. For a dramatic illustration see Messenger (1983), especially pp. 53 ff.

5   Attention is increasingly being drawn to the neglect and misunderstanding of differentiation within organisations (see, e.g., Wassell, 1986).

Documents of the late R. W. J. Irvine of the Linthouse

1. Men of Whalsay in 1576 (Peerie Lairds)

Culbein Ormesoun (Simbister), once Lawrightman
John and Antone Culbeinsoun, his sons
Magnus Petersoun (Ska)
Magnus in Neistehouss
Magnus Laurencessoun (Ska)
Magnus Sandiessoun
Magnus Mathiesoun
Magnus Androissoun (Neistehouss)
Magnus Olawsoun (Lie)
Peter Thomassoun (Houle)
Pole in Ska
Peter in Gardishouss
Erasmus in Huhsettar
Jacob in Levasetter
Christopher in Sandwijk
Olaw in Morasettar
Olaw in Scheldasettar
Magnus in Neistehouss

Note. The names Sandison (Sandiessoun); Anderson (Androissoun); and Polson or Poleson (Pole) remain prominent surnames in Whalsay. Laurenson (Laurencessoun); Peterson (Petersoun); and Thomason (Thomassoun) are surnames still common in Shetland but no longer in Whalsay. The place names referred to have all been corrupted: Ska (Skaw); Neistehouss (Nisthouse, Isbister); Lie (Lea); Houle (Houll); Gardishouss (Garderhouse, Isbister); Huhsettar (Huxter); Levasetter (Livister); Sandwijk (Sandwick); Morasettar (Marrister); Scheldasettar (Challister), and Simbister (Symbister).

2. Men of Whalsay in 1715, and the land they owned, in marks

Ska	5½ marks	Olla Blackbeard
Ska	3 marks	John Johnson
Ska	4¼ marks	Laurence Stewart
Ska	3½ marks	Malcolm Hughson
Ska	4 marks	Robert Rendall

Ska	1 mark	Kelvin Tarell
Ska	3 marks	John Gunn
Ska	3¼ marks	Henry Ollason
Huxter	3 marks	Laurence Smith
Brough, Houll & Lie	14½ marks	Wm. Leask (Laird of Lie)
Brough	3 marks	Edward Anderson
Brough	4 marks	Andrew Sinclair
Brough	2 marks	James Laureson
Brough	2½ marks	Helen Drever
Brough	1 mark	James Sutherland
Brough	2 marks	Barbara Simson
Brough	2½ marks	Theodore Kea
Brough	1 mark	George Peterson
Isbuster	4½ marks	Hugh Tarell
Isbuster	2 marks	Olla Edwardson
Isbuster	2 marks	Robert Stewart
Isbuster	3 marks	Andrew Stewart
Isbuster	6 marks	William Stewart
Isbuster	3 marks	Edward Anderson
Marasettar	4 marks	William Williamson
Marasettar	6 marks	Sheward Anderson
Clett	6 marks	Thomas Anderson
Clett	2 marks	Alex Mouat
Clett	2 marks	John Etchison
Clett	2 marks	Hynd Hughson

Note. Of these surnames, Johnson or Eunson, Stewart, Hughson, Leask, Anderson, Sinclair, Sutherland, Simpson, Kay, Williamson and Hutchinson ('Etchison', but still pronounced as Aitchison) remain extant in Whalsay.

The mark of merk was a proportional, rather than an absolute measure. A similar unit, mørk, was used in the Faroe Islands, where it has been computed as having referred on average to 'two acres of infield and 125 acres of outfield' (Jackson, 1979, p. 39). Jackson adds that the mark was used in medieval England, where, similarly, it approximated to two acres.

3. Heads of families in Whalsay, 25th June 1804

Compiled by the late John Stewart of Whalsay and Aberdeen, from a document detailing a distribution of oatmeal under 'Government Charity'. The figures in brackets refer to the number of people on behalf of whom the named person received meal and presumably, therefore, to the members of his or her household.

Ska

Laurence Anderson (7)   Henry Johnson (8)   Marion Leask (8)
Wm. Garroch Snr. (6)   Wm. Garroch Jnr. & Geo. Garroch (7)
Robert Poleson (3)   Hugh Williamson (4)   Helen Sandison (3)
Andrew Laurenceson (5)   James Irvine (5)   Martha Sinclair (1)
Elizabeth Irvine (1)

Challester

Robert Bruce Jnr. (7 or 4)   Alex Irvine (2)   Robt. Bruce Snr. (5)

Laurence Hutchison (4) George Irvine (4) John Irvine Snr. (2)
Theo. Kay (3) Thomas Kay (2) John Irvine Jnr. (6)
Ursula Park (1)

Brough

John Sybeison (7) Andrew Anderson (6) John Stewart (8)
William Johnson (5) Laurence Stewart (4) George Irvine (3)
Andrew Sinclair (5) John Johnson & Peter Henderson (5)
Mathew Robertson (8) Robert Jamieson (9) Alex. Irvine (3)
Robert Irvine (2) Thomas Henderson (9) Hugh Jamieson (6)
John Muncrief (5) Robert Sinclair (8) Robert Stewart (3)
Martha Shewardson (6) David Kay (8) James Henderson (7)
James Barchlay (10) Robert Hardie (2) Agnes Leisk (1)
Andrew Henderson (schoolmaster) (3) Margaret Irvine (1)

Marrister

Mrs Smith (3) Thomas Hughson (6) Gaun Gadie (3)

Isbister

Andrew Hutchison (4) William Leisk (5) Laurence Hutchison (5)
John Hutchison (7) James Arthur Snr. (4) Andrew Walterson (6)
Andrew Robertson (9) Robert Leisk (4) Edward Williamson (4)
Robert Robertson (5) James Arthur Jnr. (5) Wm. Anderson Jnr. (8)
Alex Irvine (9) Wm. Anderson Snr. (6) Walter Anderson (2)
Henry Anderson (5) Margaret Anderson (4) Helen Stewart (1)
Elizabeth Sinclair (1) Barbara Henry
  (Niddagoe) (1)

Treawick

Andrew Poleson (7) Laurence Irvine (5)

Huxter

John Irvine (7) John Robertson Snr. (4) Robert Leisk (3)
John Robertson Jnr. (4)

Clate

John Hutchison (4) Andrew Anderson (6) Alexander Shearer (6)
Laurence Hughson (3) James Poleson (7) John Sandison (9)
William Ewenson (6)

Sandwick

Magnus Shearer (8) Gilbert Gilbertson (5) Thos. Gilbertson (4)
Andrew Poleson (6) William Anderson (6) Isobell Thomson (2)

Simbester

John Rendall (6) Thomas Green (5) Hendry Paton (7)
Andrew Mather (7) Robert Robertson (7) James Williamson (4)
Mathew Robertson (6) Joseph Leisk (4) Laurence Henderson (4)
John Ritch (4) Lillias Rendall (3) Hugh Robertson (4)
James Rendall (9) Adam Ewenson (4) Magnus Gilbertson (3)
Magnus Robertson (6) Anne Robertson (2) Elizabeth Irvine (3)
John Henderson (4) Cathern Williamson (4) Samuel Irvine (4)
George Paton (4) James Nanson (8) Mr A. Ramsay (5)

Note. These figures cannot be treated as an accurate census of the population, since it must be presumed that there would have been a number of people absent from the island at the time at sea, fishing or otherwise engaged. If we add the twenty-one members of the laird's household who, it is expressly stated, did *not* receive any meal, we get a minimal figure for the population of 581.

By that date patronymics had generally given way to established surnames, and it is clear from this list than many families had already become established in parts of the island with which they are still associated. This is especially noticeable in the cases of Challister, Brough, Clate and Isbister. It is difficult to make a judgement about 'Simbester', since, in this list, it may include the now distinct areas of Harlsdale, Saltness and even Hamister.

Appendix B

Some Whalsay eela meyds, as used by James Arthur of Sodom and by Gilbert Stewart of Hillhead

Place	Meyd	Tidal conditions	Remarks
	1. Species: ollock (ling)		
Kirkness	Lea over kirk; Booth with Symbister Ness	South, near end of flood	Drift S. to Southerness light
do.	do.	North tide	Drift N. same distance
Holms of Skaw	Cairn over beach of inner holm; kirk with Mooaclett, point of Challister Ness	South or north	
Challister Ness	'By nort' Mooaclett' in 18 fathoms off the Ness and all round the Ness	North or south	
By East Wetherholm Bar	Kirk knowe over Holm of Skaw and Mooaclett Sound; Charlie o'Knowe's 'ower da kirk'	South	
Lunning Head	Manse o' Neap over Dragon Ness; Lunna Head with the next head (or Willie Stewart's house at Tripwell with the north end of Wetherholm) 'until da point starts opening'	North & south	Very deep. Tide and depth can exhaust the line
North end of Linga Sound	Müll (light 6 miles S. of Symbister Ness) with Heid o' Berg; Swarta Skerry in sight of Wetherholm Sound	North	Drift length of Swarta Skerry
South end of Linga	Swarta Skerry with 'Horse' of Dury Voe	North	Work at 'Calf' (of Linga) side of tide.
		South	Work at Linga side of tide

Place	Meyd	Tidal conditions	Remarks
Groyn o' Staffness	Mid. 'toog' of East Linga with Guttald; Symbister Ness with the Böd		The Böd house 'in sight of' Symbister Ness is 'spot on'
Flaeshins o' Sandwick	W. side of Flaeshins; Symbister Ness with beach of 'Crabbypool' (Linga)		Also for cod

2. Species: cod

Place	Meyd	Tidal conditions	Remarks
Symbister Ness	Anchor Cottage over lighthouse point		
Groyn of Ness	Roof of school at N. of Ramnaberg; Head of Clett over Holm of Sandwick	End of flood seems best	
'Draggin' (dredging?) Ground	By S. Skerry of Marrister; Josie Williamson's (Saltness) and the school. (Or Manse o' Neap with Symbister Ness)		

3. Species: mackerel

Place	Meyd	Tidal conditions	Remarks
'Shaklett' by N. Wetherholm	Manse o' Neap with east face of Bruseholm; northernmost Brough house with the end of Wetherholm	North and south	
N. end Linga Sound, between Southerness and Wetherholm	Müll light with Symbister Ness: 'Baith da lights in line'		
Off Symbister Ness	The Böd with Calf of Linga		The westernmost point into the light, across the tide. Fish drawn on edge of tidal-string
Bight of Dragon Ness			
Shacklett	See above	North and south	
Lunning Sound	Widespread: Manse o' Neap with Ondyaholm Sound		
West of the Ness	With Wards together: 'Ward o' Clett with Ward of Symbister Ness' and 'the Door o' Littleholm open'	South perhaps best	Approaching the east face of Bruseholm, this with the face of Littleholm gives the impression door opening and closing

Place	Meyd	Tidal conditions	Remarks
West of the Flaeshins	'Ony wye wi' Waaderholm an' Symbister Ness wi da Soond opening' (i.e. Linga Sound)	South perhaps best	Also flounder and skate
	Saffa Skerry and Heid o' Clett, and Whalsay Sound starting to open	South	
The Hairy	School over valley of Holm of Sandwick	South	
	Head of Levenwick (Hammaraheid), with Point of Staffness		Come south with the Holm of Sandwick and the school

5. Species: piltocks (saithe)

Place	Meyd	Tidal conditions	Remarks
Wetherholm Bar	'Well of Lea' over bell tower of kirk; north Ward of Linga with 'Steens' (east) of Wetherholm.		
	North end of Wetherholm, where the tide splits: about 100 yards 'be nort Waaderholm'.		An 'eela berth'
	E. and N.E. side of Marra Flaeshins		'Eela distance' — as close in as is safe.
	Swarta Skerry (N. and N.W. sides) 'Nort Hole . . .'	North	*do.*
'Heid o' Brough' and Skaw	Both ends of Sound and west side	North	
Littleholm and Bruseholm	Right around	Flood tide coming in	
Ondyaholm	South end		
Calf of Linga	Both sides of points		
Back of Linga and Flaeshins of Sandwick	All the way along		

Piltock are prolific around the shores of the island and of the holms and skerries in the Sound. Other locations they use include Saffa Skerry, Symbister Ness and the Skerry of Marrister. Tusk may occasionally be found on the *ollock* grounds, particularly those with very hard bottom. Tradition has it that the north isles of the Sound should be fished with a north tide; the south isles, with the tide going south.

References

Aberdein, J. (1986), 'The future of the Shetland fishing industry – the political solutions', *Shetland Fishing News*, 5, March.

Andersen, P. S. (1984), 'Peter Andreas Munch and the beginning of Shetland place-name research', in *Essays in Shetland History: Heidursrit to T. M. Y. Manson*, ed. B. E. Crawford, Lerwick: Shetland Times, pp. 18–32.

Andersen, R. R. (1972), 'Hunt and deceive: information management in Newfoundland deep-sea trawler fishing', in Andersen and Wadel (1972), pp. 120–40.

—— (1973), 'Those fisherman lies: custom and competition in North Atlantic fishermen communication', *Ethnos*, 38.

—— and Wadel, C., eds. (1972), *North Atlantic Fishermen: Anthropological Essays on Fishing*, St John's: ISER.

Anon. (1834), *An Account of the Present State and Capabilities of Improvement of the Herring and White Fisheries in Shetland Islands . . .*, London: John Haddon & Co.

Ardener, E. (1985), 'Social anthropology and the decline of modernism', in *Reason and Morality*, ed. J. Overing, ASA Monograph 24, London: Tavistock, pp. 47–70.

Atkinson, J. M. (1984), *Our Masters' Voices: the Language and Body Language of Politics*, London: Methuen.

Aubert, W. (1965), 'A total institution: the ship', in *The Hidden Society*, ed. W. Aubert, New Jersey: Bedminster Press.

Bailey, F. G. (1983), *The Tactical Uses of Passion: an Essay on Power, Reason and Reality*, Ithaca: Cornell University Press.

Barnes, M. (1984), 'Orkney and Shetland Norn', in *Language in the British Isles*, ed. P. Trudgill, Cambridge: Cambridge University Press, pp. 352–66.

Bateson, G. (1936), *Naven*, Cambridge: Cambridge University Press.

Berry, R. J. and Johnston, J. L. (1980), *The Natural History of Shetland*, London: Collins.

Blehr, O. (1974), 'Social drinking in the Faroe Islands: the ritual aspect of token prestations', *Ethnos*, 1–4, pp. 53–62.

Bloch, M., ed. (1975), *Political Oratory and Authority in Traditional Societies*, London: Academic Press.

Boon, J. A. (1982), *Other Tribes, other Scribes: Symbolic Anthropology in the Comparative Study of Cultures, Histories, Religions and Texts*, Cambridge: Cambridge University Press.

Bowie, H. (1981), 'Shetlandic Scotch and William Dunbar', *New Shetlander*, 135, Voar.

Breen, R. J. (1980), *Up the Airy Mountain and down the Rushy Glen: Change and Development in an Irish Rural Community, 1936–78*, unpublished Ph.D. thesis, University of Cambridge.

Brody, H. (1973), *Inishkillane: Change and Decline in the West of Ireland*, London: Allen Lane.

Brox, O. (1964), 'Natural conditions, inheritance and marriage in a north Norwegian fjord', *Folk*, 6 (1), pp. 35–45.

Byron, R. J. (1986), *Sea Change: a Shetland Society, 1970–79*, St John's: ISER.

Cargill, G., (1976), *Blockade '75: the Story of the Fishermen's Blockade of the Ports*, Glasgow: Molendinar Press.

Census (1971), *Census 1971 (Scotland): County Report (Zetland)*, Edinburgh: HMSO.

Clifford, J. (1986), 'Introduction: partial truths', in *Writing Culture: the Poetics and Politics of Ethnography*, eds. J. Clifford and G. E. Marcus, Berkeley: University of California Press, pp. 1–26.

Cohen, Abner (1977), 'Symbolic action and the structure of the self', in *Symbols and Sentiments: Cross-cultural Studies in Symbolism*, ed. I. M. Lewis, London: Academic Press, pp. 117–28.

Cohen, A. P. (1975), *The Management of Myths: the Legitimation of Political Change in a Newfoundland Community*, Manchester: Manchester University Press.

—— (1977), 'For a political ethnography of everyday life: sketches from Whalsay, Shetland', *Ethnos*, 3–4, pp. 180–205.

—— (1978a), ' "The same – but different!" The allocation of identity in Whalsay, Shetland', *Sociological Review*, 26 (3), pp. 449–69.

—— (1978b), 'Oil and the cultural account: reflections on a Shetland community', *Scottish Journal of Sociology*, 3 (1), pp. 129–41, reprinted in *The Social Impact of Oil in Scotland*, eds. R. Parsler and D. Schapiro, Farnborough: Gower Publishing Co., 1980.

—— (1978c), 'Ethnographic method in the real community', *Sociologia Ruralis*, XVIII (1), pp. 1–22.

—— (1979), 'The Whalsay croft: traditional work and customary identity in modern times', in *The Social Anthropology of Work*, ed. S. Wallman, ASA Monograph 19, London: Academic Press, pp. 249–67.

—— ed. (1982), *Belonging: Identity and Social Organisation in British Rural Cultures*, Manchester: Manchester University Press; St John's: ISER.

—— (1982a), 'A sense of time, a sense of place: the meaning of close social association in Whalsay, Shetland', in Cohen, ed. (1982), pp. 21–49.

—— (1982b), 'Blockade: a case study of local consciousness in an extra-local event', in Cohen, ed. (1982), pp. 292–321.

—— (1985a), *The Symbolic Construction of Community*, London: Tavistock, and Ellis Horwood Ltd.

—— (1985b), 'Symbolism and social change: matters of life and death in Whalsay, Shetland', *Man* (N.S.), 20, pp. 307–24.

—— (1986), 'Of symbols and boundaries, or, does Ertie's greatcoat hold the key?' in Cohen, ed. (1986), pp. 1–19.

—— ed. (1986), *Symbolising Boundaries: Identity and Diversity in British Cultures*, Manchester: Manchester University Press.

Cohen, B. J. (1983), *Norse Imagery in Shetland: an Historical Study of Intellectuals and their Use of the Past in the Construction of Shetland's Identity, with Particular Reference to the Period 1800–1914*, unpublished Ph.D. thesis, University of Manchester.

Collier, A., (1953), *The Crofting Problem*, Cambridge: Cambridge University Press.

Comaroff, J. L. (1975), 'Talking politics: oratory and authority in a Tswana chiefdom', in Bloch, ed. (1975), pp. 141–61.

Coull, J. R., Goodlad, J. H., and Sheves, G. T. (1979), *The Fisheries in the Shetland Area: a Study in Conservation and Development*, Department of Geography, University of Aberdeen.

Crapanzano, V. (1980), *Tuhami: Portrait of a Moroccan*, Chicago: University of Chicago Press.

—— (1985), *Waiting: the Whites of South Africa*, New York: Random House.

Crozier, R. M. (1985), *Patterns of Hospitality in a Rural Ulster Community*, unpublished Ph.D. thesis, Queen's University of Belfast.

Donaldson, G. (1983), 'The Scots settlement in Shetland', in *Shetland and the Outside World, 1469–1969*, ed. D. J. Withrington, Aberdeen University Studies 157, Oxford: Oxford University Press.

Dore, R. P. (1978), *Shinohata: Portrait of a Japanese Village*, New York: Pantheon Books.

Dorian, N. (1981), *Language Death: the Life Cycle of a Scottish Gaelic Dialect*, Philadelphia: University of Pennsylvania Press.

Douglas, M. (1975), *Implicit Meanings: Essays in Anthropology*, London: Routledge & Kegan Paul.

Douglass, W. A. (1969), *Death in Murélaga: Funerary Ritual in a Spanish Basque Village*, Seattle: University of Washington Press.

Dwyer, K. (1982), *Moroccan Dialogues: Anthropology in Question*, Baltimore: Johns Hopkins University Press.

Edmonston, A. (1809), *A View of the Ancient and Present State of the Zetland Isles*, etc., 2 vols, Edinburgh: Longman.

Eunson, J. (1961), 'The Fair Isle fishing marks', *Scottish Studies*, 5, pp. 81–98.

Evans-Pritchard, E. E. (1940), *The Nuer*, London: Oxford University Press.

—— (1949), *The Sanusi of Cyrenaica*, London: Oxford University Press.

Expenditure Committee (1978), *The Fishing Industry*, Minutes of Evidence, Thursday 1st December 1977, Expenditure Committee (Trade and Industry Sub-committee), London: HMSO.

Expenditure Committee, V, (1978), *Fifth Report from the Expenditure Committee: 'The Fishing Industry'*, Vol. 1, London: HMSO.

Faris, J. C. (1972), *Cat Harbour: a Newfoundland Fishing Settlement*, St John's: ISER.

Fenton, A. (1978), *The Northern Isles: Orkney and Shetland*, Edinburgh: John Donald.

Firth, J. R. (1973), *Symbols, Public and Private*, London: Allen & Unwin.

Flett, T. M. (1971), 'The auld reel, the Foula reel, and the Shaalds of Foula', in *Shetland Folk Book*, Vol. 5, ed. T. A. Robertson and J. J. Graham, Lerwick: Shetland Times, pp. 22–31.

Foster, G., *et al.*, eds. (1979), *Long-term Field Research in Social Anthropology*, London: Academic Press.

Fox, R. (1978), *The Tory Islanders: a People of the Celtic Fringe*, Cambridge: Cambridge University Press.

Frake, C. O. (1985), 'Cognitive maps of time and tide among medieval seafarers', *Man* (N.S.), 20 (2), pp. 254–70.

Frankenberg, R. J. (1957), *Village on the Border*, London: Cohen & West.

Galaty, J. G. (1981), 'Models and metaphors: on the semiotic explanation of segmentary systems', in *The Structure of Folk Models*, ed. L. Holy and M. Stuchlik, ASA Monograph 20, London: Academic Press, pp. 63–92.

Geertz, C. (1971), 'Deep play: notes on the Balinese cockfight', in *Myth, Symbol and*

Culture, ed. C. Geertz, New York: W. W. Norton & Co., pp. 1–37.

—— (1975), 'Thick description: toward an interpretive theory of culture', in *The Interpretation of Cultures*, London: Hutchinson, pp. 3–30.

—— (1984), 'Anti anti-relativism', *American Anthropologist*, 86, pp. 263–78.

Gell, A. (1985), 'How to read a map: remarks on the practical logic of navigation', *Man* (N.S.), 20, pp. 271–86.

Goodlad, C. A. (1971), *Shetland Fishing Saga*, Lerwick: Shetland Times.

Goodlad, J. H. (1983), 'Shetland's fishing industry in 1983: a review of the past year', *Shetland Life*, 38, December, pp. 4–8.

Gouldner, A. W. (1955), 'Metaphysical pathos and the theory of bureaucracy', *American Political Science Review*, 49, pp. 496–507.

Graham, J. J. (1979), *The Shetland Dictionary*, Stornoway: Thule Press.

—— (1983), 'Social changes during the quinquennium', in Withrington, ed. (1983), pp. 216–33.

Grassie, J. (1983), *Highland Experiment: the Story of the Highlands and Islands Development Board*, Aberdeen: Aberdeen University Press.

Grønneberg, R. (1981), *Jakobsen and Shetland*, Lerwick: Shetland Publishing Co.

—— (1984), 'Jakobsen and his Shetland correspondents', in *Essays in Shetland History: Heidursrit to T. M. Y. Manson*, ed. B. E. Crawford, Lerwick: Shetland Times, 225–33.

Gusfield, J. R. (1975), *Community: a Critical Response*, Oxford: Blackwell.

Hélias, P.–J. (1978), *The Horse of Pride: Life in a Breton Village*, New Haven: Yale University Press.

Hobart, M. (1985), 'Texte est un con', in *Contexts and Levels: Anthropological Essays on Hierarchy*, ed. R. H. Barnes *et al.*, Oxford: JASO, pp. 33–53.

Holy, L. (1979), 'The segmentary lineage structure and its existential status', in *Segmentary Lineage Systems Reconsidered*, ed. L. Holy, Queen's University Papers in Social Anthropology 4, Belfast: Department of Social Anthropology, Queen's University of Belfast.

—— and Stuchlik, M. (1981), 'The structure of folk models', in *The Structure of Folk Models*, ed. L. Holy and M. Stuchlik, ASA Monograph 20, London: Academic Press, pp. 1–34.

van den Hoonaard, W. (1977), *Social Context and the Evaluation of an Occupational Culture: a Study of the Shrimpers of Isafjordur, Iceland*, unpublished Ph.D. thesis, University of Manchester.

Howarth, D. (1957), *The Shetland Bus*, London: Nelson.

Hunter, J. J. (1937), 'With apologies to Thomas Moore', in *Trums an' Truss*, Lerwick: T. J. Manson.

Hunter, J. (1976), *The Making of the Crofting Community*, Edinburgh: John Donald.

Hunter, J. A. (1962), 'Weather lore', *The New Shetlander*, Summer and Hairst.

Jackson, A. (1979), 'Socio-economic change in the Faroes', in *North Atlantic Maritime Cultures*, ed. R. R. Andersen, The Hague: Mouton.

Jakobsen, J. (1928), *An Etymological Dictionary of the Norn Language in Shetland*, London: David Nutt (A. G. Berry), and Copenhagen: Vilhelm Prior, published in facsimile, Lerwick: Shetland Folk Society, 1985.

Jamieson, P. (1949), *Letters on Shetland*, Edinburgh: Moray Press.

—— (1974–5), 'Sea-speech and beliefs of Shetland fishermen', *New Shetlander*, 110 (Yule 1974) and 111 (Voar 1975).

Jorion, P. (1982), 'The priest and the fisherman: Sundays and weekdays in a former "theocracy" ', *Man* (N.S.), 17, pp. 275–86.

Knipe, E. (1984), *Gamrie: an Exploration in Cultural Ecology*, London: University Press of America.

Knox, S. A. (1985), *The Making of the Shetland Landscape*, Edinburgh: John Donald.

Kolinsky, M., ed. (1978), *Divided Loyalties: British Regional Assertion and European Integration*, Manchester: Manchester University Press.

Leach, E. R. (1964), 'Anthropological aspects of language: animal categories and verbal abuse', in *New Directions in the Study of Language*, ed. E. H. Lenneberg, Cambridge, Mass.: MIT Press.

Lee, R., and Lawrence, P. (1985), *Organizational Behaviour: Politics at Work*, London: Hutchinson.

Low, Geo. (1774), *A Tour through the Islands of Orkney and Shetland*, reprinted, Inverness: Melven Press, 1978.

MacDiarmid, H. (C. M. Grieve) (1939) *The Islands of Scotland: Hebrides, Orkneys and Shetlands*, London: B.T. Batsford.

McDonald, Rev. Fr A. (1972), *Gaelic Words and Expressions from South Uist and Eriskay*, ed. J. L. Campbell, 2nd edn, London: Oxford University Press.

Macfarlane, A. (1978), *The Origins of English Individualism: the Family, Property and Social Transition*, Oxford: Blackwell.

MacIntyre, A. (1962), 'A mistake about causality in social science', in *Philosophy, Politics and Society* (2nd series), ed. P. Laslett and W. G. Runciman, Oxford: Blackwell.

McKay, G. (1967), 'Celtic influences in Shetland', *New Shetlander*, 82, pp. 23–5.

Malinowski, B. (1948), *Magic, Science and Religion, and other Essays*, Glencoe, Ill.: Free Press.

Mandelbaum, D. G. (1976), 'Social uses of funeral rites', in *Death and Identity*, ed. R. Fulton, Maryland: Charles Press.

Manson, T. M. Y. (1978), 'Faroe and its Shetland connections', in *Scandinavian Shetland: an Ongoing Tradition?* ed. J. R. Baldwin, Edinburgh: Scottish Society for Northern Studies, pp. 13–22.

Marcus, G. E., and Cushman, D. (1982), 'Ethnographies as texts', *Annual Review of Anthropology*, 11, pp. 25–69.

Mareel, Symbister House Junior High School magazine, 1980–81.

Melchers, G. (1980), 'The Norn element in Shetland dialect today – a case of 'never-accepted' language death', *Tvåspråkighet*, ed. I. Henrysson and E. Ejerhed, Umea: Acta Universitatis Umensis, pp. 254–61.

—— (1983), *Norn: the Scandinavian Element in Shetland Dialect*, Stockholm: Department of English, University of Stockholm, mimeo.

Merton, R. K. (1957), *Social Theory and Social Structure*, rev. edn., New York: Free Press.

Messenger, J. C. (1983), *An Anthropologist at Play: Balladmongering in Ireland and its Consequences for Research*, London: University Press of America.

Mewett, P. G. (1977), 'Occupational pluralism in crofting: the influence of non-croft work on the pattern of crofting agriculture in the Isle of Lewis since about 1850', *Scottish Journal of Sociology*, 2 (1).

—— (1980), *Social Change and Migration from Lewis*, unpublished Ph.D. thesis, University of Aberdeen.

—— (1982a), 'Exiles, nicknames, social identities and the production of local consciousness in a Lewis crofting community', in Cohen, ed. (1982), pp. 222–46.

—— (1982b), 'Associational categories and the social location of relationships in a Lewis crofting community', in Cohen, ed. (1982), pp. 101–30.

Moar, P. (1947), 'Fiddle tunes', *Shetland Folk Book*, Vol. 1 ed. E. S. Reed Tait, Lerwick: Shetland Times, pp. 35–40.

Mouzelis, N. P. (1967), *Organisation and Bureaucracy: an Analysis of Modern Theories*, London: Routledge & Kegan Paul.

Mylne, C. K. (1955), 'Speak Shetland – but write English', *New Shetlander*, 41.

Nader, L. (1972), 'Up the anthropologist – perspectives gained from studying up', in *Reinventing Anthropology*, ed. D. Hymes, New York: Pantheon.

Needham, R. (1980), *Reconaissances*, Toronto: University of Toronto Press.

Nicolson, J. R. (1972), *Shetland*, Newton Abbot: David & Charles.

—— (1982), *Hay and Company: Merchants in Shetland*, Lerwick: Hay & Co.

O'Neill, B. J. (1983), 'Dying and inheriting in rural Tras-os-Montes', *J.A.S.O.*, 14, pp. 44–74.

Paine, R. P. B. (1957), *Coast Lapp Society, I. A Study of Neighbourhood in Revsboten Fjord*, Tromso: Tromso Museums Skrifter IV.

—— ed. (1981), *Politically speaking: Cross-cultural Studies in Rhetoric*, Philadelphia: ISHI; St John's: ISER.

—— (1982), *Dam a River, Damn a People? Saami (Lapp) Livelihood and the Alta/Kautokeino Hydro-electric Project and the Norwegian Parliament*, IWGIA Document 45, Copenhagen: IWGIA.

Peace's Almanac (1905), *Peace's Almanac and County Directory for 1905*, Kirkwall: William Peace & Son.

Peters, E. L. (1967), 'Some structural aspects of the feud among the camel-herding Bedouin of Cyrenaica', *Africa*, XXXVII (3), pp. 261–82.

Peterson, G. P. S. (1974), 'Da Shetland tongue', *New Shetlander*, 110.

Pitt-Rivers, J. A. (1971), *The People of the Sierra*, 2nd edn, Chicago: University of Chicago Press.

Pottinger, J. (1952), 'Seine-netting' (in favour)', *New Shetlander*, 33.

Pugh, D. S., *et al.* (1967), 'An approach to the study of bureaucracy', *Sociology*, 1 (1), pp. 61–72.

Rabinow, P. (1977), *Reflections on Fieldwork in Morocco*, Berkeley: University of California Press.

—— and Sullivan, W. (1979), 'The interpretive turn: emergence of an approach', in *Interpretive Social Science: a Reader*, ed. P. Rainbow and W. Sullivan, Berkeley: University of California Press, pp. 1–21.

Ranger, T. O., and Hobsbawm, E. (1984), *The Invention of Tradition*, Cambridge: Cambridge University Press.

Rapport, N. J. (1986), 'Cedar High Farm: ambiguous symbolic boundary. An essay in anthropological intuition', in Cohen, ed. (1986), pp. 40–9.

—— (1987), *Talking Violence: Symbolic Sameness and Difference in Scenes of St John's*, St John's: ISER.

Ratter, D. (1983), 'Herring strike', *Shetland Life*, 33, pp. 8–11.

Robertson, T. (1971), 'A list of words relating to land and agriculture', *Shetland Folk Book*, Vol. 5, ed. T. Robertson and J. J. Graham, Lerwick: Shetland Times, for Shetland Folk Society, pp. 13–21.

Robson, A. (1982), *The Saga of a Ship: the 'Earl of Zetland'*, Lerwick: Shetland Times.

Russell, Rev. J. (1887), *Three Years in Shetland*, London: Alexander Gardner.

Sahlins, M. (1961), 'The segmentary lineage: an organization of predatory expansion', *American Anthropologist*, 63, pp. 322–45.

—— (1985), *Islands of History*, Chicago: University of Chicago Press.

Sansom, B. (1981), *The Camp at Wallaby Cross*, Canberra: Australian Institute for Aboriginal Studies.

Schneider, D. M. (1980), *American Kinship: a Cultural Account*, 2nd edn, Chicago: University of Chicago Press.

Segalen, M. (1985), *Quinze Générations de Bas-Bretons: Parenté et Société dans le Pays Bigouden Sud, 1720–1980*, Paris: Presses Universitaires de France.

Shetland in Statistics (1980), *Shetland in Statistics, 1980,* Lerwick: Research and Development Department, Shetland Islands Council.

Smith, B. (1979), ' "Lairds" and "improvement" in seventeenth and eighteenth century Shetland', in *Lairds and Improvement in the Scotland of the Enlightenment,* ed. T. M. Devine, Edinburgh: Scottish Historical Association, pp. 11–20.

Smith, H. D. (1972), *The Historical Geography of Trade in the Shetland Islands, 1550–1914,* unpublished Ph.D. thesis, University of Aberdeen.

—— (1973), 'The development of Shetland fisheries and fishing communities', in *Seafarer and Community: towards a Social Understanding of Seafaring,* ed. P. Fricke, London: Croom Helm, pp. 8–29.

—— (1978), 'The Scandinavian influence in the making of modern Shetland', in *Scandinavian Shetland: an Ongoing Tradition?* ed. J. R. Baldwin, Edinburgh: Scottish Society for Northern Studies, pp. 23–33.

Spence, D. (1979), *Shetland's Living Landscape: a Study in Island Plant Ecology,* Sandwick: Thuleprint.

Sperber, D. (1975), *Rethinking Symbolism,* Cambridge: Cambridge University Press.

—— (1980), 'Is symbolic thought prerational?' in *Symbol as Sense: New Approaches to the Study of Meaning,* ed. M. LeCron Foster and S. Brandes, London: Academic Press, pp. 25–44.

—— (1985), *On Anthropological Knowledge: Three Essays,* Cambridge: Cambridge University Press.

Statistical Account (1978), *The Statistical Account of Scotland, 1791–1799,* ed. Sir John Sinclair, Vol. XIX, *Orkney and Shetland,* Reissued and repaginated, Wakefield: EP Publishing.

Stewart, H. A. (1985), 'The island of Whalsay', *The Third Statistical Account of Scotland,* Vol. XXB, *The County of Shetland,* ed. J. R. Coull, Edinburgh: Scottish Academic Press, pp. 114–120.

Stewart, J. (1943), 'Some Whalsay sea-meeads', *Shetland News,* 24th June.

Strathern, M. (1981), *Kinship at the Core: an Anthropology of Elmdon, a village in north-west Essex, in the 1960's,* Cambridge: Cambridge University Press.

—— (1984), 'The social meanings of localism', in *Locality and Rurality: Economy and Society in Rural Regions,* ed. T. Bradley and P. Lowe, Norwich: Geo Books, pp. 181–97.

—— (1986a), *Out of Context: the Persuasive Fictions of Anthropology,* Frazer Lecture, University of Liverpool, mimeo

—— (1986b), 'The limits of auto-anthropology', in *Anthropology at Home,* ed. A. Jackson, ASA Monograph 25, London: Tavistock, pp. 16–37.

Stromberg, P. G. (1986), *Symbols of Community: the Cultural System of a Swedish Church,* Tucson: University of Arizona Press.

Tambiah, S. J. (1969), 'Animals are good to think and good to prohibit', *Ethnology,* 8 (4), pp. 423–59.

Tedlock, D. (1983), *The Spoken Word and the Work of Interpretation,* Philadelphia; University of Pennsylvania Press.

Thompson, P., *et al* (1983), *Living the Fishing,* London: Routledge & Kegan Paul.

Tilly, C. (1963), 'The analysis of a counter-revolution', *History and Theory,* 3.

—— (1964), *The Vendée,* Cambridge, Mass.: Harvard University Press.

Truck Commissioners (1872), *Second Report of the Commissioners appointed to Inquire into the Truck System (Shetland),* Edinburgh: Murray & Gibb for HMSO (reprinted, Sandwick: Thuleprint, 1978).

Tunstall, J. (1962), *The Fishermen: the Sociology of an Extreme Occupation,* London: McGibbon & Kee.

Turner, V. W. (1967), *The Forest of Symbols: Aspects of Ndembu Ritual,* Ithaca:

Cornell University Press.

Underhill, R., ed. (1977), *The Future of Scotland*, London: Croom Helm for the Nevis Institute.

Vallee, F. G. (1955), 'Burial and mourning customs in a Hebridean community', *Jnl. R. Anthrop. Inst.*, pp. 119–30.

Wadel, C. (1979), 'The hidden work of everyday life', in *Social Anthropology of Work*, ed. S. Wallman, ASA Monograph 19, London: Academic Press, pp. 365–84.

Warner, W. L. (1959), *The Living and the Dead: a Study of the Symbolic Life of Americans*, New Haven: Yale University Press.

Warner, W. W. (1984), *Distant Water: the Fate of the North Atlantic Fisherman*, Harmondsworth, Penguin.

Warrack, A. (1911), *A Scots Dialect Dictionary*, Edinburgh: W. & R. Chambers.

Wassell, P. (1986), 'Partly politics', *Times Higher Education Supplement*, 22nd August.

Williamson, K. (1948), *The Atlantic Islands: a Study of the Faroese Life and Scene*, London: Collins.

Wills, J. W. G. (1975), *Of Laird and Tenant: a Study of the Social and Economic Geography of Shetland in the Eighteenth and Early Nineteenth Centuries*, unpublished Ph.D. thesis, University of Edinburgh.

—— (1984), 'The Zetland method', in *Essays in Shetland History: Heidursrit to T. M. Y. Manson*, ed. B. E. Crawford, Lerwick: Shetland Times, pp. 161–78.

Withrington, D. J., ed. (1983), *Shetland and the outside World, 1469–1969*, Aberdeen University Studies Series 157, Oxford: Oxford University Press.

Worsley, P. M. (1966), 'The end of anthropology?' presented to the Sociology and Social Anthropology Working Group, *6th World Congress of Sociology*.

Zulaika, J. (1981), *Terranova: the Ethos and Luck of Deep Sea Fishermen*, Philadelphia: ISHI; St John's: ISER.

Index